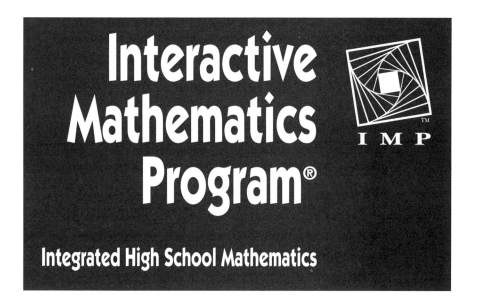

# Interactive Mathematics Program®

## Integrated High School Mathematics

Dan Fendel and Diane Resek
with
Lynne Alper and Sherry Fraser

KEY CURRICULUM PRESS
Innovators in Mathematics Education

This material is based upon work supported by the National Science Foundation under award number ESI-9255262. Any opinions, findings, and conclusions or recommendations expressed in this publication are those of the authors and do not necessarily reflect the views of the National Science Foundation.

Key Curriculum Press
1150 65th Street
Emeryville, CA 94608

10 9 8 7 6 5 4     05
ISBN 1-55953-344-7
Printed in the
United States of America

Publisher
Steven Rasmussen

Editorial Director
John Bergez

Project Editor
Casey FitzSimons

Project Administrator
Jeff Gammon

Additional Editorial Development
Masha Albrecht, Mary Jo Cittadino

Art Developer
Ellen Silva

Production Editors
Caroline Ayres, Kristin Ferraioli

Project Assistants
Stefanie Liebman, Beck Finley

Copyeditor
Thomas L. Briggs

Cover and Interior Design
Terry Lockman
Lumina Designworks

Production and Manufacturing Manager
Diana Jean Parks

Production Coordinator
Laurel Roth Patton

Art Editor
Kelly Murphy

Photo Researcher
Laura Murray

Technical Graphics
Tom Webster, Lineworks, Inc.

Illustration
Alan Dubinsky, Tom Fowler, Nikki Middendorf, Evangelia Philippidis, Paul Rogers, Sara Swan, Martha Weston, April Goodman Willy, Amy Young

MATHEMATICS REVIEW
Lynn Arthur Steen, St. Olaf College,
    Northfield, Minnesota

MULTICULTURAL REVIEWS
Genevieve Lau, Ph.D., Skyline College,
    San Bruno, California
Luis Ortiz-Franco, Ph.D., Chapman University,
    Orange, California
Marilyn E. Strutchens, Ph.D., University of Maryland,
    College Park, Maryland

TEACHER REVIEWS
Kathy Anderson, Aptos, California
Dani H. Brutlag, Mill Valley, California
Robert E. Callis, Oxnard, California
Susan Schreibman Ford, Stockton, California
Mary L. Hogan, Arlington, Massachusetts
Jane M. Kostik, Minneapolis, Minnesota
Brian R. Lawler, Carson, California
Brent McClain, Portland, Oregon
Michelle Novotny, Aurora, Colorado
Barbara Schallau, San Jose, California
James Short, Oxnard, California
Kathleen H. Spivack, New Haven, Connecticut
Linda Steiner, Escondido, California
Marsha Vihon, Chicago, Illinois
Edward F. Wolff, Glenside, Pennsylvania

# ACKNOWLEDGMENTS

Many people have contributed to the development of the IMP™ curriculum, including the hundreds of teachers and many thousands of students who used preliminary versions of the materials. Of course, there is no way to thank all of them individually, but the IMP directors want to give some special acknowledgments.

We want to give extraordinary thanks to these people who played unique roles in the development of the curriculum.

- **Bill Finzer** was one of the original directors of IMP, helped develop the concept of a problem-based unit, and contributed important ideas for *High Dive*.

- **Matt Bremer** pilot-taught the entire curriculum, did the initial revision of every unit after its pilot testing, and did major work on subsequent revisions.

- **Mary Jo Cittadino** became a high school student once again during the piloting of the curriculum, which gave her a unique perspective on the curriculum.

- **Lori Green** left the classroom as a regular teacher after piloting Year 1 and became a traveling resource for IMP classroom teachers. She has compiled many of her classroom insights in the *Teaching Handbook for the Interactive Mathematics Program®*.

- **Celia Stevenson** developed the charming and witty graphics that graced the prepublication versions of the IMP units.

In creating this program, we needed help in many areas other than writing curriculum and giving support to teachers.

The National Science Foundation (NSF) has been the primary sponsor of the Interactive Mathematics Program. We want to thank NSF for its ongoing support, and we especially want to extend our personal thanks to Dr. Margaret Cozzens, who was Director of NSF's Division of Elementary, Secondary, and Informal Education during IMP's development period, for her encouragement and her faith in our efforts.

We also want to acknowledge here the initial support for curriculum development from the California Postsecondary Education Commission and the San Francisco Foundation, and the major support for dissemination from the Noyce Foundation and the David and Lucile Packard Foundation.

Keeping all of our work going required the help of a first-rate office staff. This group of talented and hard-working individuals worked tirelessly on many tasks, such as sending out units, keeping the books balanced, helping us get our message out to the public, and handling communications with schools, teachers, and administrators. We greatly appreciate their dedication.

- Barbara Ford—Secretary
- Tony Gillies—Project Manager
- Marianne Smith—Communications Manager
- Linda Witnov—Outreach Coordinator

## IMP National Advisory Board

We have been further supported in this work by our National Advisory Board—a group of very busy people who found time in their schedules to give us more than a piece of their minds every year. We thank them for their ideas and their forthrightness.

**David Blackwell**
Professor of Mathematics and
    Statistics
University of California, Berkeley

**Constance Clayton**
Professor of Pediatrics
Chief, Division of Community
    Health Care
Medical College of Pennsylvania

**Tom Ferrio**
Manager, Professional Calculators
Texas Instruments

**Andrew M. Gleason**
Hollis Professor of Mathematics
    and Natural Philosophy
Department of Mathematics
Harvard University

**Milton A. Gordon**
President and Professor of
    Mathematics
California State University,
    Fullerton

**Shirley Hill**
Curator's Professor of Education
    and Mathematics
School of Education
University of Missouri

**Steven Leinwand**
Mathematics Consultant
Connecticut Department of
    Education

**Art McArdle**
Northern California Surveyors
    Apprentice Committee

**Diane Ravitch** (1994 only)
Senior Research Scholar,
    Brookings Institution

**Roy Romer** (1992-1994 only)
Governor
State of Colorado

**Karen Sheingold**
Research Director
Educational Testing Service

**Theodore R. Sizer**
Chairman
Coalition of Essential Schools

**Gary D. Watts**
Educational Consultant

We want to thank Dr. Norman Webb of the Wisconsin Center for Education Research for his leadership in our evaluation program, and our Evaluation Advisory Board, whose expertise was so valuable in that aspect of our work.

- David Clarke, University of Melbourne
- Robert Davis, Rutgers University
- George Hein, Lesley College
- Mark St. John, Inverness Research Associates

Finally, we want to thank Steven Rasmussen, President of Key Curriculum Press, John Bergez, Key's Executive Editor for the IMP curriculum, Casey FitzSimons, Project Editor, and the many others at Key whose work turned our ideas and words into published form.

*Dan Fendel      Diane Resek      Lynne Alper      Sherry Fraser*

"I hated math" is an often-heard phrase that reflects an unfortunate but almost socially acceptable adult prejudice. One hears it from TV announcers, politicians, and even football coaches. I'll bet they didn't start their education feeling that way, however. According to the Third International Mathematics and Science Study, American fourth graders score near the top of their international peers in science and math. Surely mathphobia hasn't broken out by that grade level. By twelfth grade, however, students in the United States score among the lowest of the 21 participating nations in both mathematics and science general knowledge. Even our advanced math students—the ones we like to think are the best in the world—score at the very bottom when compared to advanced students in other countries. What happened? Is there something different about our students? Not likely. Is there an opportunity for improvement in our curriculum? You bet.

Traditional mathematics teaching continues to cover more repetitive and less challenging material. For the majority of students, rote memorization, if not too difficult, is certainly an unenlightening chore. The learning that does result tends to be fragile. There is little time to gain deep knowledge before the next subject has to be covered. American eighth-grade textbooks cover five times as many subjects in much less depth than student materials found in Japan. Because there is no focus on helping students discover fundamental mathematical truths, traditional mathematics education in the United States fails to prepare students to apply knowledge to problems that are slightly different and to situations not seen before.

As an engineering director in the aerospace industry, I'm concerned about the shrinking supply of talented workers in jobs that require strong math and science skills. In an internationally competitive marketplace, we desperately need employees who have not only advanced academic skills, but also the capability to discover new, more cost-effective ways of doing business. They need to design with cost as an independent variable. They need to perform system trades that not only examine the traditional solutions, but explore new solutions through lateral, "out of the box" thinking. They need to work in teams to solve the most difficult problems and present their ideas effectively to others.

Programs like IMP foster these skills and fulfill our need as employers to work with educators to strengthen the curriculum, making it more substantive and challenging. I can attest to the value of IMP because, as the father of a student who has completed four years of the program, I've discovered that something *different* is going on here. My son is given problems around a theme, each one a little harder than the one before. This is not much different from the way I was taught. What is different is that he is not given the basic math concept ahead of time, nor is he shown how to solve upcoming problems by following the rule. By attacking progressively harder problems in many different ways, he often learns the basic mathematical concepts through discovery. He is taught to think for himself. He says that the process "makes you feel like you are actually solving the problem, not just repeating what the teacher says."

This process of encouraging discovery lies at the heart of IMP. Discovery is not fragile learning; it is powerful learning. My son thinks it can be fun, even if he won't admit it to other students.

I have another window on IMP as well. As the husband of a teacher who helped to pioneer the use of IMP in her district, I've learned that teaching IMP is a lot more than letting the students do their own thing. Lessons are carefully chosen to facilitate the discovery process. Points are given for finding the correct answer, and points are given for carefully showing all work, which is as it should be. Because the curriculum encourages different ways of solving a problem, my wife spends more than the typical amount of time teachers spend in reading and understanding students' efforts. The extra time doesn't seem to burden her, however. I think she thinks it's fun. She even gets excited when she sees that the focus on communicating and presenting solutions is measurably improving her students' English skills.

Let me conclude with a word of encouragement to all of you who are using this book. I congratulate you for your hard work and high standards in getting to this, the fourth and final year of IMP. IMP students have performed well in SAT scores against their peers in traditional programs. Colleges and universities accept IMP as a college preparatory mathematics sequence. I know that your efforts will pay off, and I encourage you to take charge of your future by pursuing advanced math and science skills. Even if you don't become an aerospace engineer or computer programmer, this country needs people who think logically and critically, and who are well prepared to solve the issues yet to be discovered.

Larry Gilliam
Scotts Valley, California

*Larry Gilliam is a parent of two IMP students and works as the chief test engineer for Lockheed Martin Missiles & Space in Sunnyvale, California.*

# CONTENTS

# DAYS 26–30: Components of Velocity ......... 78

# DAYS 31–32: High Dive Concluded ........... 91

# Appendix: Supplemental Problems ......... 97

# As the Cube Turns

## Know How

# The World of Functions

# DAYS 21–26: Composing Functions . . . . . . . . . . .315

# DAYS 27–28: Transforming Functions . . . . . . . .335

# DAYS 29–30: Back to the Beginning . . . . . . . . . .341

# Appendix: Supplemental Problems . . . . . . . . . .346

## The Pollster's Dilemma

### DAYS 1–3: What's a Pollster to Think? . . . . . . . .365

### DAYS 4–5: Polls and Pennant Fever . . . . . . . . .377

### DAYS 6–10: Normal Distributions Revisited . . . .386

# Note to Students

This textbook represents the last year of a four-year program of mathematics learning and investigation. As in the first three years, the program is organized around interesting, complex problems, and the concepts you learn grow out of what you'll need to solve those problems.

## If you studied IMP Year 1, 2, or 3

If you studied IMP Year 1, 2, or 3, then you know the excitement of problem-based mathematical study. The Year 4 program extends and expands the challenges that you worked with previously. For instance:

- In Year 1, you began developing a foundation for working with variables. In Year 2, you learned how to solve linear equations algebraically, and in Year 3, you worked with quadratic equations. In Year 4, you'll solve a quadratic equation as part of the process of finding out when a diver should be dropped from a Ferris wheel in order to land in a moving tub of water.

- In Year 1, you used the normal distribution to help predict the period of a 30-foot pendulum. In Year 2, you learned about the chi-square statistic to understand statistical comparisons of populations, and in Year 3, you learned about the binomial distribution. In Year 4, you'll use the context of election polls to see the connection between the binomial distribution and the normal distribution, and you'll use ideas such as margin of error and confidence level to study how sample size affects poll reliability.

You'll also use ideas from geometry, trigonometry, and matrix algebra to develop a calculator program that shows a cube rotating in space, you'll prove the quadratic formula as part of a unit on ways to learn mathematics on your own, and you'll synthesize your IMP experience with functions by examining a variety of methods for creating functions that fit specific real-world problems.

*If you didn't study IMP Year 1, 2, or 3*

If this is your first experience with the Interactive Mathematics Program (IMP), you can rely on your classmates and your teacher to fill in what you've missed. Meanwhile, here are some things you should know about the program, how it was developed, and how it is organized.

The Interactive Mathematics Program is the product of a collaboration of teachers, teacher-educators, and mathematicians who have been working together since 1989 to reform the way high school mathematics is taught. About one hundred thousand students and five hundred teachers used these materials before they were published. Their experiences, reactions, and ideas have been incorporated into this final version.

Our goal is to give you the mathematics you need in order to succeed in this changing world. We want to present mathematics to you in a manner that reflects how mathematics is used and that reflects the different ways people work and learn together. Through this perspective on mathematics, you will be prepared both for continued study of mathematics in college and for the world of work.

This book contains the various assignments that will be your work during Year 4 of the program. As you will see, these problems require ideas from many branches of mathematics, including algebra, geometry, probability, graphing, statistics, and trigonometry. Rather than present each of these areas separately, we have integrated them and presented them in meaningful contexts, so you will see how they relate to each other and to our world.

Each unit in this four-year program has a central problem or theme, and focuses on several major mathematical ideas. Within each unit, the material is organized for teaching purposes into "days," with a homework assignment for each day. (Your class may not follow this schedule exactly, especially if it doesn't meet every day.)

At the end of the main material for each unit, you will find a set of supplementary problems. These problems provide you with additional opportunities to work with ideas from the unit, either to strengthen your understanding of the core material or to explore new ideas related to the unit.

Although the IMP program is not organized into courses called "Algebra," "Geometry," and so on, you will be learning all the essential mathematical concepts that are part of those traditional courses. You will also be learning concepts from branches of mathematics—especially statistics and probability—that are not part of a traditional high school program.

To accomplish your goals, you will have to be an active learner, because the book does not teach directly. Your role as a mathematics student will be to experiment, to investigate, to ask questions, to make and test conjectures, and to reflect, and then to communicate your ideas and conclusions both orally and in writing. You will do some of your work in collaboration with fellow students, just as users of mathematics in the real world often work in teams. At other times, you will be working on your own.

We hope you will enjoy the challenge of this new way of learning mathematics and will see mathematics in a new light.

*Dan Fendel    Diane Resek*

*Lynne Alper    Sherry Fraser*

High Dive

# Going to the Circus

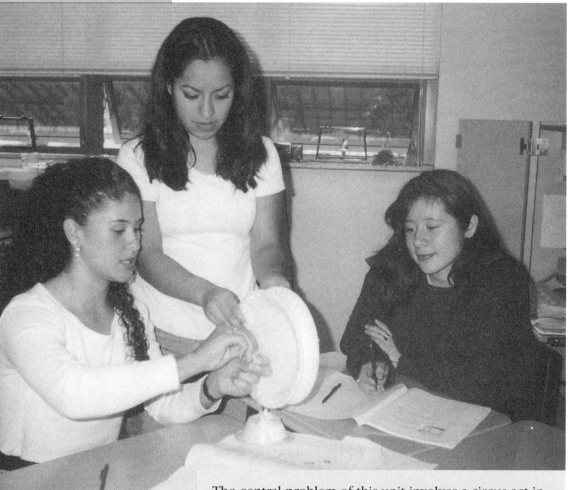

*Maribel DeLoa, Vivian Barajas, and Caroline Moo build a physical model as a first step toward solving the unit problem.*

The central problem of this unit involves a circus act in which a diver falls from a turning Ferris wheel into a tub of water carried by a moving cart. The problem involves various kinds of motion, and you will need to learn quite a bit of mathematics before the unit is over in order to solve this problem.

# High Dive

## The Circus Act

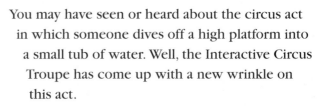

You may have seen or heard about the circus act in which someone dives off a high platform into a small tub of water. Well, the Interactive Circus Troupe has come up with a new wrinkle on this act.

They have attached the diver's platform to one of the seats on a Ferris wheel, so that it sticks out horizontally, perpendicular to the plane of the Ferris wheel. The tub of water is on a moving cart that runs along a track, parallel to the plane of the Ferris wheel, and passes under the end of the platform.

As the Ferris wheel turns, an assistant holds the diver by the ankles. The assistant must let go at exactly the right moment, so that the diver will land in the moving tub of water.

If you were the diver, would you want to trust your assistant's on-the-spot judgment? A slight error and you could get a "splat!" instead of a "splash!"

## Your Task

The diver has insisted that the circus owners hire your group to advise the assistant. You need to figure out exactly when the assistant should let go. (Your analysis will be tested carefully on a dummy before it is used with a human being.)

1. Make a physical model of the problem, using materials that your teacher has provided.

*Continued on next page*

**2.** Specify any other information you need to know about the circus act to determine when the assistant should let go.

*Historical note:* The first Ferris wheel was created for the 1893 Chicago World's Fair and was the brainchild of George Washington Gale Ferris. This creation was much larger than the Ferris wheels of today. It stood 265 feet high and was 250 feet in diameter. It carried 36 cars, each of which could hold 60 people. A single revolution took about 20 minutes, and admission was 50 cents, ten times the cost of any other ride at the fair.

The Ferris wheel was dismantled after the fair and made brief appearances at other major events. It was sold for scrap metal in 1906.

# The Standard POW Write-up

The standard POW write-up for Year 4 includes the same five categories that you used in Year 3.

1. *Problem statement:* State the problem clearly in your own words. Your problem statement should be clear enough that someone unfamiliar with the problem could understand what it is that you are being asked to do.

2. *Process:* Describe what you did in attempting to solve this problem, using your notes as a reminder. Include things that didn't work out or that seemed like a waste of time. Do this part of the write-up even if you didn't solve the problem.

   If you get assistance of any kind on the problem, you should indicate what the assistance was and how it helped you.

3. *Solution:* State your solution as clearly as you can. Explain how you know that your solution is correct and complete. (If you only obtained a partial solution, give that. If you were able to generalize the problem, include your more general results.)

   Your explanation should be written in a way that will be convincing to someone else—even someone who initially disagrees with your answer.

*Continued on next page*

4. *Evaluation:* Discuss your personal reaction to this problem. For example, you might comment on these questions:

- Did you consider the problem educationally worthwhile? What did you learn from it?

- How would you change the problem to make it better?

- Did you enjoy working on it?

- Was it too hard or too easy?

5. *Self-assessment:* Assign yourself a grade for your work on this POW, and explain why you think you deserved that grade.

# The Tower of Hanoi

## The Legend of the Golden Discs

Buddhism, one of the world's major religions, has roots in India and is practiced by over three hundred million people throughout the world. An ancient legend describes an important task once given to a group of Buddhist monks.

According to the legend, a Buddhist temple contained a pile of 64 large golden discs, one on top of another, with each successive disc slightly smaller than the one below it. This pile of discs sat upon a golden tray. Two empty golden trays lay next to the one with the pile of discs.

The monks' task was to move the pile of 64 discs from its original tray to one of the other trays. But according to the rules of the task, the monks could move only one disc at a time, taking it off the top of a pile. They could then place this disc either on an empty tray or on the top of an existing pile on one of the trays. Moreover, a disc placed on the top of an existing pile could not be larger than the disc below it.

The legend concludes with the promise that when the monks finish this task, the world will be filled with peace and harmony.

## The Puzzle

As you will see, the monks could not possibly have finished the task. (How unfortunate for the state of the world!) But there is a mathematical puzzle, known as "The Tower of Hanoi," that is based on this legend. (Hanoi is the capital of Vietnam, which is located in southeast Asia. Many people in Vietnam are Buddhists.)

*Continued on next page*

The puzzle consists of three pegs and a set of discs of different sizes, as shown in the accompanying diagram. The discs all have holes in their centers. To begin with, the discs are all placed over the peg at the left, with the largest disc on the bottom and with the discs in decreasing size as they go up, as shown here. (This diagram uses only 5 discs instead of 64.)

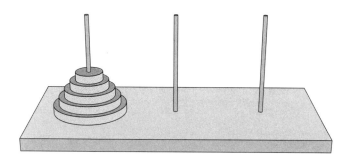

The task in this puzzle is to transfer all of the discs to the peg on the right. As in the legend, the discs must be moved according to certain rules.

- Only one disc can be moved at a time.

- The disc being moved must be the top disc on its peg.

- The disc being moved must be placed either on an empty peg or on top of a larger disc on a different peg.

## Getting Started

In a sense, your POW is to answer this question.

> *If the monks had moved one disc every second, how long would it have taken them to complete the task?*

But don't start with this question. Instead, start with two or three discs and work your way up, finding the *least number* of moves that are required to transfer the pile of discs from the peg on the left to the peg on the right.

*Continued on next page*

As you work, consider these questions. (The notation $a_n$ represents the number of moves required to move $n$ discs from the peg on the left to the peg on the right.)

- If you knew how many moves were needed to move 20 discs, how could you find the number of moves needed to move 21 discs? Can you generalize this process into a formula? (That is, if you know $a_n$, how can you find $a_{n+1}$?) Can you explain why this formula holds true?

- Look for a formula that gives $a_n$ directly in terms of $n$, and test your formula with specific cases. If you knew that this formula worked for $n = 20$, could you prove that it worked for $n = 21$? Can you prove the formula in general?

When you have answered these questions as best you can, go back to the question about the monks and their 64 discs.

## Write-up

1. *Process*

2. *Results:* Give the results of your investigation, including

   - the number of moves required for any specific cases you studied

   - the amount of time required for the monks to move the 64 discs

   - any general formulas or procedures that you found, even if you aren't sure of them

3. *Solutions:* Explain your results, including how you know that the number of moves for each number of discs is the smallest possible. Also give any explanations you found for your generalizations.

4. *Evaluation*

5. *Self-assessment*

# The Ferris Wheel

Al and Betty have gone to the amusement park to ride on a Ferris wheel. The wheel in the park has a radius of 15 feet, and its center is 20 feet above ground level.

You can describe various positions in the cycle of the Ferris wheel in terms of the face of a clock, as indicated in the accompanying diagram. For example, the highest point in the wheel's cycle is the 12 o'clock position, and the point farthest to the right is the 3 o'clock position.

For simplicity, think of Al and Betty's location as they ride as simply a point on the circumference of the wheel's circular path. That is, ignore the size of the Ferris wheel seats, Al and Betty's own heights, and so on.

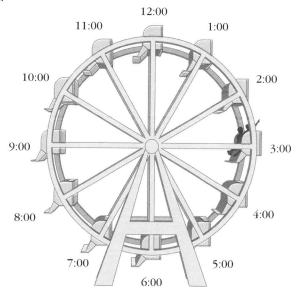

1. How far off the ground are Al and Betty when they are at each of the following positions?

   a. the 3 o'clock position

   b. the 12 o'clock position

   c. the 9 o'clock position

   d. the 6 o'clock position

2. How far off the ground are Al and Betty when they are at the 2 o'clock position? (*Caution:* Their height at the 2 o'clock position is *not* a third of the way between their height at the 3 o'clock position and their height at the 12 o'clock position.)

3. Pick two other clock positions and figure out how far off the ground Al and Betty are when they reach each of those positions.

# As the Ferris Wheel Turns

In order to understand what happens when a diver is released from a moving Ferris wheel, you need precise information about the position of the diving platform as the Ferris wheel turns.

In this assignment, you will be looking only at the *height* of the platform. Later, you will consider how far the platform is to the left or right of the center of the Ferris wheel.

*Continued on next page*

You will need this information about the Ferris wheel.

- The radius of the Ferris wheel is 50 feet.

- The Ferris wheel turns at a constant speed, makes a complete turn every 40 seconds, and moves counterclockwise.

- The center of the Ferris wheel is 65 feet off the ground.

You should use these facts throughout the unit unless a problem specifically gives different information. *Reminder:* The circumference of a circle can be found from its radius using the formula $C = 2\pi r$.

1. At what speed is the platform moving (in feet per second) as it goes around on the Ferris wheel?

2. Through what angle (in degrees) does the Ferris wheel turn each second? (The rate at which an object turns is called **angular speed,** because it measures how fast an angle is changing. Angular speed does not depend on the radius.)

3. How many seconds does it take for the platform to go each of these distances?

    a. from the 3 o'clock to the 11 o'clock position

    b. from the 3 o'clock to the 7 o'clock position

    c. from the 3 o'clock to the 4 o'clock position

4. What is the platform's height off the ground at each of these times?

    a. 1 second after passing the 3 o'clock position

    b. 6 seconds after passing the 3 o'clock position

    c. 10 seconds after passing the 3 o'clock position

    d. 14 seconds after passing the 3 o'clock position

    e. 23 seconds after passing the 3 o'clock position

    f. 49 seconds after passing the 3 o'clock position

# The Height and the Sine

**Jason Weinstock presents the formula his group developed to express Al and Betty's height off the ground as the Ferris wheel turns.**

You've seen that trigonometric functions can be helpful in describing where the platform is as it goes around on the Ferris wheel. But the basic right-triangle definitions of these functions only work for acute angles.

In the next portion of this unit, you'll explore how to extend the definition of the sine function to arbitrary angles and how to use this extended definition to get a general formula for the platform's height.

# At Certain Points in Time

In *Homework 2: As the Ferris Wheel Turns*, you found the height of the platform after it had turned for specific amounts of time. You probably saw that this was easiest to do if the platform was in the first quadrant.

Your task in this activity is to generalize that work for the case of the first quadrant. (*Reminder:* The basic facts about the Ferris wheel are the same as in *Homework 2: As the Ferris Wheel Turns.* In particular, the period is 40 seconds, so the platform remains in the first quadrant for the first 10 seconds.)

1. Suppose the Ferris wheel has been turning for $t$ seconds, with $0 < t < 10$. Represent the platform's height off the ground as $h$, and find a formula for $h$ in terms of $t$.

2. Verify your "first-quadrant formula" using your results from Questions 4a ($t = 1$) and 4b ($t = 6$) of *Homework 2: As the Ferris Wheel Turns.*

# A Clear View

As you may remember, the Ferris wheel at the amusement park where Al and Betty like to ride has a radius of 15 feet, and its center is 20 feet above ground level. (This is not the same Ferris wheel as the one at the circus.)

The Ferris wheel turns with a constant angular speed and takes 24 seconds for a complete turn.

There is a 13-foot fence around the amusement park, but once you get above the fence, there is a wonderful view.

1. What percentage of the time are Al and Betty above the height of the fence? (You may want to find out how long they are above the height of the fence during each complete turn of the Ferris wheel.)

2. How would the answer to Question 1 change if the period were different from 24 seconds?

# Extending the Sine

If the Ferris wheel turns counterclockwise at a constant angular speed of 9 degrees per second and the platform passes the 3 o'clock position at $t = 0$, then the platform will remain in the first quadrant through $t = 10$.

During this time interval, the platform's height above the ground is given by the formula

$$h = 65 + 50 \sin 9t$$

But the right-triangle definition of the sine function makes sense only for acute angles. To make this formula work for all values of $t$, we need to extend the definition of the sine function to include all angles.

## The Coordinate Setting

Although the context of the Ferris wheel could be used to develop this extended definition, the standard approach uses a more abstract setting, which makes it easier to apply the definition to other situations.

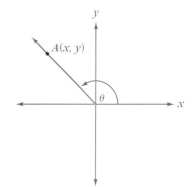

Specifically, the angle is placed within a coordinate system, with its vertex at the origin, and is measured counterclockwise from the positive direction of the $x$-axis. The goal is to express $\sin \theta$ in terms of the $x$- and $y$-coordinates of a point on the ray defining the angle, such as the point $A$ shown in the first diagram. ($A$ is assumed to be different from the origin.)

When $\theta$ is an acute angle, we get a diagram like the second one. It's helpful to introduce the letter $r$ to represent the distance from $A$ to the origin, which is also the length of the hypotenuse of the right triangle.

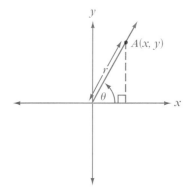

*Continued on next page*

Based on the right-triangle definition of the sine function, we get

$$\sin \theta = \frac{y}{r}$$

Mathematicians use this equation to extend the definition of the sine function to arbitrary angles. That is, they define $\sin \theta$ as the ratio $\frac{y}{r}$ for *any* angle $\theta$. (*Comment:* This automatically means that the new definition agrees with the old one for acute angles.)

## The Ferris Wheel Analogy

You can think of $A$ as a point on the circular path of the Ferris wheel, as shown in this diagram. In this context, $r$ corresponds to the radius of the Ferris wheel, and $y$ corresponds to the platform's height *relative to the center of the Ferris wheel*.

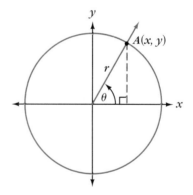

# Testing the Definition

You've seen that the sine function can be extended to all angles using the *xy*-coordinate system. The big question is this.

> *If you use this coordinate definition of the sine function, does the platform height formula work for all angles?*

Your task in this activity is to investigate that question.

1. If the platform has been turning for 25 seconds, then it has moved through an angle of 225° and is now in the third quadrant of its cycle.

   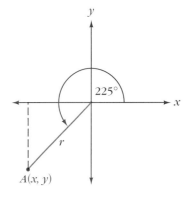

   **a.** Use a diagram like the one shown here to find the value of sin 225° based on the coordinate definition of the sine function. (*Suggestion:* Choose a specific value for *r*. Then find the value of *y* using the right triangle in the third quadrant.)

   **b.** Substitute your answer from Question 1a into the expression 65 + 50 sin 225°.

   **c.** Explain why your answer in Question 1b is a reasonable answer for the position of the platform after 25 seconds.

   **d.** Verify that your calculator gives the same value for sin 225° that you found in Question 1a.

2. Go through a sequence of steps like those in Question 1, but use the value *t* = 32, which places the platform in the fourth quadrant. ( You will first need to find the actual height of the platform for *t* = 32.)

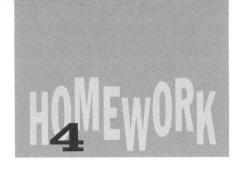

# HOMEWORK 4

# Graphing the Ferris Wheel

1. Plot individual points to create a graph showing the platform's height, $h$, as a function of the time elapsed, $t$. Explain how you get the value for $h$ for each point you plot. Your graph should show the first 80 seconds of the Ferris wheel's movement.

   *Reminder:* Use the same basic information about the Ferris wheel as in *Homework 2: As the Ferris Wheel Turns.*

2. Describe in words how this graph would change if you made each of the changes described in Questions 2a through 2c. Treat each question as a separate problem, changing only the item mentioned in that problem and keeping the rest of the information as in Question 1.

   **a.** How would the graph change if the radius of the Ferris wheel was smaller?

   **b.** How would the graph change if the Ferris wheel was turning faster (that is, if the period was shorter)?

   **c.** How would the graph change if you measured height with respect to the center of the Ferris wheel instead of with respect to the ground? (For example, if the platform was 40 feet above the ground, you would treat this as a height of $-25$, because 40 feet above the ground is 25 feet below the center of the Ferris wheel.)

# Ferris Wheel Graph Variations

In Question 1 of *Homework 4: Graphing the Ferris Wheel*, you made a graph showing how the height of the platform depends on the amount of time that has elapsed since the Ferris wheel began moving. That graph was based on the "standard" Ferris wheel, which has a radius of 50 feet and a period of 40 seconds and whose center is 65 feet off the ground. The accompanying diagram shows two periods of that graph.

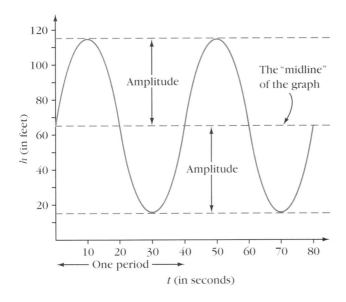

The dashed line at $h = 65$ shows the "midline" of the graph. The graph is as much above this line as it is below. The other dashed lines, at $h = 115$ and $h = 15$, show the maximum and minimum of the graph. The distance from the midline to the maximum or minimum is called the **amplitude** of the graph, so the amplitude here is 50.

In Question 2 of *Homework 4: Graphing the Ferris Wheel*, you described in words how the graph would

*Continued on next page*

change if you made certain changes in the Ferris wheel itself. In this assignment, you will look at those changes in more detail.

Treat each question as a separate problem, changing only the item mentioned in that problem and keeping the rest of the information as in the standard Ferris wheel. Use the same scale for all of your graphs so that you can make easy visual comparisons.

1. a. Pick a specific new value, less than 50 feet, for the radius, and draw the graph.

   b. Give an equation for your new graph, expressing $h$ (the height of the platform, in feet) in terms of $t$ (the time elapsed, in seconds).

   c. Pick a specific value for $t$ and verify that your equation from Question 1b gives the value you used in your graph for that value of $t$.

2. a. Pick a specific new value, less than 40 seconds, for the period, and draw the graph.

   b. Give an equation for your new graph, expressing $h$ in terms of $t$.

   c. Pick a specific value for $t$ and verify that your equation from Question 2b gives the value you used in your graph for that value of $t$.

3. Suppose the Ferris wheel were set up inside a large hole so that its center was exactly level with the ground.

   a. Draw the graph based on this change.

   b. Give an equation for your new graph, expressing $h$ in terms of $t$.

   c. Pick a specific value for $t$ and verify that your equation from Question 3b gives the value you used in your graph for that value of $t$.

# The "Plain" Sine Graph

The height of the Ferris wheel platform is given by a formula that involves the sine function. In previous assignments, you've graphed this height function and examined how the graph changes as various details of the Ferris wheel itself are changed.

In this activity, you'll look at the graph of the "plain" sine function.

1. Draw the graph of the function defined by the equation $z = \sin \theta$ for values of $\theta$ from $-360°$ to $720°$. (*Note:* To avoid confusion with $x$- and $y$-coordinates or the idea that $t$ represents time and $h$ represents height on the Ferris wheel, we are introducing new variables here.)

2. What is the amplitude of this function?

3. What is the period of this function? Why is the sine function periodic?

4. What are the $\theta$-intercepts of the graph?

5. What values of $\theta$ make $\sin \theta$ a maximum? What values of $\theta$ make $\sin \theta$ a minimum?

6. If the equation $h = \sin t$ describes the "platform height function" for some Ferris wheel, what are the specifications of that Ferris wheel? (That is, what are its radius, its period, and the height of its center?) Indicate any ways in which it differs from the "standard" Ferris wheel described in *Homework 2: As the Ferris Wheel Turns*.

# Sand Castles

Shelly loves to build elaborate sand castles at the beach. Her big problem is that her sand castles take a long time to build, and they often get swept away by the in-coming tide.

Shelly is planning another trip to the beach next week. She decides to pay attention to the tides so that she can plan her castle building and have as much time as possible.

The beach slopes gradually up from the ocean toward the parking lot. Shelly considers the waterline to be "high" if the water comes farther up the beach, leaving less sandy area visible. She considers the waterline to be "low" if there is more sandy area visible on the beach. Shelly likes to build as close to the water as possible because the damp sand is better for building.

According to Shelly's analysis, the level of the water on the beach for the day of her trip will fit this equation.

$$w(t) = 20 \sin 29t$$

In this equation, $w(t)$ represents how far the waterline is above or below its average position. The distance is measured in feet, and $t$ represents the number of hours elapsed since midnight.

In the case shown in the accompanying diagram, the water has come up above its average position, and $w(t)$ is positive.

*Continued on next page*

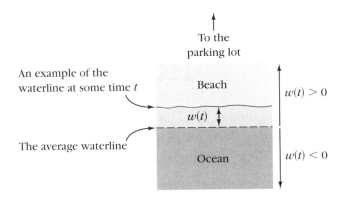

An example of the
waterline at some time $t$

Beach

$w(t) > 0$

$w(t)$

The average waterline

Ocean

$w(t) < 0$

To the
parking lot

1. Graph the waterline function for a 24-hour period.

2. **a.** What is the highest up the beach (compared to its average position) that the waterline will be during the day? (This is called *high tide*.)

   **b.** What is the lowest that the waterline will be during the day? (This is called *low tide*.)

3. Suppose Shelly plans to build her castle right on the average waterline just as the water has moved below that line. How much time will she have to build her castle before the water returns and destroys her work?

4. Suppose Shelly wants to build her castle 10 feet below the average waterline. What is the maximum amount of time she can arrange to have to make her castle?

5. Suppose Shelly decides she needs only two hours to build and admire her castle. What is the lowest point on the beach where she can build it?

# More Beach Adventures

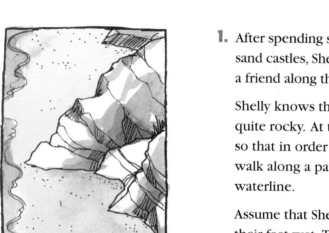

1. After spending some of the day at the beach building sand castles, Shelly wants to take an evening walk with a friend along the shoreline.

   Shelly knows that at one place along the shore, it is quite rocky. At that point, the rocks jut into the ocean so that in order to pass around them, a person has to walk along a path that is 14 feet below the average waterline.

   Assume that Shelly and her friend don't want to get their feet wet. Therefore, they need to take their walk during the time when the waterline is 14 feet or more below the average waterline.

   What is the time period during which they can take their walk?

   (Recall that the position of the waterline over the course of the day is given by the equation $w(t) = 20 \sin 29t$, where the distance is measured in feet and $t$ represents the number of hours elapsed since midnight.)

*Continued on next page*

**2.** Shelly often finds herself looking for numbers whose sine is a given value. This question asks you to do the same. Your solutions should all be between $-360°$ and $360°$. In Questions 2a and 2b, find exact values for $\theta$. In Questions 2c and 2d, give $\theta$ to the nearest degree.

  **a.** Find three values of $\theta$, other than $15°$, such that $\sin \theta = \sin 15°$.

  **b.** Find three values of $\theta$ such that $\sin \theta = -\sin 60°$.

  **c.** Find three values of $\theta$ such that $\sin \theta = 0.5$.

  **d.** Find three values of $\theta$ such that $\sin \theta = -0.71$.

# Paving Patterns

Al and Betty are hard at work. They are helping Al's family lay paving stones for a path along the side of their house.

The path is to be exactly 2 feet wide. Each paving stone is rectangular, with the dimensions 1 foot by 2 feet.

You might think this would be easy: simply lay one stone after another across the path. But there is more than one way to lay out the stones.

For example, a 3-foot section of the path could use any of the three arrangements shown here.

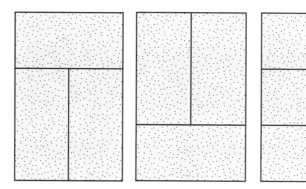

*Important:* These arrangements are all considered different, even though the first two are very similar.

So, of course, Al and Betty want to know how many different ways there are to lay out the stones. The path is 20 feet long altogether.

Al and Betty started to analyze this situation by using 1-inch-by-2-inch plastic tiles set out within a 2-inch-by-20-inch rectangle, but they soon were overwhelmed by all the possibilities.

*Continued on next page*

Can you help? You might want to start with shorter paths and look for patterns in the number of cases.

*Note:* You do not need to show the patterns themselves, except to explain your thinking. Your focus should be on *how many* patterns there are for a given length path.

## Write-up

1. *Problem statement*

2. *Process*

3. *Results*

   - Give the numerical results for any specific cases you studied.

   - Give any general formulas that you found, even if you aren't sure of them.

   - Give any explanations you found for your formulas.

4. *Evaluation*

5. *Self-assessment*

# Falling, Falling, Falling

*Dan Medina and Mike Rodricks add to their carefully kept notes a formula for the height of an object falling from rest.*

The diver on the Ferris wheel doesn't simply go round and round. At some point, the assistant lets go and the diver begins his fall.

How long will the diver be in the air? You'll have to learn some principles of physics, as well as use some mathematics, to answer this question. The question is complicated by the fact that the diver does not fall at a constant speed.

# Distance with Changing Speed

**1.** Curt drove from 1 p.m. to 3 p.m. at an average speed of 50 miles per hour and then drove from 3 p.m. to 6 p.m. at an average speed of 60 miles per hour.

   **a.** Draw a graph showing Curt's speed as a function of time for the entire period from 1 p.m. to 6 p.m., treating his speed as constant for each of the two time periods—from 1 p.m. to 3 p.m. and from 3 p.m. to 6 p.m.

   **b.** Describe how to use areas in this graph to represent the total distance he traveled.

**2.** Consider a runner who is going at a steady 20 feet per second. At exactly noon, he starts to increase his speed. His speed increases at a constant rate so that 20 seconds later, he is going 30 feet per second.

   **a.** Graph the runner's speed as a function of time for this 20-second time interval.

   **b.** Calculate his average speed for this 20-second interval.

   **c.** Explain how to use area to find the total distance he runs during this 20-second interval.

# Acceleration Variations and a Sine Summary

## Part I: Acceleration Variations

In Question 2 of *Distance with Changing Speed*, you considered the case of a person running with constant acceleration. In other words, the runner's speed was increasing at a constant rate.

In that problem, the runner's speed went from 20 feet per second to 30 feet per second over a 20-second time interval. The accompanying diagram shows a graph of the speed as a function of time.

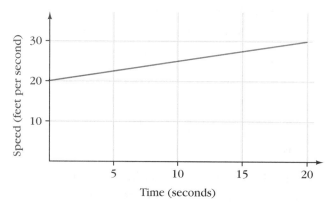

That problem illustrated an important principle.

**If an object is traveling with constant acceleration, then its average speed over any time interval is the average of its beginning speed and its final speed during that time interval.**

*Continued on next page*

According to this principle, the runner's average speed for the 20-second interval was exactly 25 feet per second, which is the average of 20 feet per second (the beginning speed) and 30 feet per second (the final speed).

Your task in Part I of this assignment is to describe three variations on this situation. In each case, the runner's speed should increase, as before, from 20 feet per second to 30 feet per second over the same 20-second time interval. But in your examples, *the runner's acceleration should not be constant*.

For each example, show a graph of the runner's speed in terms of time.

- Give an example in which the runner's average speed is *more than* the average of the beginning speed and the final speed.

- Give an example in which the runner's average speed is *less than* the average of the beginning speed and the final speed.

- Give an example in which the runner's average speed is *equal to* the average of the beginning speed and the final speed. (Remember that even with this example, the runner's acceleration should not be constant.)

## Part II: A Sine Summary

The idea of extending the sine function to all angles—not merely acute angles—is an important concept. Your task in Part II of this assignment is to reflect on your work with the sine function. Your written work should include these things.

- A summary of what you have learned so far about this idea

- Any questions you still have about this extended sine function

- An explanation of how the extension of the sine function helps with the solution of the unit problem

# Free Fall

As long as people can remember, objects have been falling. But it wasn't until the sixteenth and seventeenth centuries that scientists fully understood the physics and mathematics of falling objects.

The Italian physicist Galileo Galilei (1564-1642) is one of those credited with figuring out the laws of gravitational fall based on experiments. The English physicist Isaac Newton (1642-1727) developed a broader theory of gravitation to explain Galileo's observations.

## Free-Falling Objects

Using both experiments and theoretical analysis, physicists have confirmed this principle.

**Falling objects have constant acceleration.**

This principle assumes that there is no air resistance or other complicating factor to interfere with the object's fall. That is, the principle describes the behavior of *free-falling* objects. In this unit, you should assume, unless told otherwise, that all falling objects are falling freely.

The analysis by physicists is even more precise than this broad principle.

> **The instantaneous speed of a freely falling object increases approximately 32 feet per second for each second of its fall.**

*Continued on next page*

## Starting from Rest

The simplest case occurs when the object starts from rest, that is, when its speed is zero when $t = 0$. In this case, the object's instantaneous speed after 1 second is 32 feet per second; after 2 seconds, its instantaneous speed is 64 feet per second; and so on.

## From Acceleration to Distance

Your task in this activity is to use the principles just stated to express the distance an object falls in terms of the amount of time it has been falling. You should assume that the object is dropped from rest and falls freely.

1. **a.** How fast is the object going at $t = 5$?

   **b.** How far does the object fall in its first 5 seconds?

2. Generalize your work from Question 1 to develop a formula for how far the object falls in its first $t$ seconds.

3. Suppose the object starts from a height of $h$ feet. What is its height after $t$ seconds? (Assume that the object has not yet reached the ground.)

4. Use your result from Question 3 to find an expression in terms of $h$ for the amount of time it would take for the object to reach the ground.

Now apply your work to a simple version of the circus act.

5. Suppose the platform is fixed at 90 feet above the ground, the diver falls freely from rest, and the level of the water in the tub is 8 feet above the ground. How long will it take for the diver to reach the water?

# Not So Spectacular

The circus owner decided that to save money, he would fill in for the diver from time to time.

This did not end up being a very good idea because the owner was not an experienced diver, so he could not safely fall large distances. In fact, he refused to be dropped from more than 25 feet above the ground. He also insisted that there be a huge tub of water under him at all times.

Your task is to find all possible times when the owner will be 25 feet from the ground. You may want to describe the complete set of possibilities by writing an algebraic expression for $t$.

*Reminder:* Here are the basic facts about the Ferris wheel.

• The radius is 50 feet.

• The center of the Ferris wheel is 65 feet off the ground.

• The Ferris wheel turns counterclockwise at a constant angular speed, with a period of 40 seconds.

• The Ferris wheel is at the 3 o'clock position when it starts moving.

# A Practice Jump

After some not-so-high practice dives by the circus owner, the circus decided to do a practice run of the show with the diver himself. But they decided to set it up so that they would not have to worry about a moving cart.

Instead, the cart containing the tub of water was placed directly under the Ferris wheel's 11 o'clock position. As usual, the platform passed the 3 o'clock position at $t = 0$.

1. How many seconds will it take for the platform to reach the 11 o'clock position?

2. What is the diver's height off the ground when he is at the 11 o'clock position?

One purpose of this practice run was to see how long it would take for the diver to fall into the water. You should be able to predict this, based on the formula that an object falling freely from rest takes $\sqrt{\frac{h}{16}}$ seconds to fall $h$ feet. (Assume that the diver is falling freely from rest.)

3. How long will it take from the time the diver is released until he hits the water? (Don't forget that the water level in the cart is 8 feet above the ground.)

4. More generally, suppose the assistant lets go $W$ seconds after the Ferris wheel starts turning. (Here, $W$ stands for "wheel time.") Assuming that the cart is in the right place, how long will the diver be in the air before he hits the water?

# Moving Left and Right

*Ken Hoffman and Jeff Tung address the fact that the turning Ferris wheel also involves horizontal movement of the diver's platform.*

Thus far, you have mostly been considering the platform's position and the diver's motion in the vertical dimension. But as the Ferris wheel turns, the platform is also moving to the left or right, and the cart is moving steadily to the right (once it gets started).

The key to a successful dive is to have the cart at the right place at the right time, which means it's now time for you to consider the horizontal dimension of the Ferris wheel problem.

# Cart Travel Time

Thus far in the unit, you've focused mainly on the position and motion of the diver. So where's the cart of water in all this?

Recall that the cart starts moving when the Ferris wheel passes the 3 o'clock position. The goal is to have the cart be in the correct position when the diver reaches the level of the water in the cart. In this activity, you will consider only the cart's *travel time*.

Suppose the assistant lets go of the diver $W$ seconds after the Ferris wheel passes the 3 o'clock position. Write an expression in terms of $W$ for the length of time the cart will have traveled from the moment it starts until the moment when the diver reaches the level of the water.

---

# Where Does He Land?

Earlier in the unit, you found that the expression
$65 + 50 \sin 9t$ gives the diver's height off the ground
while he is still on the platform. But what about the diver's
*horizontal* position? This will be crucial in determining
whether he lands in the tub of water on the moving cart.

To describe the diver's horizontal position, we will use a
horizontal coordinate system as shown below, in which an
object's $x$-coordinate is based on its distance (in feet) to
the right or left of the center of the Ferris wheel, with
objects to the right of the Ferris wheel considered as
having positive $x$-coordinates.

For instance, in this coordinate system, the platform and
diver have an $x$-coordinate of 50 when the platform
passes the 3 o'clock position. Similarly, the cart starts its
motion with an $x$-coordinate of $-240$, because it is
initially 240 feet to the left of the center of the base of
the Ferris wheel.

As usual, assume that the platform passes the 3 o'clock
position at $t = 0$. Recall also that the Ferris wheel turns
counterclockwise at a constant rate with a period
of 40 seconds. Further, assume that the diver falls straight
down once he is released.

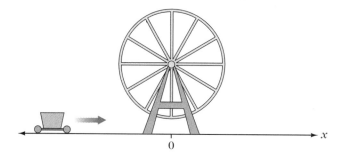

*Continued on next page*

1. Where will the diver land if he is released at each of these times?

   **a.** at $t = 3$

   **b.** at $t = 7$

   **c.** at $t = 12$

   **d.** at $t = 26$

   **e.** at $t = 37$

2. Sketch a graph giving the platform's $x$-coordinate as a function of $t$. Your graph should cover two complete turns of the Ferris wheel—that is, from $t = 0$ to $t = 80$.

   *Note:* Although the platform's $x$-coordinate represents its horizontal position, in this context $x$ is a function of $t$. That is, $t$ is the independent variable and $x$ is the dependent variable. Therefore, the value of $t$ should be shown on the horizontal axis of your graph, and the value of $x$ on the vertical axis.

# First-Quadrant Platform

In Question 1 of *Homework 11: Where Does He Land?*, you found the $x$-coordinate of the diver's landing position for a variety of specific cases.

At the moment when the diver is released, his $x$-coordinate is the same as the $x$-coordinate of the platform, and in Question 2 of that assignment, you sketched a graph of the platform's $x$-coordinate as a function of $t$.

Now focus specifically on values of $t$ between 0 and 10, so that the platform is still in the first quadrant. Develop an equation that gives the platform's $x$-coordinate in terms of $t$.

# Carts and Periodic Problems

## Part I: Where's the Cart?

In *Homework 11: Where Does He Land?*, you looked at the horizontal coordinate of the diver as he falls. You also need to know where the cart is while the diver is falling and, especially, where it is when the diver reaches the water.

Recall that the cart begins 240 feet to the left of the base of the Ferris wheel, so its $x$-coordinate at $t = 0$ is $-240$. The cart moves to the right at 15 feet per second and begins moving at that speed at $t = 0$.

Based on this information, find the cart's $x$-coordinate at the moment when the diver reaches the water level.

## Part II: Periodic Problems

In this unit, you have seen that the height of a platform on a Ferris wheel represents a periodic function. You have encountered periodic functions before. For instance, the swinging of a pendulum is periodic motion, and the bob's

distance from the center line is a periodic function of time (assuming that the pendulum isn't slowing down).

1. Describe three other situations that you believe are periodic. For each example, explain what is repeating and give the period for the repetition.

2. Sketch graphs of at least two of the periodic situations you described in Question 1.

# Generalizing the Platform

If the Ferris wheel platform starts at the 3 o'clock position, with the Ferris wheel turning counterclockwise at a constant angular speed of 9 degrees per second, then the platform will remain in the first quadrant through $t = 10$.

During this time interval, the platform's $x$-coordinate is given by the formula

$$x = 50 \cos 9t$$

This formula specifically uses the fact that the radius of the Ferris wheel is 50 feet and that the angular speed is 9 degrees per second. But the right-triangle definition of the cosine function applies only to acute angles, so this formula isn't defined if $t$ is greater than 10. Your task in this activity is to explore how to extend the definition of the cosine function.

## Specific Cases

1. Consider the case $t = 12$.

   **a.** Find the platform's $x$-coordinate when $t = 12$. (This was Question 1c of *Homework 11: Where Does He Land?*) You may want to express your answer in terms of the cosine of some acute angle.

   **b.** What value should you assign to $\cos (9 \cdot 12)$ so that the formula $x = 50 \cos 9t$ gives your answer from Question 1a when you substitute 12 for $t$?

*Continued on next page*

**2.** Consider the case $t = 26$.

    **a.** Find the platform's $x$-coordinate when $t = 26$. (This was Question 1d of *Homework 11: Where Does He Land?*) You may want to express your answer in terms of the cosine of some acute angle.

    **b.** What value should you assign to cos (9 · 26) so that the formula $x = 50 \cos 9t$ gives your answer from Question 2a when you substitute 26 for $t$?

## The General Case

**3.** How can you define cos $\theta$ in a way that makes sense for all angles and that gives the results you needed in Questions 1b and 2b? ( You may want to look at *Extending the Sine.*)

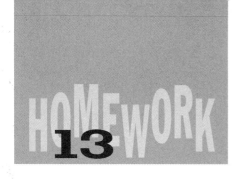

# HOMEWORK 13

# Planning for Formulas

You now have all the parts to the puzzle. You simply have to put the pieces together.

You have formulas that tell you each of these things.

• The diver's height at the moment when he is released

• The diver's $x$-coordinate at the moment when he is released

• The amount of time the diver is falling

• The cart's $x$-coordinate when the diver reaches the water level

All of these quantities can be expressed in terms of $W$, which represents the amount of time the Ferris wheel has been turning at the moment when the diver is released.

Write out each of the formulas just described, and explain each of them clearly, including how the general definitions of sine and cosine and principles about falling objects are used in your formulas.

*Continued on next page*

Also discuss how each of these facts fits into your formulas.

- The Ferris wheel has a radius of 50 feet.

- The center of the Ferris wheel is 65 feet above the ground.

- The Ferris wheel turns counterclockwise at a constant rate, making a complete turn every 40 seconds.

- When the cart starts moving, it is 240 feet to the left of the base of the Ferris wheel.

- The cart moves to the right along the track at a constant speed of 15 feet per second.

- The water level in the cart is 8 feet above the ground.

- When the cart starts moving, the platform is at the 3 o'clock position.

# Finding the Release Time

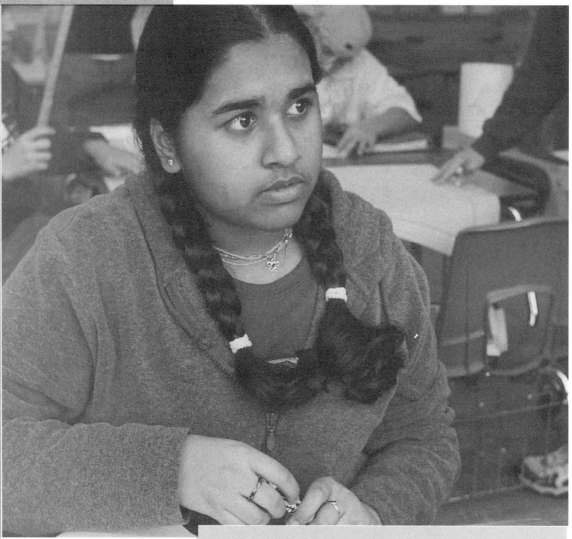

*Shaleen Nand ponders how to pull together all the information she's developed and the different formulas she's collected.*

You have developed a large collection of formulas that explain specific parts of the Ferris wheel problem. Now the time has come to put them all together.

# Moving Cart, Turning Ferris Wheel

Your job is to figure out when the assistant should let go of the diver. Let $t = 0$ represent the moment when the platform passes the 3 o'clock position. Let $W$ represent the number of seconds until the release of the diver. You need to determine the right value for $W$.

In addition to giving the value of $W$, you should also determine these things.

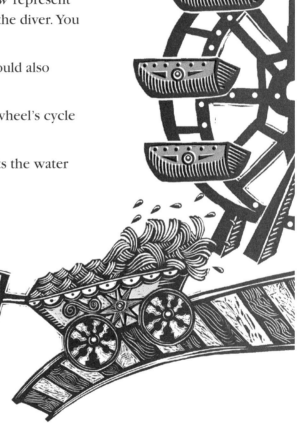

- Where the platform will be in the Ferris wheel's cycle when the diver is dropped

- Where the cart will be when the diver hits the water

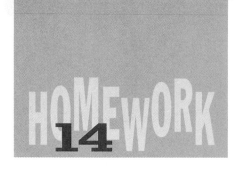

# Putting the Cart Before the Ferris Wheel

What if you could change where the cart started? That might make things a little easier.

In this assignment, assume that all the facts about the Ferris wheel and the cart are the same as usual except for the cart's initial position.

Suppose the diver is released exactly 25 seconds after the Ferris wheel began turning from its 3 o'clock position.

1. What is his $x$-coordinate as he falls?

2. Where should the cart start out so that the diver will fall into the tub of water on the cart? (Assume that the cart still starts to the left of the Ferris wheel and travels to the right at 15 feet per second.)

# What's Your Cosine?

You have seen that we define the cosine function in a manner similar to that for the sine function. If $\theta$ is any angle, we draw a ray from the origin, making a counterclockwise angle of that size with the positive $x$-axis, pick a point $(x, y)$ on the ray (other than the origin), and define $r$ as the distance from $(x, y)$ to the origin, so $r = \sqrt{x^2 + y^2}$. We then define the cosine function for all angles by the equation

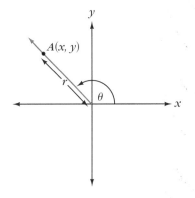

$$\cos \theta = \frac{x}{r}$$

As with the sine function, this definition gives the same values for acute angles as the right-triangle definition. Also like the sine function, the extended cosine function can give the same value for different angles.

**1.** Draw the graph of the function defined by the equation $z = \cos \theta$ for values of $\theta$ from $-360°$ to $720°$, and answer these questions.

    **a.** What is the amplitude of this function?

    **b.** What is the period of this function? Why is the cosine function periodic?

    **c.** What are the $\theta$-intercepts of the graph?

    **d.** What values of $\theta$ make $\cos \theta$ a maximum? What values of $\theta$ make $\cos \theta$ a minimum?

*Continued on next page*

**2.** The questions here are similar to questions about the sine function in *Homework 7: More Beach Adventures.* As in that assignment, your solutions should all be between $-360°$ and $360°$. In Questions 2a and 2b, find exact values for $\theta$. In Questions 2c and 2d, give $\theta$ to the nearest degree.

**a.** Find three values of $\theta$, other than $81°$, such that $\cos \theta = \cos 81°$.

**b.** Find three values of $\theta$ such that $\cos \theta = -\cos 20°$.

**c.** Find three values of $\theta$ such that $\cos \theta = 0.3$.

**d.** Find three values of $\theta$ such that $\cos \theta = -0.48$.

# Find the Ferris Wheel

**1.** Imagine that the equations in Questions 1a and 1b are each thought of as describing the $x$-coordinate of a rider on some Ferris wheel in terms of time, where the rider is at the 3 o'clock position when $t = 0$. (Here, $t$ is in seconds and $x$ is in feet.)

Give the radius, period, and angular speed of the Ferris wheel that each expression represents. (Recall that *angular speed* is the rate at which the Ferris wheel turns and in this situation is given in degrees per second.)

  **a.** $x = 25 \cos 10t$

  **b.** $x = 100 \cos 3t$

**2. a.** Write an expression that would give the $x$-coordinate of a rider on a Ferris wheel that has a smaller radius than the Ferris wheel in Question 1a but a greater angular speed.

  **b.** Describe how the graph for the expression in Question 2a would differ from the graph in Question 1a.

# A Trigonometric Interlude

*The Ferris wheel problem gives Vick Chandra a meaningful context in which to develop trigonometric identities.*

Congratulate yourself on a major achievement — finding out when the assistant should release the diver. Unfortunately, the work in the unit thus far has involved a significant simplification of the problem. If the assistant uses the solution from *Moving Cart, Turning Ferris Wheel,* it could cost the diver his life. So there's still quite a bit of work to do on the Ferris wheel situation.

Before turning to that more complex version of the problem, the unit digresses with some further study of trigonometry, including the introduction of polar coordinates and the development of some important general principles, called *identities*.

# Some Polar Practice

Polar coordinates and rectangular coordinates provide two ways to describe points in the plane. The questions in this activity focus on the relationships between the two systems.

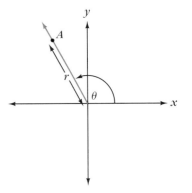

1. **a.** Find the rectangular coordinates for the point whose polar coordinates are $(2, 30°)$.

   **b.** Find the rectangular coordinates for the point whose polar coordinates are $(5, 140°)$.

2. **a.** Find a pair of polar coordinates for the point whose rectangular coordinates are $(8, 2)$.

   **b.** Find a pair of polar coordinates for the point whose rectangular coordinates are $(4, -9)$.

# A Polar Summary

You know that the position of a point in the plane is usually described in terms of coordinates $x$ and $y$, which are called its **rectangular coordinates** (or *Cartesian coordinates*). But a point's position in the plane can also be described in terms of **polar coordinates,** usually represented by the letters $r$ and $\theta$.

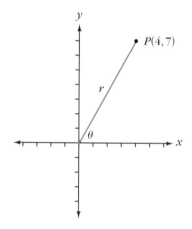

For example, in the accompanying diagram, the point $P$ is shown with rectangular coordinates $(4, 7)$. The variable $r$ represents the distance from $P$ to the origin, and the variable $\theta$ represents the angle made between the positive direction of the $x$-axis and the ray from the origin through $P$ (measured counterclockwise).

You can use the Pythagorean theorem to see that $r = \sqrt{4^2 + 7^2} = \sqrt{65} \approx 8.06$, and you can use one of the trigonometric functions to get $\theta$.

For example, you can use the sine function, whose general definition is $\sin \theta = \frac{y}{r}$. For the point $P$, this equation becomes $\sin \theta = \frac{7}{\sqrt{65}} \approx 0.868$, which gives $\theta \approx 60°$. In other words, the point $P$ can be represented approximately in polar coordinates as $(8.06, 60°)$.

The process can be reversed, starting from the polar coordinates of a point and finding its rectangular coordinates. For instance, in the next diagram, the point $Q$ is shown with polar coordinates $(10, 240°)$.

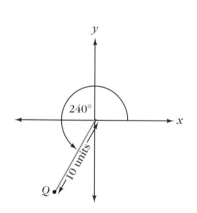

You can use the general definitions of the sine and cosine functions to find the rectangular coordinates of $Q$.

For example, $\sin \theta = \frac{y}{r}$, so $y = r \sin \theta$. Therefore, the $y$-coordinate of $Q$ is $10 \sin 240°$, or approximately $-8.7$.

*Continued on next page*

Similarly, $\cos \theta = \frac{x}{r}$, which gives $x = r \cos \theta$. Therefore, the $x$-coordinate of $Q$ is $10 \cos 240°$, which equals $-5$. Thus, the rectangular coordinates of $Q$ are approximately $(-5, -8.7)$.

## Angles Greater Than 360°

The concept of polar coordinates is complicated by the fact that we do not restrict $\theta$ to angles between $0°$ and $360°$. An angle of $360°$ or more is simply interpreted as representing more than a complete rotation around the origin. For instance, point $P$ could also be represented in polar coordinates as $(8.06, 420°)$, because a counterclockwise rotation of $420°$ from the positive $x$-axis leads to the same ray from the origin as a rotation of $60°$. Similarly, point $Q$ could be represented as $(10, 600°)$, $(10, 960°)$, $(10, 1320°)$, and so on.

## Negative Angles

We also allow the polar coordinate $\theta$ to be negative, by interpreting a negative angle as a *clockwise* rotation from the positive direction of the $x$-axis. For example, the point $Q$ whose polar coordinates are given as $(10, 240°)$ could also be described by the polar coordinates $(10, -120°)$. The negative sign for the angle of $120°$ means that we are going $120°$ in the *clockwise* direction.

*Continued on next page*

## Negative Values for *r*

The final complication for polar coordinates is that we allow negative values for *r*. If *r* is negative, the point lies in the opposite direction from the point with the corresponding positive *r*-value.

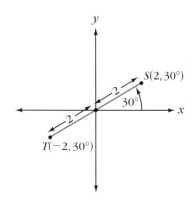

For example, consider the diagram shown here. Suppose point *S*, in the first quadrant, has polar coordinates (2, 30°), and suppose point *T*, in the third quadrant, is in the direction from the origin opposite to *S*, but is also 2 units from the origin. Then *T* can be described by the polar coordinates (−2, 30°).

*Comment:* Point *T* can also be described by the polar coordinates (2, 210°).

## Summary: Multiple Representations

The use of arbitrary angles for θ and of both positive and negative values for *r* means that every point in the plane has infinitely many ways to be represented in polar coordinates. This definitely creates some problems in working with polar coordinates, but it also leads to flexibility. Because points have more than one representation, we sometimes speak of "a polar representation" of a point rather than "the polar coordinates" of the point. For convenience, you might refer to the representation with *r* positive and with θ between 0° and 360° as the "standard" polar representation.

# Polar Coordinates on the Ferris Wheel

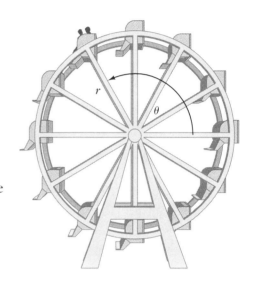

You may find it helpful to think of polar coordinates in terms of the Ferris wheel. To do so, picture the Ferris wheel with its center at the origin of the coordinate system. Then picture a rider on the circumference of the Ferris wheel, starting on the positive part of the $x$-axis and going counterclockwise.

In this model, the rider's $r$-coordinate gives the radius of the Ferris wheel and the rider's $\theta$-coordinate gives the angle through which the rider has turned (starting from the 3 o'clock position). For example, a person on a 30-foot Ferris wheel who has gone one-fourth of the way around has polar coordinates $(30, 90°)$.

1. Suppose a Ferris wheel has a radius of 40 feet and a period of 20 seconds, and the rider passes the 3 o'clock position at $t = 0$. Find both the rectangular coordinates and the "standard" polar coordinates for the rider when $t = 3$ (using the center of the Ferris wheel as the origin).

2. **a.** Find a value of $t$ different from 3 seconds for which the rider would be at the same position as in Question 1.

   **b.** Use your answer to Question 2a to find a different pair of polar coordinates for the position in Question 1.

3. Find general expressions for both the rectangular coordinates and the polar coordinates of a rider's position at time $t$ (using the Ferris wheel from Question 1 with radius 40 feet and period 20 seconds).

# Pythagorean Trigonometry

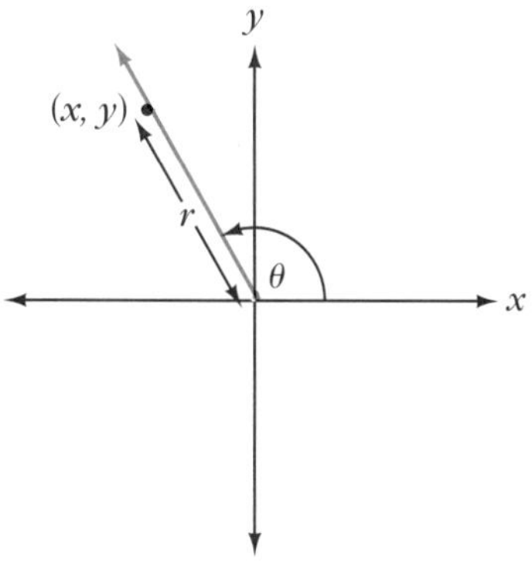

As you have seen, the definitions of the sine and cosine functions are based on a coordinate diagram like the one shown here.

Specifically, to define $\sin \theta$ and $\cos \theta$, we draw a ray from the origin that makes a counterclockwise angle $\theta$ with the positive $x$-axis. Then we pick some point on that ray (other than the origin). We use $r$ to represent the distance from the point to the origin, so $r = \sqrt{x^2 + y^2}$.

If the point has rectangular coordinates $(x, y)$, then we define $\sin \theta$ as the ratio $\frac{y}{r}$ and define $\cos \theta$ as the ratio $\frac{x}{r}$.

Because the ratios $\frac{y}{r}$ and $\frac{x}{r}$ are the same no matter which point on the ray is chosen, we can choose any point that is convenient. One common simplification is to pick the point that lies on the unit circle, which is the circle with radius 1 and center at the origin. Choosing this point simplifies matters because it means that $r = 1$.

1. If the point $(x, y)$ is chosen so that it is on the unit circle, how can you express $x$ and $y$ in terms of $\sin \theta$ and $\cos \theta$?

2. What is the equation of the unit circle? That is, what condition must $x$ and $y$ satisfy if $(x, y)$ is 1 unit from the origin?

3. Use your answers to Questions 1 and 2 to write an equation relating $\sin \theta$ and $\cos \theta$ for points on the unit circle.

4. Choose four different values of $\theta$, one in each quadrant, and verify on a calculator in each case that your equation in Question 3 holds true.

# Coordinate Tangents

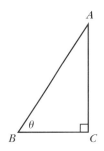

You've developed a way to define the sine and cosine functions for arbitrary angles. Now it's time to look at the tangent.

*Reminder:* For a right triangle such as the one shown here, we define $\tan \theta$ by the formula

$$\tan \theta = \frac{\text{opposite}}{\text{adjacent}}$$

where "opposite" means the length of $\overline{AC}$ and "adjacent" means the length of $\overline{BC}$.

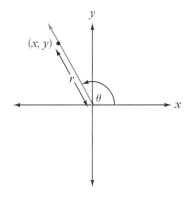

1. Suppose a point in the plane has rectangular coordinates $(x, y)$ and polar coordinates $(r, \theta)$, as in the next diagram. How would you define $\tan \theta$ in terms of $x$ and $y$? Explain and justify your decision.

2. It's helpful to have equations connecting the different trigonometric functions. How can you express $\tan \theta$ in terms of $\sin \theta$ and $\cos \theta$, rather than in terms of the coordinates $x$ and $y$? (*Hint:* Think about how $x$ and $y$ might be expressed in terms of sine, cosine, and $r$.)

3. Find each of these values, based on your definition in Question 1.

   **a.** $\tan 120°$

   **b.** $\tan 230°$

   **c.** $\tan (-50°)$

   **d.** $\tan 385°$

4. Sketch a graph of the equation $z = \tan t$, using $t$ for the horizontal axis and $z$ for the vertical axis. Your graph should include values for $t$ from $-180°$ through $360°$.

# Positions on the Ferris Wheel

In *Pythagorean Trigonometry,* you developed the equation $\cos^2 \theta + \sin^2 \theta = 1$. You saw that this equation is true no matter what value is substituted for the angle $\theta$.

Equations with variables that are true no matter what values are substituted for the variables are called **identities.** In this assignment and in *Homework 19: More Positions on the Ferris Wheel,* you will look at other identities involving the sine and cosine functions. The Ferris wheel model can help in developing and understanding these identities.

The diagram below shows two riders on a Ferris wheel, one at the 1 o'clock position and the other at the 11 o'clock position. The first rider has turned 60° from the 3 o'clock position, and the second has turned 120°.

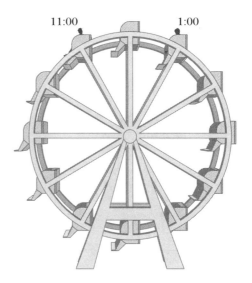

*Continued on next page*

If the radius of the Ferris wheel is 50 feet, then a rider's height, compared to the center of the Ferris wheel, is given by the expression 50 sin $\theta$. But these two riders are at the same height, so 50 sin 60° = 50 sin 120°. Dividing by 50 gives the relationship

$$\sin 60° = \sin 120°$$

The equation sin 60° = sin 120° can be generalized, using the next diagram, to get an identity involving the sine function.

In this diagram, points $A$ and $B$ represent the positions of two riders on a Ferris wheel, so $A$ and $B$ are the same distance from the origin.

The angle $\theta$ represents the angle of turn for a rider at point $A$. You should assume that $A$ and $B$ are at the same height on the Ferris wheel, so the two points have the same $y$-coordinate.

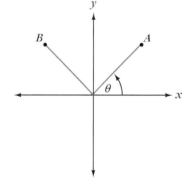

1. Find the angle through which the rider at point $B$ has turned. You should express your answer in terms of $\theta$. (*Hint:* Consider an example, such as $\theta = 20°$, find the angle for point $B$, and then generalize.)

2. Use the fact that $A$ and $B$ are at the same height to write a generalization of the equation sin 60° = sin 120°.

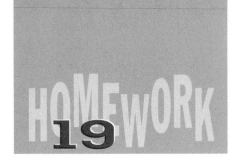

# More Positions on the Ferris Wheel

This assignment continues the topic of trigonometric identities.

## Part I: Clockwise and Counterclockwise

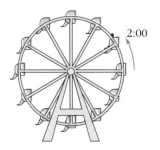

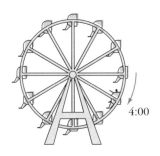

The diagrams here show two Ferris wheel riders. Both started from the 3 o'clock position, but the first turned 30° and is now at the 2 o'clock position, while the second turned −30° and is now at the 4 o'clock position. (Recall that negative angles are interpreted as clockwise motion.)

Assume that the radius of the Ferris wheel is 50 feet, and recall that if a rider turns through an angle $\theta$, then his $x$-coordinate is given by the expression 50 cos $\theta$. Thus, the first rider's $x$-coordinate is 50 cos 30° and the second rider's $x$-coordinate is 50 cos (−30°).

1. **a.** Explain why these two riders have the same $x$-coordinate. That is, why are they the same distance to the right of the center of the Ferris wheel?

   **b.** What does the result in Question 1a tell you about cos 30° and cos (−30°)?

Now consider the general situation. In the diagram shown on the next page, points $C$ and $D$ represent two positions on the same Ferris wheel. In the case of point $C$, the rider has turned through an angle $\theta$. For point $D$, the rider has turned through an angle $-\theta$.

*Continued on next page*

**2. a.** Explain why points $C$ and $D$ have the same $x$-coordinate.

 **b.** Use the diagram and Question 2a to explain why $\cos\theta$ and $\cos(-\theta)$ must be equal.

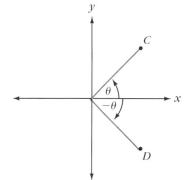

# Part II: From Identity to the Ferris Wheel

In Part I, you started with a situation on the Ferris wheel and generalized it to get a trigonometric identity. In this part of the assignment, your task is to start with the identity and create a Ferris wheel explanation.

Consider the equation $\sin(-\theta) = -\sin\theta$.

 **3.** Substitute specific values for $\theta$ to confirm that the equation is true for those values. Try a variety of values, including angles that are negative and angles that are greater than $360°$.

 **4.** Create a Ferris wheel situation to explain the equation in a manner similar to that used in Part I.

 **5.** Create a coordinate system diagram like that used in Part I to illustrate the situation.

# Initial Motion from the Ferris Wheel

When you finished the activity *Moving Cart, Turning Ferris Wheel,* you may have thought that you had solved the main unit problem. And you were right, sort of. But that activity involved a simplified version of the unit problem, and now you're ready to tackle a more complicated version.

The complication is that when the diver is released from the turning Ferris wheel, he does not fall as if dropped from a stationary Ferris wheel. He is actually moving when he is dropped, and this fact can affect both the speed and

*Continued on next page*

the path of his fall. The final aspect of the unit problem, then, is to figure out how to take this into account.

To get started, the first problem in this assignment is about a situation that involves circular motion but does not involve gravity.

1. You are a skateboard rider. You go to a park that has a merry-go-round such as the one shown in the picture on the preceding page. You hold onto the railing while the merry-go-round spins rapidly, so you are moving in a circular path. Suddenly, you let go of the railing.

   What is the path of your motion?

   (Assume that your skateboard has perfect ball bearings and that the merry-go-round is surrounded by an ideal surface so that there is no friction anywhere to slow you down.)

2. Now think about the Ferris wheel. You are holding onto a railing on the circumference of a Ferris wheel that is turning rapidly. Suddenly, you let go.

   Sketch the path of your fall for at least one position in each quadrant.

# A Falling Start

**Mark Martin tries to visualize what effect the motion of the Ferris wheel will have on the diver's path upon release.**

In *Moving Cart, Turning Ferris Wheel*, you analyzed the Ferris wheel problem as if the diver had fallen "from rest," that is, with no initial velocity. But the diver is moving while he's still on the Ferris wheel, because the platform itself is moving. This means that the diver will have some initial speed at the moment when he is released.

The simplest cases are those in which the diver's initial motion is vertical—either straight up or straight down. These cases require a new look at the formulas related to falling objects, as well as some new ideas about solving equations.

# Look Out Below!

It was Thanksgiving vacation, and many students were going home for the holiday. Maxine heard a voice shout, "Hey, up there! Could you toss me my pillow?"

She glanced out the floor-to-ceiling window of her room in the high-rise dormitory, just in time to see the pillow fly past.

Because pillows are comparatively light for their size, the effect of air resistance on a falling pillow cannot be ignored. For this activity, assume that the falling pillow accelerates at a rate of only 20 feet per second for each second it falls (although this is an oversimplification), and assume that the pillow was traveling at an instantaneous speed of 30 feet per second when Maxine saw it.

**1.** What was the pillow's *instantaneous* speed 1 second after Maxine saw it? Two seconds after Maxine saw it?

**2.** What was the pillow's *average* speed for the first 2 seconds after Maxine saw it?

**3.** How far did the pillow fall during the first 2 seconds after Maxine saw it?

Maxine walked over to the window, looked down to the sidewalk, and saw someone reach over to pick up the pillow. The sidewalk was 200 feet below Maxine's window.

**4.** How long did it take for the pillow to reach the ground from the time Maxine saw it? Give your answer to the nearest tenth of a second.

**5.** Find a general expression for the height of the pillow *t* seconds after Maxine saw it.

---

# So What Happens to the Diver?

You have seen something about what happens to objects when they start out moving in a circular path and are then released. In this assignment, you will look at how these principles affect our circus diver.

In thinking about the questions in this assignment, you may want to pay special attention to the cases in which the diver is released from the 3 o'clock, 6 o'clock, 9 o'clock, or 12 o'clock position.

1. From what release positions will the diver's falling time be increased by his initial motion from the Ferris wheel? From what release positions will it be made shorter?

2. From what release positions will the diver land to the left of his release position? From what release positions will he land to the right?

3. In *Moving Cart, Turning Ferris Wheel*, using the assumption that the diver fell straight down as if dropped from rest, you found that the assistant should hold onto the diver for about 12.3 seconds. (This means the diver will be released between the 12 o'clock and 11 o'clock positions on the Ferris wheel.)

    If you take into account the effect of the Ferris wheel's motion on the diver's fall, do you think the assistant should hold onto the diver longer than 12.3 seconds or let go sooner than that? Explain your reasoning.

# Big Push

Earlier in this unit, you solved the Ferris wheel problem based on the simplifying assumption that once the diver was released, he would fall as if the Ferris wheel had not been moving. But that was a simplification. In this assignment, you will examine in a specific case how the motion of the Ferris wheel would affect the diver's fall.

Here is a summary of some important facts about the Ferris wheel and the cart.

• The Ferris wheel has a radius of 50 feet.

• The center of the Ferris wheel is 65 feet above the ground.

• The Ferris wheel turns counterclockwise at a constant rate, making a complete turn every 40 seconds.

• The water level in the cart is 8 feet above the ground.

Imagine that the assistant lets go of the diver at the 9 o'clock position. Because the platform is moving downward at that moment, the diver will also be moving downward as he is released. His initial speed when released is equal to the speed with which he was moving when he was on the platform, which you already have found to be $2.5\pi$ feet per second, or approximately 7.85 feet per second.

Once released, the diver's speed will increase, just as with any object falling freely, so that his speed increases by 32 feet per second for each second that he falls. For now, assume that the tub of water is in a fixed position, directly below the diver's point of release.

*Continued on next page*

1. What is the diver's height *t* seconds after he is released?

2. How long will it take from the time the diver is released until he reaches the water?

3. How long would it take the diver to fall to the water level if the Ferris wheel was not moving and the diver was simply dropped, with no initial speed, from the 9 o'clock position?

4. Compare the answers to Questions 2 and 3, and determine how far the cart would travel during a time interval equal to the difference between those answers.

# Finding with the Formula

Sometimes, when repeating the same process over and over, it becomes easier simply to develop a formula that gives you the same result.

Solving quadratic equations is one of those situations. You can use the method of completing the square for individual examples, but there is a general formula that saves the trouble of repeating the steps each time.

The **general quadratic equation** is usually written in the form $ax^2 + bx + c = 0$, where the coefficients $a$, $b$, and $c$ can be any numbers except that $a$ cannot be 0. If you apply the method of completing the square to the general quadratic equation, you get an expression, called the **quadratic formula,** that gives the solutions in terms of the coefficients $a$, $b$, and $c$. The general result says

If $ax^2 + bx + c = 0$, and $a \neq 0$,

then $x = \dfrac{-b \pm \sqrt{b^2 - 4ac}}{2a}$

That is, if $x$ is a solution to the equation $ax^2 + bx + c = 0$, then $x$ must be equal to either $\dfrac{-b + \sqrt{b^2 - 4ac}}{2a}$ or $\dfrac{-b - \sqrt{b^2 - 4ac}}{2a}$. (You will develop a proof for this formula as part of the unit *Know How* later in Year 4.)

1. Use the quadratic formula to solve the equation $x^2 - 3x - 28 = 0$, and check your answers.

2. Use the quadratic formula to solve the equation $3x^2 + 7x = 5$, and check your answers.

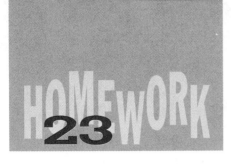

# Using Your ABC's

**1.** Find all the solutions to each of these equations using the quadratic formula. Give exact solutions, using square roots if necessary. Also approximate the solutions to the nearest tenth, and use the equations to confirm that these solutions seem correct.

**a.** $x^2 + 7x + 12 = 0$

**b.** $x^2 - 3x - 8 = 0$

**c.** $2x^2 + 5x - 1 = 0$

**d.** $2x^2 - 3x + 4 = 0$

**2.** Set up and solve quadratic equations to answer each of these questions.

**a.** A rectangle with one side 5 feet longer than the other has an area of 126 square feet. What are the dimensions of the rectangle?

**b.** A right triangle has one leg 6 inches shorter than the other, and its hypotenuse is 13 inches long. How long are the legs of the right triangle?

**c.** An object is thrown up into the air off the roof of a building so that its height $h$ in feet after $t$ seconds is given by the equation $h = 90 + 50t - 16t^2$. When will the object be 120 feet high?

# Three O'Clock Drop

In *Homework 22: Big Push*, you found the falling time for the diver if he was released from the 9 o'clock position. In that problem, the motion of the Ferris wheel gave him an initial downward velocity as he was released, and you saw that it took him less time to fall than if he had been dropped from a stationary Ferris wheel.

Now consider what happens if he is released from the 3 o'clock position. Because the platform is moving upward at that moment, the diver will start off with an initial upward motion. As in *Homework 22: Big Push*, his initial speed is equal to the speed with which he was moving when he was on the platform.

Assume again that the cart is in a fixed position, directly below the diver's point of release.

1. How long will it take from the time the diver is released until he reaches the water?

2. How long would it have taken him to reach the water if he had been released from a motionless Ferris wheel (at the 3 o'clock position)?

# Up, Down, Splat!

Melissa's science class is having a contest. The contest is to see who can build a container that will keep an egg from breaking when dropped from the school window.

Melissa is quite confident of her contraption. She leans out the window, which is 25 feet off the ground, and hurls her egg container straight up in the air with an initial velocity of 35 feet per second. (Consider velocity upward to be positive.)

Assume that the egg container's velocity is affected by gravity in the usual way. That is, the velocity decreases by 32 feet per second for each second the egg container travels.

1. How long does it take for the egg container to hit the ground?

2. At what speed does the egg container hit the ground?

# Falling Time for Vertical Motion

In each of several recent problems, you figured out how long it took for an object to fall a certain distance if it started with a certain initial velocity.

When an object is falling freely, its height after $t$ seconds is given by the expression $h + vt - 16t^2$, where $h$ is the object's initial height and $v$ is the object's initial velocity (where upward motion is considered positive). Finding out when the object hits the ground is equivalent to solving the equation $h + vt - 16t^2 = 0$.

In specific cases, you might be able to solve the equation (or get a good estimate) by guess-and-check or with a graph. But when you solve the main unit problem, you will not have numerical values for $h$ or $v$, because those coefficients will be expressed in terms of the variable $W$. In preparation for dealing with that complication, your task here is to solve the equation $h + vt - 16t^2 = 0$ *in terms of h and v.*

1. Rewrite the equation $h + vt - 16t^2 = 0$ so that it is in the form $ax^2 + bx + c = 0$, with a positive value for $a$.

2. Use the quadratic formula to solve the equation from Question 1. Your answer should give $t$ in terms of $h$ and $v$.

3. Which of the two solutions you found in Question 2 will give you a positive value for $t$? (*Hint:* Assume that $h$ is a positive number.)

# 26-30

# Components of Velocity

*Stephanie Skangos and DeAnna DelCarlo consider what other directions are possible for the diver upon release from a moving Ferris wheel.*

In several recent problems, you've considered objects with either positive or negative initial *vertical* velocity. But when the Ferris wheel diver is released by his assistant, he might go sideways as well as up or down.

How do you take this into consideration? How do the vertical and horizontal parts of his motion work together? How does gravity fit into the picture? These are the sorts of questions you need to answer next.

# High Noon

At the moment when the diver reaches the 12 o'clock position, his motion on the Ferris wheel is purely horizontal. So if he were released at that moment, he would not be moving up or down at all, but only to the side.

Because of this, the diver's falling time is the same as if he had fallen from a motionless Ferris wheel. But the diver will continue to move sideways throughout his fall. His sideways motion will be at the same rate as the platform was moving.

Use these facts, together with everything else you know about the Ferris wheel and the motion of falling objects, to answer these questions.

1. How long will it take for the diver to reach the water level?

2. How far to the left of center will the diver be when he is 8 feet off the ground? In other words, what is his $x$-coordinate when he reaches the water level?

# Leap of Faith

"Fire! Fire!" someone yells from down the hall. You reach for the doorknob to look out the door, but remember to feel the door first. It's a good thing you did, because the door is extremely hot, and the fire is working its way through the door.

You are able to go out the window and make your way up to the roof, which is flat. As you contemplate your situation, the firefighters arrive.

"Jump! Jump!" they shout, and they hold out a rescue net. The net is 30 feet below you, and its center is 15 feet out from the edge of the roof.

You decide to run straight off the edge of the roof, hoping to go just far enough out so as to land in the middle of the net.

1. At what speed should you be going as you leave the roof in order to hit the center of the net? (*Hint:* First figure out how long it will take you to fall the 30 feet.)

2. If the net is 10 feet across, then what range of speeds will allow you to hit the net?

# The Ideal Skateboard

Let's consider a skateboard situation like the one you looked at in *Homework 20: Initial Motion from the Ferris Wheel*. Imagine a skateboarder holding onto a spinning platform in the middle of a skateboard park.

Here are some more details.

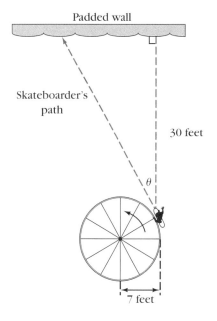

- The platform has a 7-foot radius and makes a complete turn every 6 seconds.

- The skateboarder lets go from the 2 o'clock position, as shown in the diagram.

The skateboarder will eventually crash into the padded wall. At the moment of release from the platform, the skateboarder is 30 feet from this wall.

1. How fast will the skateboarder travel? (Assume as before that there is no friction.)

2. What is the angle shown in the diagram as θ?

3. How much closer will the skateboarder be to the wall after each second? In other words, what is the "toward the wall" component of the skateboarder's velocity?

4. Use your answer to Question 3 to find out how long it takes for the skateboarder to reach the wall.

5. Find the actual distance the skateboarder travels, and use that information (and the answer to Question 1) as an alternate way to find out how long it takes for the skateboarder to reach the wall.

# Racing the River

One year, as part of their River Days Festival, the citizens of River City were looking for a new event to raise money for charity.

Someone had the idea of having groups of swimmers from the two local high schools, River High and New High, compete in a race across the river. The town would raise money by charging admission to watch the race.

The river was generally quite calm during the time when the festival was held, so the planners could safely assume that the current would not affect the swimmers. The race was set to take place along a straight stretch where the river was 200 meters across.

Representatives of New High pointed out that the River City swim team was based at River High, so most of the best swimmers attended that school. To even things out, the planners decided to make the River High swimmers swim farther. The arrangement they agreed on was that the New High swimmers would swim directly across the river while the River High swimmers would swim at an angle of 45° off from the direct route across the river, as shown here.

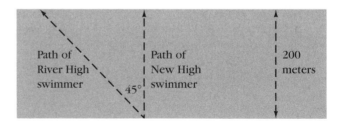

*Continued on next page*

---

Interactive Mathematics Program

1. If a River High swimmer swims at a rate of 1.5 meters per second, how long will it take the swimmer to get to the other side? (*Hint:* How far does a swimmer from River High need to swim to get across?)

2. How fast must a New High swimmer swim to get to the other side at the same time as the River High swimmer?

The next year, the planners decided that the New High swimmers did not need such a big advantage. They changed the path for the River High swimmers so it would make only a 30° angle with the direct route, as shown here.

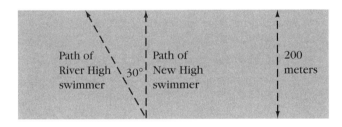

3. Assume that a River High swimmer still swims at a rate of 1.5 meters per second. Based on this new rate and new angle, answer these questions.

   a. How far does a swimmer from River High need to swim to get across?

   b. How long will it take a River High swimmer to get to the other side?

   c. How fast must a New High swimmer swim to get to the other side at the same time as the River High swimmer?

# One O'Clock Without Gravity

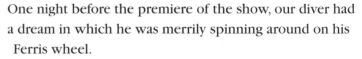

One night before the premiere of the show, our diver had a dream in which he was merrily spinning around on his Ferris wheel.

In this dream, the assistant decided to let go when the diver was at the 1 o'clock position. But in the diver's dream, there was no gravity, so he sailed up and to the left at a constant speed, in a direction that was tangent to the Ferris wheel's circumference at the 1 o'clock position.

Of course, his speed was the same as his speed when he was on the platform. As you know, that speed is $2.5\pi$ feet per second, which is approximately 7.85 feet per second.

**1.** What was the vertical component of his velocity? That is, how much height did he gain each second? (As in other recent problems, you will need to find the angle labeled $\theta$.)

**2.** What was the horizontal component of his velocity? (Remember that movement to the left is considered negative.)

# General Velocities

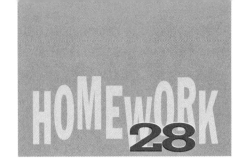

As you have seen, although the speed of the Ferris wheel is constant, the vertical and horizontal components of the diver's velocity are different for different positions in the cycle.

1. What are the horizontal and vertical components of the diver's initial velocity if he is released after 8 seconds on the Ferris wheel? (*Reminder:* The period for the Ferris wheel is 40 seconds. Also remember that for horizontal velocity, the positive direction is to the right.)

To generalize the situation, suppose that the diver is released after $W$ seconds.

2. First, assume that $W$ is less than 10, so that the diver is still in the first quadrant when he is released. Write an expression in terms of $W$ for the vertical and horizontal components of the diver's initial velocity.

3. Now consider all values of $W$ from 0 to 40.

   a. For which values of $W$ is the vertical component of velocity positive? For which values is it negative? For which values is it zero?

   b. For which values of $W$ is the horizontal component of velocity positive? For which values is it negative? For which values is it zero?

# Release at Any Angle

In *Homework 28: General Velocities*, you examined the components of the diver's initial velocity if he was released within the first quadrant, perhaps using a diagram like the one shown here. This analysis leads to these two equations.

• Vertical component of velocity = 7.85 cos 9*W*

• Horizontal component of velocity = −7.85 sin 9*W*

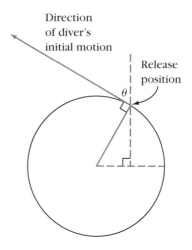

Direction of diver's initial motion

Release position

$\theta$

Here, *W* is the time elapsed between when the platform passes the 3 o'clock position and when the diver is released, so the angle of turn is 9*W*.

If the diver is still in the first quadrant, then *W* is less than 10 seconds. But what if *W* is more than 10 seconds? Do these formulas still work?

1. a. Assume for the moment that the formula for the vertical component of the diver's initial velocity is correct for all values of *W*. Use that formula to make a graph showing this vertical component of velocity as a function of *W*, from *W* = 0 to *W* = 40.

*Continued on next page*

**b.** In Question 3a of *Homework 28: General Velocities,* you examined how the sign of the vertical component of velocity depends on *W.* Is your graph consistent with your results from that question? Explain.

**c.** For values of *W* between 10 and 20, the diver is released in the second quadrant. Describe how the *size* of the vertical component of velocity changes as *W* increases from 10 to 20. Is your graph consistent with your description? Explain.

**d.** Find the vertical component of velocity for *W* = 11 and *W* = 12. (Use diagrams as needed to show how to get these values. Do not simply rely on the formula.) Are these values consistent with your conclusions in Question 1c? Explain.

**2.** Go through a sequence of steps for the horizontal component of velocity similar to Questions 1a through 1d.

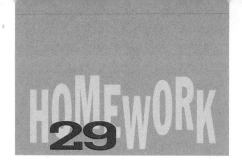

# A Portfolio of Formulas

To find the correct release time for the circus act, you could take a guess, see what would happen if the diver were released after that much time, and then adjust your guess until you got a "close enough" answer. Or you could develop an equation whose solution would be the answer to the question of when to release the diver.

In preparation for the second approach, your assignment here is to compile a portfolio of all the formulas that have been developed in this unit that might be helpful in solving the unit problem. This portfolio of formulas will be included in your general portfolio for this unit.

Each formula should be appropriately labeled and each variable clearly defined so that you will know what the formula represents.

# Moving Diver at Two O'Clock

In *Three O'Clock Drop,* you were asked how long it would take for the diver to reach the water level if he were released at the 3 o'clock position. In that problem, the diver's initial velocity had only a vertical component.

In *High Noon,* you answered the same question for a situation in which the initial velocity was all horizontal.

In this activity, you will examine a Ferris wheel situation in which the diver's initial velocity is a blend of vertical and horizontal motion. Specifically, suppose the diver is released after a 30° turn on the Ferris wheel, at the moment when the platform reaches the 2 o'clock position.

1. How long does it take for the diver to reach the water level?

2. What is the diver's *x*-coordinate when he reaches the water level? (Remember that you are using a horizontal coordinate system in which the base of the Ferris wheel is zero and the positive direction is to the right.)

3. What is the cart's *x*-coordinate when the diver reaches the water level?

# The Danger of Simplification

In *Moving Cart, Turning Ferris Wheel*, you found that the assistant should release the diver after approximately 12.3 seconds. But that analysis was based on the idea that the diver would fall straight down as if released from a stationary platform.

You've now seen that the motion of the Ferris wheel would cause the diver to have an initial speed of $2.5\pi$ feet per second (or about 7.85 feet per second), and that this initial speed has both a vertical and a horizontal component. This initial velocity affects both the amount of time the diver is in the air and the diver's $x$-coordinate at the moment when he reaches the water level.

To learn whether the initial velocity really matters, suppose the diver were released after 12.3 seconds (the time found in *Moving Cart, Turning Ferris Wheel*), and answer these questions, taking the initial velocity into account.

1. How long would it take for the diver to fall to the level of the water in the cart?

2. What would the diver's $x$-coordinate be at the moment when he reached the water level?

3. What would the cart's $x$-coordinate be at the moment when the diver reached the water level?

4. Would the diver land in the tub of water?

# High Dive Concluded

*Stephanie Wood, Elizabeth Graf, Sharon Wang, and Rochak Nevpane work on their group's presentation of the unit's final solution.*

At last! It's time to put all the formulas and ideas together and figure out when the assistant should let go of the diver. The diver will certainly appreciate your hard work and careful analysis.

# High Dive Concluded

It's now time, once again, to solve the main unit problem. Although you solved a simplified version in *Moving Cart, Turning Ferris Wheel,* now you will take into account that the diver leaves the Ferris wheel with some initial velocity, with both horizontal and vertical components.

Again, here are the details about the setup for the act.

• The Ferris wheel has a radius of 50 feet.

• The center of the Ferris wheel is 65 feet above the ground.

• The Ferris wheel turns counterclockwise at a constant rate, making a complete turn every 40 seconds.

• When the cart starts moving, it is 240 feet to the left of the base of the Ferris wheel.

• The cart moves to the right along the track at a constant speed of 15 feet per second.

• The water level in the cart is 8 feet above the ground.

• The cart starts moving as the platform passes the 3 o'clock position.

As before, let $t = 0$ represent the time when the Ferris wheel passes the 3 o'clock position, which is also when the cart begins moving. Let $W$ represent the number of seconds that elapse between $t = 0$ and the moment when the diver is released. Your assignment is to answer this question.

> *For what choice of W will the diver land in the tub of water?*

*Continued on next page*

Interactive Mathematics Program

Feel free to use all the accumulated formulas and shortcuts that you have developed over the course of this unit.

Your group should prepare an oral report on your conclusions and how you reached them. You should also prepare your own write-up of your solution.

*Suggestion:* You may want to give variable names to complex expressions that are part of your solution. If you use a calculator to graph an equation, you can define some of these expressions as preliminary functions and then express your main equation or function in terms of these.

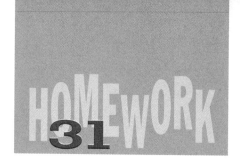

# A Trigonometric Reflection

While you're pondering the final details of the solution to the unit problem, take time to think about what you have learned about trigonometry in this unit.

In addition to the general definitions of the sine and cosine functions, you have also learned some things about graphs, trigonometric identities, and polar coordinates.

Compile a summary of these ideas. You should include diagrams as needed to explain any formulas. You do not need to include formulas that relate only to the unit problem, but you should use ideas about the Ferris wheel to explain ideas about trigonometry.

# *High Dive* Portfolio

Now that *High Dive* is completed, it is time to put together your portfolio for the unit. Compiling this portfolio has three parts.

* Writing a cover letter in which you summarize the unit

* Choosing papers to include from your work in this unit

* Discussing your personal mathematical growth in this unit

## Cover Letter for *High Dive*

Look back over *High Dive* and describe the central problem of the unit and the main mathematical ideas. This description should give an overview of how the key ideas, such as extending the sine and cosine functions and finding falling-time functions, were developed and how they were used to solve the central problem.

In compiling your portfolio, you will select some activities that you think were important in developing the key ideas of this unit. Your cover letter should include an explanation of why you selected the particular items.

*Continued on next page*

## Selecting Papers from *High Dive*

Your portfolio for *High Dive* should contain these items:

• *"High Dive" Concluded*

• A Problem of the Week

Select one of the POWs you completed in this unit (*Tower of Hanoi* or *Paving Patterns*)

• *Homework 29: A Portfolio of Formulas*

• *Homework 31: A Trigonometric Reflection*

• Other key activities

Identify two concepts that you think were important in this unit. For each concept, choose one or two activities that helped improve your understanding, and explain how the activity helped.

## Personal Growth

Your cover letter for *High Dive* describes how the mathematical ideas develop in the unit. As part of your portfolio, write about your own personal development during this unit. You may want to address this question.

> *How do you feel about your ability to solve a problem that is as complex and that has as many components as the "High Dive" problem?*

You should include here any other thoughts about your experiences with this unit that you want to share with a reader of your portfolio.

# Appendix

# Supplemental Problems

The supplemental problems in *High Dive* focus primarily on the trigonometric functions and their relationship with the Ferris wheel situation. Other activities look at the use of derivatives to understand issues in this unit. Here are some examples.

- *A Shifted Ferris Wheel* examines how changing the "starting time" for the Ferris wheel would affect the function describing the platform's height.

- *Polar Equations* and *Circular Sine* continue the work with polar coordinates.

- *The Derivative of Position* uses derivatives to get insight into the formula for the height of a falling object, while *Derivative Components* uses derivatives to understand the vertical and horizontal components of the diver's initial velocity.

# Mr. Ferris and His Wheel

The Ferris wheel is named after its inventor, George Washington Gale Ferris.

Most of us have probably either ridden on or watched a Ferris wheel at some point in our lives. But even though the Ferris wheel turns within our own memories, it's unlikely that we have looked into its fascinating history. Here are some questions about the Ferris wheel that you may want to research. Who was George Ferris? Where was he raised and educated? How did he come to invent the Ferris wheel? What was the first Ferris wheel made of? How did the invention of the Ferris wheel change Ferris's life? Did Ferris make any other notable inventions?

You may want to expand this topic to a broader study of amusement park rides or some other aspect of carnivals and fairs.

# A Shifted Ferris Wheel

In the main unit problem, the diver's platform is at the 3 o'clock position when the cart starts moving. Based on using this moment as $t = 0$, the platform's height after $t$ seconds is given by the expression $65 + 50 \sin 9t$.

Suppose instead that at $t = 0$, the platform was at the 6 o'clock position.

1. Find an expression that would give the platform's height as a function of $t$.

2. Sketch the graph of the height function, and compare it to the graph for the main unit problem.

3. Consider other positions for the Ferris wheel at $t = 0$, and describe in general how changing the position affects the function describing the platform's height.

---

# Prisoner Revisited

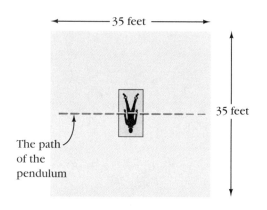

35 feet

35 feet

The path of the pendulum

Do you remember the prisoner from the Year 1 unit *The Pit and the Pendulum*? Well, he's back.

This time, he is lying on the table in the middle of a square prison cell that is 35 feet by 35 feet, again with a pendulum moving back and forth above him, as shown here. (There are no rats in this cell.) As before, the pendulum has a blade at its end. This time, the length of the pendulum does not change, but the table is gradually rising, moving the prisoner up toward the blade.

As he lies there, the prisoner notices that the pendulum's motion is following a sine-like pattern as it swings back and forth. Specifically, the pendulum's horizontal distance $p(t)$ from the center of the cell (measured in feet) is given by the function

$$p(t) = 15 \sin 60t$$

where $t$ is the number of seconds the pendulum has been swinging.

The accompanying diagram shows this horizontal distance, viewed from the front of the cell. (This diagram is not drawn to scale.)

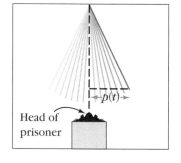

$p(t)$

Head of prisoner

*Continued on next page*

Suddenly, a friend of the prisoner appears in the adjacent cell. The friend rushes over to the bars that separate the two cells, so that the pendulum swings alternately toward him and away from him, as shown below. (This is an overhead view.)

The prisoner's friend realizes that if the pendulum comes within 3 feet of the bars between the cells, he can reach through the bars, grab onto the pendulum, and stop its motion.

1. Will the pendulum come close enough to the bars between the cells so that the prisoner's friend can reach it? Explain your answer.

2. If so, for how long will the pendulum be in the friend's range each time it comes by?

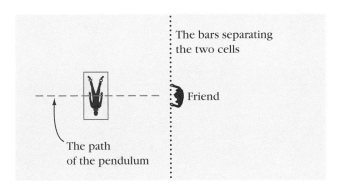

Interactive Mathematics Program

# Lightning at the Beach on Jupiter

As you may have noticed, the three variables of *rate*, *time*, and *distance* are closely related to one another.

In the problems in this assignment, you are given information about two of these variables. Your task is to find out the value for the third.

*Continued on next page*

1. Light travels at about 186,000 miles per second. Jupiter is about 483,000,000 miles from the sun. (It's sometimes closer and sometimes farther away, but we'll use this average distance.)

   How long does it take for light to get from the sun to Jupiter?

2. Amparo wants to spend the day at the beach, which is 100 miles away. She leaves at 8:00 in the morning and needs to be home by 7:00 that evening.

   If she wants to have 6 hours at the beach, what should be her average speed for the trip?

3. You see a flash of lightning. About 6 seconds later, you hear the crash of thunder. Assume that the light reaches you instantly and that the sound travels at about 1100 feet per second. (The exact speed of sound depends on atmospheric conditions like temperature.)

   How far away was the lightning?

4. What general relationships exist among rate, distance, and time?

5. How do the concepts of rate, distance, and time relate to the main unit problem?

# SUPPLEMENTAL PROBLEM

# The Derivative of Position

In *Free Fall*, you developed an important general principle about free-falling objects. Here is the principle.

> **If an object falls freely from rest from a height of $h$ feet, then its height after $t$ seconds is approximately $h - 16t^2$ feet.**

This principle builds on the fact from physics that a free-falling object accelerates at approximately 32 feet per second for each second it falls.

Your task in this activity is to confirm the formula $h - 16t^2$ using derivatives, by showing that if an object's height fits this formula, then its acceleration will actually be 32 feet per second for each second it falls.

1. Suppose, as just described, that a certain object is moving downward so that its height $f(t)$ after $t$ seconds is given by the equation $f(t) = h - 16t^2$.

   **a.** At what rate is the object's height changing at $t = 1$? That is, what is the object's instantaneous velocity at $t = 1$?

   **b.** Explain why the number you found in Question 1a is the same as the derivative of $f$ at $t = 1$.

2. **a.** Find the derivative of $f$ at $t = 2$, at $t = 5$, and at $t = 10$.

   **b.** Based on your answers to Questions 1a and 2a, give a general expression for $f'(t)$ in terms of $t$.

3. What does your result from Question 2b say about the object's acceleration?

# Polar Equations

Over the years, you've worked with many equations involving $x$ and $y$ and found the graphs of those equations. The graph of such an equation consists of all those points whose rectangular coordinates fit the equation.

For example, the point with rectangular coordinates $(3, 4)$ is on the graph of the equation $5x - 2y = 7$ because $5 \cdot 3 - 2 \cdot 4 = 7$.

You can also find the graphs for equations involving polar equations. As with equations using $x$ and $y$, the graph of an equation involving $r$ and $\theta$ consists of those points whose polar coordinates fit the given equation.

For example, the point with polar coordinates $(3, 90°)$ is on the graph of the equation $r + \sin \theta = 4$ because $3 + \sin 90° = 4$.

For each of these equations, first find some number pairs for $r$ and $\theta$ that fit the equation. Then use those number pairs as polar coordinates and plot the points they represent. Finally, use these points to sketch a graph of the equation. Find more solutions if you need them in order to get a good idea of what the graph should look like.

**1.** $r = \theta$

**2.** $r = \cos \theta$

**3.** $r = 2$ (*Hint:* Where's $\theta$? Think about equations like $x = 3$.)

**4.** $\theta = 20°$ (*Hint:* See the hint for Question 3.)

# SUPPLEMENTAL
PROBLEM

# Circular Sine

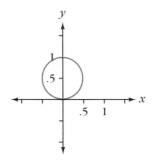

If you were to plot some points for the polar coordinate equation $r = \sin \theta$ and then connect them, you might find that the graph looked something like the diagram shown here. It appears to be a circle, but it's hard to tell for sure merely from plotting a bunch of points and connecting them with a freehand sketch.

Your challenge in this problem is to show that the graph of the polar equation $r = \sin \theta$ is definitely a circle.

1. If this graph is a circle, what are the rectangular coordinates of its center and what is its radius?

2. What is the rectangular equation for the circle whose center and radius you found in Question 1? (*Hint:* Suppose a point $(x, y)$ is on this circle. Use the Pythagorean theorem to get an equation for the distance from this point to the center of the circle.)

3. How can you use the relationships between rectangular and polar coordinates to see that the rectangular equation for Question 2 is equivalent to the polar equation $r = \sin \theta$?

# A Polar Exploration

If you worked on the supplemental problem *Polar Equations*, you may have seen that the graphs of simple polar equations, such as $r = \theta$, can give very different graphs from simple equations with rectangular coordinates.

The diagram below shows one of the interesting graphs that you can get from a fairly simple polar equation.

Your assignment on this problem is to investigate graphs and equations using polar coordinates.

Feel free to consult a trigonometry textbook for ideas of interesting equations to explore. Your report on this problem should indicate any references you used and show clearly which ideas came from other books and which were your own.

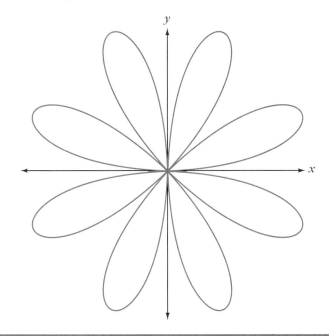

# SUPPLEMENTAL
## PROBLEM

# A Shift in Sine

You have observed that the graphs of the functions $z = \sin t$ and $z = \cos t$ are quite similar. One way to describe the relationship is that if you "shift" the graph of the sine function 90° to the left, you get the graph of the cosine function.

**1.** Express this relationship between the graphs as a trigonometric identity, writing $\sin \theta$ as the cosine of a different angle.

**2.** Prove the identity you found in Question 1. (*Suggestion:* Use the relationship $\sin \theta = \cos (90° - \theta)$.)

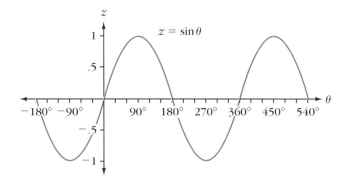

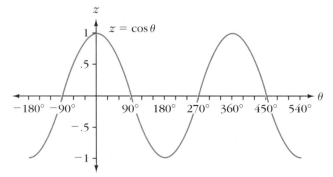

# More Pythagorean Trigonometry

The Pythagorean theorem states that in a right triangle such as the one shown here, the lengths of the sides satisfy the equation $a^2 + b^2 = c^2$.

The sine and cosine functions are defined for right triangles by the equations $\sin \theta = \frac{b}{c}$ and $\cos \theta = \frac{a}{c}$.

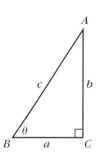

In *Pythagorean Trigonometry,* you developed an identity involving the sine and cosine functions that resembles the statement of the Pythagorean theorem.

1. State that identity and explain it for acute angles based on the equations $a^2 + b^2 = c^2$, $\sin \theta = \frac{b}{c}$, and $\cos \theta = \frac{a}{c}$.

2. Develop similar identities involving the other trigonometric functions—tangent, cotangent, secant, and cosecant—based on the definitions $\tan \theta = \frac{b}{a}$, $\cot \theta = \frac{a}{b}$, $\sec \theta = \frac{c}{a}$, and $\csc \theta = \frac{c}{b}$.

# SUPPLEMENTAL
## PROBLEM

# Derivative Components

In our standard Ferris wheel, the radius is 50 feet, the Ferris wheel turns counterclockwise at a constant rate with a period of 40 seconds, the center of the Ferris wheel is 65 feet off the ground, and the platform is at the 3 o'clock position at $t = 0$.

Based on these facts, you developed the formula that the platform's height off the ground after $t$ seconds is given by the equation $h(t) = 65 + 50 \sin 9t$.

Of course, this platform is moving, so its height is constantly changing. You found that the vertical component of the platform's velocity is given by the expression $2.5\pi \cos 9t$. Your task in this activity is to confirm this relationship using derivatives.

1. **a.** Pick a specific value for $t$.

   **b.** Find $h(t)$ for that value of $t$.

   **c.** Find the rate at which the height is changing by finding $h'(t)$ for that value of $t$.

2. Compare your answer to Question 1c with the value of the expression $2.5\pi \cos 9t$.

3. Repeat Questions 1 and 2 for a different value of $t$.

4. Explain why the observations you made in Questions 2 and 3 should hold true.

5. Develop a similar sequence of steps to confirm that the horizontal component of the platform's velocity is $-2.5\pi \sin 9t$.

# As the Cube Turns

# Picture This!

*Stephanie Wood and Elizabeth Graf begin the unit by conferring about how to draw pictures on the graphing calculator.*

Did you ever wonder how animators create all of those wonderful effects you see on the movie screen? In this unit, you will learn the mathematics behind computer animation and create your own animation programs on a graphing calculator.

You begin this unit by discovering how to use your calculator to draw pictures.

# Picture This!

Your goal today is to learn about drawing pictures on your graphing calculator, which is the first step toward making a turning cube on the calculator.

You can begin simply by experimenting with different keys or menus on the calculator. You may want to read parts of the calculator instruction manual or look up ideas in its index or table of contents. You can also ask other students for ideas.

Take careful notes on your own discoveries and on ideas you get from fellow students. You may appreciate these notes later in the unit as you work on the turning cube program or on your project.

# "A Sticky Gum Problem" Revisited

Do you remember Ms. Hernandez and her twins? They were the main characters in a Year 1 POW called "A Sticky Gum Problem" (in the unit *The Game of Pig*). This POW involves a variation on that POW.

## The Original POW

To refresh your memory, here's the initial scenario from the Year 1 POW.

> Every time Ms. Hernandez passed a gum ball machine, her twins each wanted to get a gum ball, and they insisted on getting gum balls of the same color. Gum balls cost a penny each, and Ms. Hernandez had no control over which color she would get.

First, Ms. Hernandez and the twins passed a gum ball machine with only two colors. Then they came across a machine with three colors. In each case, you needed to find out the maximum amount Ms. Hernandez might have to spend in order to satisfy her twins.

Then Mr. Hodges came by the three-color gum ball machine. He had triplets, and so he needed to get three gum balls that were the same color. You needed to find the maximum amount Mr. Hodges might have to spend in order to satisfy his triplets.

Finally, you were asked to generalize the problem. Your goal was to find a formula that would work for any number of colors and any number of children. Your formula needed to tell you the maximum amount that the parent might have to spend to provide each of the children with a gum ball of the same color.

*Continued on next page*

1. Before starting on the new problem, re-create the generalization for the old one.

   a. Find a formula for the maximum amount a parent might have to spend in terms of the number of colors and the number of children.

   b. Provide a proof of your generalization. That is, give a convincing argument to show that your formula is correct.

## Some New Gum Ball Problems

Ms. Hernandez' twins have grown up a bit in the last three years, and they have changed in some ways. Now they each insist on getting a gum ball of a *different* color from the other twin. (Gum balls are still a penny each.)

One day, Ms. Hernandez and the twins passed a gum ball machine that contained exactly 20 gum balls: 8 yellow, 7 red, and 5 black. As before, Ms. Hernandez could not control which gum ball would come out of the machine.

2. If each twin wanted one gum ball, what's the maximum amount that Ms. Hernandez might have to spend so that the twins could each get a different color? Prove your answer.

3. Because the twins have grown, they now have bigger mouths, so sometimes they each want two gum balls. The two gum balls each twin gets must be the same color, so the flavors match, but one twin's pair of gum balls have to be a different color from the pair the other twin gets.

What's the maximum amount that Ms. Hernandez might have to spend? Prove your answer.

*Continued on next page*

# New Generalizations

Now, make at least three generalizations about these new problems. You get to decide exactly what you want to generalize. Here are some options.

- Generalize the number of children.

- Generalize the number of gum balls each child wants.

- Generalize the number of gum balls of each color.

- Generalize the number of colors in the machine.

Your formula or procedure should tell you how to find the maximum amount that the parent might have to spend to provide all the children with the particular number of gum balls with each child getting gum balls of a different color.

Write a proof for each generalization you create. As a grand finale, try to generalize all of these variables.

# Write-up

Your write-up for this problem should begin with the formula and proof for Question 1 and the answers (with proofs) for Questions 2 and 3.

Then present each generalization you found for the new type of problem, with a proof for each generalization. Also explain how you arrived at each generalization and how you discovered your proof.

Adapted from "A Sticky Gum Problem" in *aha! Insight* by Martin Gardner, W. H. Freeman and Company, New York City/San Francisco, 1978.

# Starting Sticky Gum

Read *POW 3: "A Sticky Gum Problem" Revisited*.

Assume that a parent comes across a gum ball machine containing many gum balls of several colors, and needs to provide each of several children with a gum ball of the same color.

**1.** (This is Question 1 of the POW.)

    **a.** Find a formula for the maximum amount a parent might have to spend in terms of the number of colors in the gum ball machine and the number of children.

    **b.** Provide a proof of your generalization. That is, give a convincing argument to show that your formula is correct.

Suppose Ms. Hernandez and the twins passed a gum ball machine that contained 20 gum balls: 8 yellow ones, 7 red ones, and 5 black ones.

    **2.** (This is Question 2 of the POW.) If each twin wanted one gum ball, what's the maximum amount that Ms. Hernandez might have to spend so that the twins could each get a *different* color? Prove your answer.

    **3.** Identify any questions you have about what is expected in the POW.

# Programming Without a Calculator

Every programming language uses very specific syntax and commands. This formal programming language is often called *programming code,* and the code for a particular task is likely to vary from one calculator model to another.

Programmers often begin with "plain-language" descriptions of what they want to do. Then they turn those descriptions into programming code.

Over the course of this unit, you will have several assignments asking you to write or interpret plain-language programs. Each of these programs will begin with a title line, and each command will begin on a new line. You will also sometimes be asked to turn a plain-language program into programming code, as in Question 2 of this assignment.

1. Read through the steps of the plain-language program shown on the next page, and then draw on graph paper what should appear on the calculator screen when the program is run. (Assume that the calculator has an appropriate viewing rectangle.)

*Continued on next page*

**Program: LINES**

Clear the screen

Draw a line segment connecting (−4, −2)
to (2, −2)

Draw a line segment connecting (−4, 2) to (−1, 3)

Draw a line segment connecting (−1, 3) to (1, 5)

Draw a line segment connecting (2, −2) to (4, 0)

Draw a line segment connecting (1, 5) to (4, 4)

Draw a line segment connecting (1, 5) to (−2, 4)

Draw a line segment connecting (−4, 2) to (−2, 4)

Draw a line segment connecting (4, 4) to (4, 0)

Draw a line segment connecting (−1, 3) to (2, 2)

Draw a line segment connecting (−4, 2)
to (−4, −2)

Draw a line segment connecting (2, 2) to (4, 4)

Draw a line segment connecting (2, −2) to (2, 2)

*Note:* If you don't get something that looks like a real picture, you've probably made a mistake somewhere and should check your work.

2. Turn the plain-language program of Question 1 into programming code. In other words, write the program lines you would enter into your calculator to get the drawing you got for Question 1.

3. Add some more commands to the program you wrote in Question 2 in order to improve the rather dull picture. Then draw what should appear on the calculator screen when you run your improved program.

# Programming Loops

*Rebecca Yaeger writes a report about her work so far in determining how to rotate a cube.*

You may think of a loop as something you make with a shoelace or a piece of string, but it is also a handy device in writing programs for computers or calculators. Loops allow you to repeat the same set of instructions as many times as you like.

Over the next several days, you will use loops to simplify the work of writing a program and to create the illusion of motion.

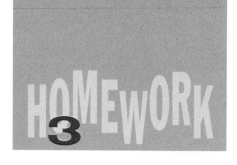

# Learning the Loops

The For/End combination of instructions can be used to do lots of interesting things. Your job is to figure out how it all works, both in the plain-language version and in the version using programming code for your calculator.

*Note:* To show the overall structure of the program more clearly, it's helpful to indent the body of the loop. The plain-language programs in this and later assignments use that format, and start each step of the body of the loop with a bullet (the symbol •).

1. Describe what will happen when you run a calculator program based on this plain-language program.

---
**Program: LOOP1**

For T from 1 to 5
  • Display "HELLO" on the screen
End the T loop

2. Describe what will happen when you run a calculator program based on this plain-language program.

---
**Program: FRUITLOOP**

For A from 1 to 5
  • Display "LEMON" on the screen
  • For B from 1 to 3
    • Display "LIME" on the screen
  • End the B loop
End the A loop

*Continued on next page*

**3.** Sketch what the calculator should show when you run a program based on this plain-language description.

### Program: LOOP2

For G from 3 to 10
- Draw a line segment from (G, G) to (G+3, G+1)

End the G loop

**4.** Write a short program (in programming code, using a For/End loop) that you think will draw something interesting. Describe in words what you think it will draw.

# An Animated Shape

Your task in this activity is to write a program to create and animate a shape on your calculator. As you progress, write down any questions you have about writing programs for animation. Keep in mind that you are trying to create the illusion of motion.

1. First, draw your shape on graph paper. Make it very simple! Your picture should have no more than five line segments or pieces.

2. Next, write out the program code to have the calculator draw your shape. (You may want to begin with a plain-language program.)

3. a. Draw the same shape on graph paper in a new location, near the first.

   b. Write additional program instructions to make it appear that your shape has moved to its new location.

   c. Repeat steps 3a and 3b several times, changing the position of your shape slightly each time.

4. Enter your program into the calculator and run it. Locate and correct errors if the program doesn't run as you would like.

# A Flip Book

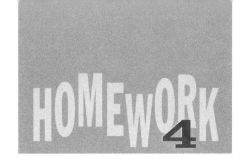

A *flip book* is a device consisting of a series of pictures, each slightly different from the previous one. The pictures are drawn on index cards (or something similar) so that you can flip through them to create the illusion of movement like animation.

1. Create a simple flip book of your own. (You don't have to be a great artist to complete this assignment. A moving rectangle or a rolling ball is okay. On the other hand, if you like drawing, let yourself have fun with this.)

2. Explain how you think this assignment is related to the unit.

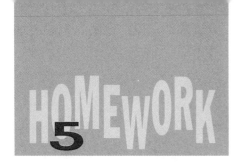

# Movin' On

It's often helpful to have a "setup" program at the beginning of a calculator program. This setup program might adjust the viewing window, clear the screen, and so on.

From now on, we will include a line that simply says "Setup program" in all plain-language programs that involve screen graphics. When you translate such programs into code, you will need to give details for the setup program.

1. **a.** Use drawings on graph paper to describe the result of this plain-language calculator program.

   ### Program: SEGMENTS

   Setup program

   For S from 1 to 5

   - Clear the screen
   - Let T be 3 more than S
   - Let U be 6 more than S
   - Draw a line segment from (S, S) to (T, T)
   - Draw a line segment from (T, T) to (U, S)
   - Draw a line segment from (U, S) to (S, S)
   - Delay

   End the S loop

   **b.** Create programming code for the plain-language program in Question 1a. Include an appropriate setup program. (You can write the setup program using plain-language instructions, if necessary.)

2. Make a general list of components that you would include in a setup program. (This may include items that were not needed in Question 1b.)

# Some Back and Forth

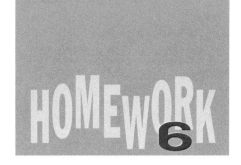

1. The sequence of graphs here shows a line segment going back and forth between two positions. Use a loop to write a plain-language program to produce an animation showing the line segment in these positions, one position after the other. (Your program does not need to draw the coordinate axes or scales. They are shown here merely to indicate the changing position of the line segment.)

First position of segment:

Second position of segment:

Third position of segment:

Fourth position of segment:

*Continued on next page*

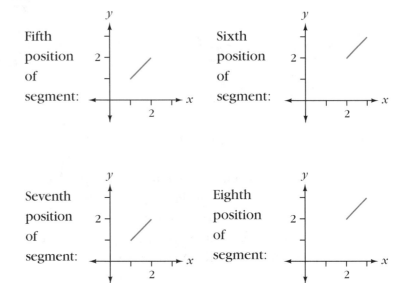

Fifth position of segment:

Sixth position of segment:

Seventh position of segment:

Eighth position of segment:

**2.** Create programming code for the plain-language program you wrote for Question 1, including an appropriate setup program.

# Arrow

This plain-language program describes the animation of a flying arrow. Create programming code for this plain-language program, enter the code into your calculator, run the program, and then find ways to improve it.

### Program: ARROW

Setup Program

For A from 1 to 8

- Clear the screen
- Make B 3 less than A
- Make C 1 less than A
- Draw a line from (B, B) to (A, A)
- Draw a line from (C, A) to (A, A)
- Draw a line from (A, C) to (A, A)
- Delay

End the A loop

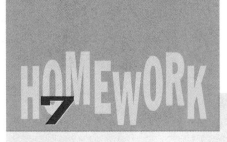

# Sunrise

In this assignment, you will create a program that displays a rising sun by showing a circle "moving" up and across the screen.

There are three parts to this assignment.

• Make a sequence of drawings on graph paper to show what you want to appear on the screen. You should show at least four different positions for the circle.

• Write a plain-language program describing how to create your sequence of drawings.

• Write programming code for your plain-language program. Be sure to include settings for the viewing window so that your circles will be visible.

# A Wider Windshield Wiper, Please

Imagine! Straight out of high school and you land a job at Better Design Ideas, Inc. Your boss is just starting to explain the company's project to design a car windshield wiper that will clean more area than the standard wiper.

The standard wiper consists of a 12-inch blade attached rigidly to a 12-inch arm. The middle of the blade is at the end of the arm, and the arm rotates back and forth, making a 45° angle with the horizontal at each end of its motion. The path swept out by the blade of the standard wiper is shown by the shaded area in the first diagram on the next page.

While your boss is talking, two men in white coats rush in with another model. "It's better!" exclaims one. "It's worse," shouts the other.

*Continued on next page*

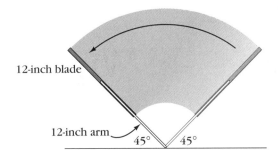

12-inch blade

12-inch arm

45° 45°

The new model also has a 12-inch blade attached at its midpoint to a 12-inch arm. But in this case, the blade pivots so that it's always vertical. The arm rotates 90° as in the standard model. The next diagram shows the path swept out by the blade of the new wiper.

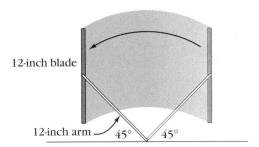

12-inch blade

12-inch arm

45° 45°

The two men keep shouting, but your boss merely rolls her eyes, hands you a white coat, and tells you to find out who's right. Just as you are racing out the door, she calls after you, "In any case, make a better one—one that will clean more area."

You know you are limited to 12-inch blades, which are an industry standard, and that any rotating arm can rotate only 90°. You also know your job is at stake, so go to it!

As your write-up for this POW, write a report for the boss. Be sure to state any further assumptions that you make.

# Translation in Two Dimensions

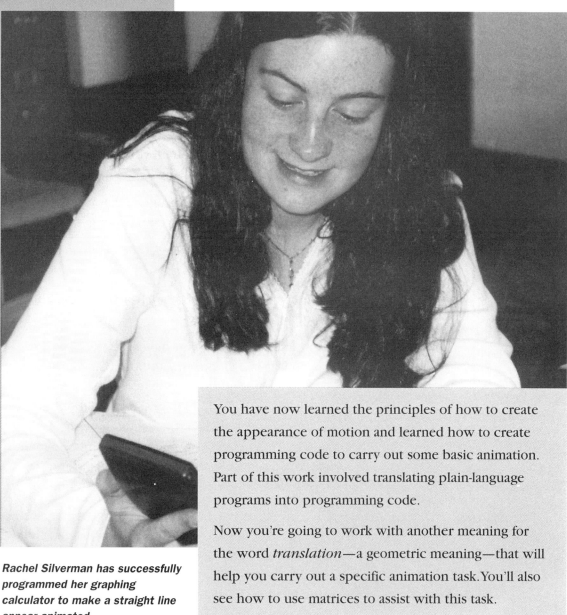

*Rachel Silverman has successfully programmed her graphing calculator to make a straight line appear animated.*

You have now learned the principles of how to create the appearance of motion and learned how to create programming code to carry out some basic animation. Part of this work involved translating plain-language programs into programming code.

Now you're going to work with another meaning for the word *translation*—a geometric meaning—that will help you carry out a specific animation task. You'll also see how to use matrices to assist with this task.

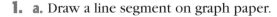

# Move That Line!

Your task in this activity is to write a program that will make a line segment move across the screen by repeating the same translation. After you have done this for a single line segment, you will do it for a more complex picture.

**1. a.** Draw a line segment on graph paper.

   **b.** Choose a translation and draw the result of applying that translation to your line segment.

   **c.** Apply the same translation to the segment you got in Question 1b, and then apply it again to your new result, and so on, until you have applied the translation five times altogether.

**2. a.** Write a plain-language program that will produce the results you drew on graph paper in Question 1.

   **b.** Write programming code for the plain-language program of Question 2a.

   **c.** Enter and test your program from Question 2b, and modify it if necessary.

**3.** If you didn't use a loop in Question 2, redo those programs using a loop. (*Suggestion:* Use variables for the coordinates of the endpoints, and use steps before you start the loop to give the initial values for these variables. Then think about how the coordinates for each new pair of endpoints are found from the coordinates of the preceding pair, and put steps in your loop to make these changes in the variables.)

**4.** Once you know how to write a program using a loop to make a single line segment move, make a simple picture out of four or five segments. Then write a program to make that whole picture move through several identical translations.

# Double Dotting

This is another homework assignment that presents plain-language calculator programs and asks you to predict their results. In each of Questions 1 and 2, read the program and show on graph paper what should appear on the calculator screen.

1. **Program: DOTS**

   Setup program

   Set A equal to 3

   Set B equal to 2

   Set C equal to 9

   Set D equal to 2

   For P from 1 to 7

   - Draw dots at (A, B) and (C, D)
   - Increase A, B, and D by 1 each
   - Decrease C by 1

   End the P loop

*Continued on next page*

2. **Program: MOREDOTS**

Setup program

Set A equal to 3

Set B equal to 5

Set C equal to 3

Draw a dot at (A, B)

For P from 1 to 5

- Decrease A and B by 1
- Increase C by 1
- Draw dots at (A, B) and (C, B)

End the P loop

3. Write a program of your own that uses variables in loops to draw dots.

# Memories of Matrices

Do you remember matrices?

"How could we possibly forget matrices?" you might reply. But just in case, this assignment begins with part of an activity from the Year 3 unit *Meadows or Malls?* to help jog your memory.

It turns out that matrices can be helpful in expressing geometric translations, and you'll be using them to do that in later assignments.

1. (From *Meadows or Malls?*) A matrix could be used to keep track of students' points in a class. Each row could stand for a different student: Clarabell, Freddy, Sally, and Frashy. The first column might be for homework, the second for oral reports, and the third for POWs.

   Suppose the results for the first grading period were represented by this table.

   |          | Homework | Reports | POWs |
   |----------|----------|---------|------|
   | Clarabell | 18      | 54      | 30   |
   | Freddy    | 35      | 23      | 52   |
   | Sally     | 46      | 15      | 60   |
   | Frashy    | 60      | 60      | 60   |

   A matrix representation of this information might look like this.

   $$\begin{bmatrix} 18 & 54 & 30 \\ 35 & 23 & 52 \\ 46 & 15 & 60 \\ 60 & 60 & 60 \end{bmatrix}$$

*Continued on next page*

Here, in table form, are the students' points in each category for the second grading period.

|  | Homework | Reports | POWs |
|---|---|---|---|
| Clarabell | 10 | 60 | 0 |
| Freddy | 52 | 35 | 58 |
| Sally | 42 | 20 | 48 |
| Frashy | 60 | 60 | 60 |

a. Write these second-grading-period scores in a matrix.

b. Figure out each student's total points *in each assignment category* for the two grading periods combined, and write the totals in matrix form.

c. Congratulations! If you completed Question 1b, you have added two matrices. Based on your work, write an equation showing two matrices being added to give the matrix you got in Question 1b.

With this brief review of matrix addition, now look at how matrix addition relates to translations.

2. Suppose you have a diagram of a house set up in a coordinate system like the one shown here.

a. Make a matrix *A* out of the coordinates of the five points that are at the corners of the house, using a separate row of the matrix for each point.

Now suppose you want to translate this diagram, moving it so that the lower left-hand corner of the house ends up at (4, 2).

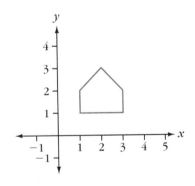

*Continued on next page*

Interactive Mathematics Program

**b.** Make a matrix $B$ out of the coordinates of the translated house.

**c.** Find a matrix $C$ so that $A + C = B$. (The matrix $C$ is called a *translation matrix*.)

**3.** Let's use the letter $A$ for the matrix shown in Question 1. $A$ has 4 rows and 3 columns, so it has 12 entries altogether.

$$A = \begin{bmatrix} 18 & 54 & 30 \\ 35 & 23 & 52 \\ 46 & 15 & 60 \\ 60 & 60 & 60 \end{bmatrix}$$

You will need to be familiar with notation used to represent individual entries of a matrix. Mathematicians use the symbol $a_{ij}$ to refer to the entry in the $i^{th}$ row and $j^{th}$ column (with the lower-case letter $a$ indicating that the entry is from the matrix represented by upper-case $A$). For example, $a_{32}$ refers to the entry in the third row and second column of matrix $A$, so $a_{32}$ is 15.

*Note:* The context makes clear that the numbers 3 and 2 here are separate subscripts, and not the number 32. For larger matrices, you would need to use commas to separate the two subscripts. For instance, $a_{12,34}$ would represent the entry in the 12th row and 34th column.

**a.** What is $a_{23}$ in the matrix $A$ shown above?

**b.** Write the entry 30 from matrix $A$ in the form $a_{ij}$.

**c.** Write a new matrix $B$ with entries defined by this set of equations:

$$b_{11} = 3, b_{12} = 6, b_{13} = 2$$
$$b_{21} = 5, b_{22} = 1, b_{23} = 3$$

# Cornering the Cabbage

Did you ever read about Peter Rabbit and his siblings, Flopsie, Mopsie, and Cottontail?

Actually, it doesn't matter whether you did or not. All you need to know is that Peter used to steal cabbages from a local farmer, Mr. McGregor. But now Peter and his sibling Flopsie are working for Mr. McGregor.

Peter and Flopsie usually got paid in cabbages, but Mr. McGregor decided that because they had been working so hard, he'd pay them by giving them some land. That would allow them to grow some of their own cabbages. Peter and Flopsie thought this was a great idea.

Two poles were lying nearby, and Mr. McGregor gave one to Peter and one to Flopsie. He said they could hold them together at the ends and spread them out at any angle they wanted. Then he'd connect the two other ends, forming a triangle. They'd get all the land inside the triangle.

*Continued on next page*

It turned out Peter's pole was approximately 2 meters long and Flopsie's was approximately 3 meters long. Of course, they wanted the most land they could get, and they weren't sure what angle to choose, or even if it mattered. Can you help them?

1. **a.** Figure out what the area would be if the angle formed by the two poles was 25°.

   **b.** Figure out what the area would be if the angle was 100°.

2. Pick two other angles to try. Figure out what area Peter and Flopsie would get if they used each of those angles.

3. Develop a general formula for the area of the triangle. Use *t* and *u* for the lengths of the two given sides and θ for the angle they form, as in the diagram at the right.

4. Determine what value for the angle θ would give Peter and Flopsie the largest area, and justify your answer.

# Rotating in Two Dimensions

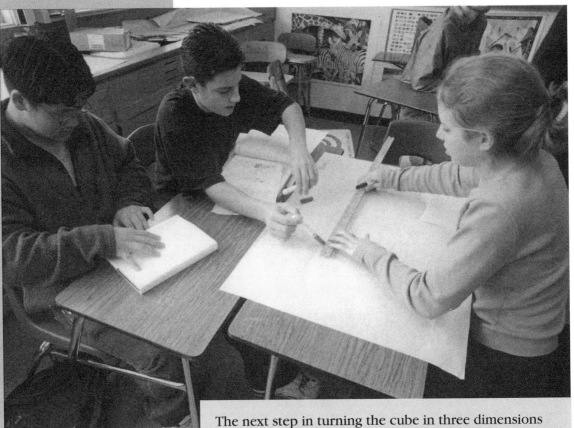

*Jeff Tung, Ken Hoffman, and Audrey Rae use coordinates to help them work in two and three dimensions.*

The next step in turning the cube in three dimensions is learning to turn things in two dimensions. To accomplish this, you will need to develop some trigonometric formulas. You probably won't be surprised to learn that with rotations, as with translations, matrices can also prove very useful.

# Goin' Round the Origin

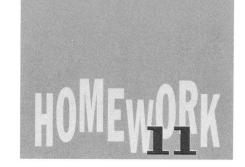

Being able to rotate pictures around the origin will be useful when trying to create interesting graphics. And, of course, this will be important in turning a cube.

This assignment begins the task by examining a specific problem and its generalization.

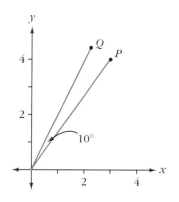

**1.** Consider the point $P$ in the accompanying diagram, whose coordinates are $(3, 4)$. Suppose this point is rotated 10° counterclockwise around the origin to the position shown as point $Q$.

What are the coordinates of $Q$? (*Hint:* You may find trigonometry useful.)

**2.** Next, consider the point $R$ with coordinates $(2, 5)$. As in Question 1, rotate this point 10° counterclockwise around the origin. What are the coordinates of its new location?

**3.** Now generalize Questions 1 and 2. Begin with a point with coordinates $(x, y)$. Rotate that point 10° counterclockwise around the origin. Develop a formula or procedure for getting the coordinates of the new point in terms of $x$ and $y$.

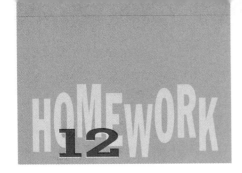

# Double Trouble

Do you remember Woody from the *Shadows* unit in Year 1? As you may recall, Woody was very fond of measuring trees. He was especially happy to learn how to use trigonometry so he could avoid climbing trees.

One time, Woody leaned a ladder between the branches so that its tip just reached the top of a tree. Next, he measured the angle that the ladder made with the ground. He wrote down the angle and headed home to do the computation to find the tree's height. (He knew the length of the ladder.)

When he got home, he grabbed his scientific calculator, punched in sin 40°, and got 0.643. Then he punched in cos 40°, just in case he might want to know how far the foot of the ladder had been from the tree. He found that cos 40° was about 0.766.

When he did the calculation, he realized that his answer seemed way off. He ran back to the scene, and measured the angle again. Lo and behold, it was really 80°!

When Woody returned home, he couldn't find his calculator anywhere. His friend Elmer suggested that Woody simply multiply sin 40° by 2 to get sin 80°.

1. Is Elmer's suggestion correct? That is, is sin 80° equal to 2 sin 40°?

2. How could you decide if he was right if you had no way to look up sin 80°?

*Continued on next page*

Interactive Mathematics Program

In *Homework 10: Cornering the Cabbage*, you saw that the area of a triangle such as the one shown here is given by the expression $\frac{1}{2}tu \sin \theta$. Use this formula in Questions 3a and 3b.

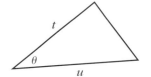

**3.** The first diagram below shows an isosceles triangle with two sides of length $x$ and an angle of $80°$ formed by those sides. The second diagram shows the same triangle with the altitude drawn. The altitude has length $z$ and splits the original triangle into two smaller triangles.

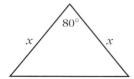 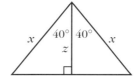

   **a.** Find the area of the original triangle (in terms of $x$).

   **b.** Find the area of each of the two small triangles (in terms of $x$ and $z$).

**4. a.** Use the fact that the large triangle is made up of the two smaller triangles to get an expression for $\sin 80°$. This expression may involve $\sin 40°$ and both $x$ and $z$.

   **b.** Work with your answer to Question 4a to get an expression for $\sin 80°$ that involves neither $x$ nor $z$, but may involve both $\sin 40°$ and $\cos 40°$.

# The Sine of a Sum

You have seen that when a point is rotated 10° around the origin, the rectangular coordinates for its new location involve the expressions cos $(\theta + 10°)$ and sin $(\theta + 10°)$.

It would be helpful if you knew how to find the sine or cosine of two angles added together, using their individual sines and cosines. In this activity, you'll begin with sine.

Your task is to develop a formula for sin $(A + B)$, where $A$ and $B$ are two angles. You can use sin $A$, cos $A$, sin $B$, and cos $B$ in your formula.

*Suggestion:* Modify your work on *Homework 12: Double Trouble* using a diagram like the one shown here.

# A Broken Button

Elmer's phone rang. He knew it would be Woody even before he picked it up. Ever since Woody had lost his calculator, he'd been pestering Elmer.

This time, Woody wanted to know the value of cos 50°. But when Elmer went to find out on his own calculator, he discovered that the cosine key was broken.

Fortunately, the sine key was working. Elmer offered to give Woody the value of sin 50° if that would help. Woody thanked him, wrote down the value of sin 50°, hung up, and proceeded to find cos 50° using the Pythagorean identity, $\sin^2 x + \cos^2 x = 1$.

1. Show how Woody might have used the Pythagorean identity and the numerical value of sin 50° to determine the value of cos 50°.

Later, Elmer called to tell Woody that he'd found an easy, no-computation way to get cos 50°, by using a right triangle and simply finding the sine of a different angle.

2. How do you think Elmer's method worked?

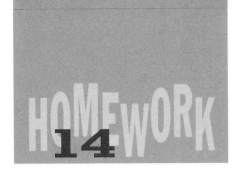

# Oh, Say What You Can See

In recent work, you may have used the trigonometric identity $\cos \theta = \sin (90° - \theta)$. (*Reminder:* An *identity* is an equation that holds true no matter what values are substituted for the variables.)

Your task in this activity is to give specific examples illustrating this and other identities, and then to explain each identity in one or more of these two ways:

• Using the situation of the Ferris wheel (from *High Dive*)

• Using the graphs of the equations $y = \sin \theta$ and $y = \cos \theta$, which are shown here for your reference

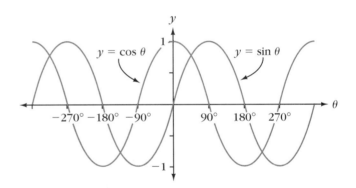

1. Consider the equation $\cos \theta = \sin (90° - \theta)$.

   a. Choose two values for $\theta$, in different quadrants, and verify that the equation holds true for those values.

   b. Write an explanation of the equation in terms of the Ferris wheel model.

   c. Write an explanation of the equation in terms of the graphs of the sine and cosine functions.

*Continued on next page*

**2.** Consider the equation $\cos(-\theta) = \cos\theta$.

    **a.** Choose two values for $\theta$, in different quadrants, and verify that the equation holds true for those values.

    **b.** Write an explanation of the equation using either the Ferris wheel model or the graph of the cosine function.

**3.** Consider the equation $\sin(-\theta) = -\sin\theta$.

    **a.** Choose two values for $\theta$ in different quadrants, and verify that the equation holds true for those values.

    **b.** Write an explanation of the equation using either the Ferris wheel model or the graph of the sine function.

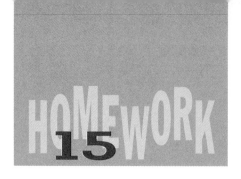

# Comin'
# Round Again
# (and Again ...)

To write a calculator program to rotate pictures, you need to be able to rotate points.

You have seen that when a point $(x, y)$ is rotated counterclockwise through an angle $\phi$, the coordinates $(x', y')$ of its new location are given by the equations

$$x' = x \cos \phi - y \sin \phi$$
$$y' = x \sin \phi + y \cos \phi$$

To see how to use these formulas, make a small picture on a coordinate grid. Use only line segments in your picture to connect points. Use at least five points to get an interesting picture.

**1.** Write the $x$- and $y$-coordinates of the points in your picture.

**2.** Rotate your picture 60° around the origin by rotating each point. Don't guess about the new coordinates. Calculate them and show your work. Round off to the nearest tenth.

**3.** Based on your answers to Question 2, draw the rotated picture. (Be sure to keep track of which pairs of points you should connect by line segments.)

**4.** Rotate your new picture another 60° as you did previously, showing your work.

# More Memories of Matrices

In *Homework 9: Memories of Matrices,* you reviewed the idea of addition of matrices and saw how to apply that idea to the geometric translation of points.

Guess what? It's time to review some more about matrices and then to use them for rotations. Once again, the first question is based on an assignment from *Meadows or Malls?*

1. (From *Meadows or Malls?*) Linda Sue has a transport plane and delivers goods for two customers. One is Charley's Chicken Feed and the other is Careful Calculators. Here are some important facts about these two customers.

   • Charley's Chicken Feed packages its product in containers that weigh 40 pounds and are 2 cubic feet in volume.

   • Careful Calculators packages its materials in cartons that weigh 50 pounds and are 3 cubic feet in volume.

   a. Organize this information into a matrix, using the first row for Charley's Chicken Feed and the second row for Careful Calculators. Call this matrix *A*.

   b. Suppose that on Monday, Linda Sue transports 500 containers of chicken feed and 200 cartons of calculators. Put those facts into a row matrix (that is, a matrix with one row). Call this matrix *B*.

*Continued on next page*

**c.** Use the information in your two matrices to find out the total weight carried and the total volume used. Put those two answers into a row matrix. Call this matrix *C*.

Congratulations! If you completed Question 1c, you have multiplied two matrices. The matrix *C* is the product $B \cdot A$.

**2.** Based on your work in Question 1, write a description of how to multiply matrices. Your description should include a statement about when it is *possible* to multiply two matrices.

**3.** In Question 1, you found the matrix product $B \cdot A$. Now try to find the matrix product $A \cdot B$. Did you get the same result as in Question 1? Explain.

**4.** Suppose that on Tuesday, Linda Sue transports 400 containers of chicken feed and 300 cartons of calculators, and on Wednesday, she transports 250 containers of chicken feed and 350 cartons of calculators.

   **a.** Make a matrix showing Linda Sue's transportation record for all three days, using a different row for each day. Call this matrix *D*.

   **b.** Describe how you would use matrix multiplication to get a matrix showing the weight and volume carried each day.

**5.** Use the idea of matrix multiplication to express rotations. That is, find a way to use matrices to get from the ordered pair $(x, y)$ to the ordered pair $(x \cos \phi - y \sin \phi, x \sin \phi + y \cos \phi)$.

# Taking Steps

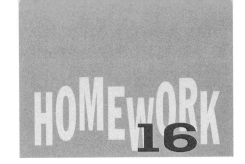

You've seen how the For/End instructions can be used to create a programming loop in which the loop variable increases by 1 each time the program goes through the loop.

For example, consider this plain-language program.

> For A from 4 to 8
>   • Show A on the screen
> End the A loop

This program will print the numbers 4, 5, 6, 7, and 8 on the calculator screen.

*Continued on next page*

It's possible to make the loop variable increase by something other than 1 each time. For example, you can probably use an instruction on your calculator that looks something like this.

For C from 2 to 11, step 3

This instruction will start the variable *C* at 2 and then increase it by 3 each time the program comes back to this instruction. The number 3 is called the *increment* or *step value*.

1. What do you think will appear on the screen when this program is run?

**PROGRAM: STEP3**

For C from 2 to 11, step 3
 • Show C on the screen
End the C loop

2. Write a plain-language program that will show the calculator counting by 5's from 30 to 50.

3. What do you think would happen in each of these programs?

a. **PROGRAM: MISSTEP**

For W from 2 to 10, step 3
 • Show W on the screen
End the W loop

b. **PROGRAM: FRACSTEP**

For S from 3 to 6, step 0.7
 • Show S on the screen
End the S loop

4. How might you get the calculator to count backwards? For example, write a plain-language program (using a For/End loop) that you think would display the values 5, 4, 3, 2, and 1, in that order.

# How Did We Get Here?

In this unit, you have worked with several different mathematical concepts. Before you go on, it might be a good idea for you to sort things out. This assignment gives you a chance to reflect on where you have been and think about where you are going.

1. Make a list of the important mathematical terms and formulas you've learned or used so far in the unit. Write a definition of each of the key terms.

2. Write out the purpose of this unit, as clearly as you can.

3. For each item you listed in Question 1, discuss how it fits into the purpose of this unit.

# Swing That Line!

In this activity, your task is to write a program for the calculator that will take a line segment and rotate it counterclockwise around the origin a certain number of degrees. Your program should repeat this rotation several times, allowing you to see each segment briefly before erasing it and showing the next one.

1. Make a careful sketch on graph paper of the lines you want your calculator to draw.

2. Write a plain-language program to create the animation.

3. Turn your program from Question 2 into programming code for your calculator.

4. Enter and run your program from Question 3.

5. Once your program is successful, modify it to work with a more complicated picture.

Write down your completed programs on paper once you are satisfied with them on the calculator.

*Suggestion:* Use what you can of the *Move That Line!* program, simply making the necessary changes.

# Doubles and Differences

You have developed formulas for the sine and cosine of the sum of two angles, writing sin $(A + B)$ and cos $(A + B)$ in terms of sin $A$, cos $A$, sin $B$, and cos $B$. In this assignment, you'll develop some variations on those formulas.

**1.** Develop a formula for the sine of the difference between two angles. That is, find a formula for sin $(A - B)$ in terms of sin $A$, cos $A$, sin $B$, and cos $B$. (*Hint:* Think of sin $(A - B)$ as sin $[A + (-B)]$.)

**2.** Check the formula you got in Question 1 by choosing several pairs of values for $A$ and $B$ and seeing if your formula works.

**3.** Find a formula for cos $(A - B)$ in terms of sin $A$, cos $A$, sin $B$, and cos $B$. Then check your formula by substituting pairs of values for $A$ and $B$.

**4.** In *Homework 12: Double Trouble*, you got a formula for sin $80°$ in terms of sin $40°$ and cos $40°$ using ideas about area. Now, use the formula for sin $(A + B)$ to develop a formula for sin $2A$, in terms of sin $A$ and cos $A$. Then check your formula by substituting values for $A$.

**5.** Use the formula for cos $(A + B)$ to develop a formula for cos $2A$. Then check your formula by substituting values for $A$.

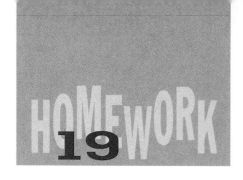
# What's Going On Here?

Once again, your task is to figure out what a certain plain-language program does. You should show on graph paper what would appear on the calculator screen after someone executes the program MYSTERY.

### Program: MYSTERY

Setup program

Clear the screen

Let A be the matrix $\begin{bmatrix} 2 & 2 \\ 5 & 2 \\ 2 & 6 \\ 5 & 6 \\ 3.5 & 9 \end{bmatrix}$

Let B be the matrix $\begin{bmatrix} \cos 30 & \sin 30 \\ -\sin 30 & \cos 30 \end{bmatrix}$

For C from 1 to 12

- Draw a line from $(a_{11}, a_{12})$ to $(a_{21}, a_{22})$
- Draw a line from $(a_{21}, a_{22})$ to $(a_{41}, a_{42})$
- Draw a line from $(a_{41}, a_{42})$ to $(a_{51}, a_{52})$
- Draw a line from $(a_{11}, a_{12})$ to $(a_{31}, a_{32})$
- Draw a line from $(a_{31}, a_{32})$ to $(a_{51}, a_{52})$
- Replace matrix A by the product A · B

End the C loop

# Projecting Pictures

*Cassie Burniston and Sam Ellison are enmeshed in how to create a two-dimensional drawing of a three-dimensional cube.*

You are now ready to move on to three dimensions. You will need to review some things you learned in *Meadows or Malls?* about three-dimensional graphs. You will also need to adapt some of the two-dimensional geometry you learned in the Year 3 unit *Orchard Hideout* to three dimensions.

# An Animated POW

Your assignment in this POW is to create an interesting animation program for the graphing calculator. You will work with a partner.

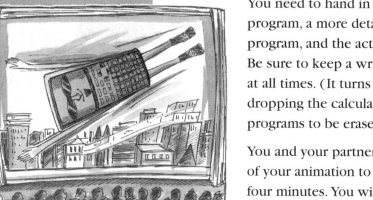

You need to hand in a general outline of the program, a more detailed plain-language program, and the actual code for the program. Be sure to keep a written copy of your work at all times. (It turns out that even merely dropping the calculator can cause all of its programs to be erased!)

You and your partner will make a presentation of your animation to the class, lasting three to four minutes. You will show your animation on the overhead projector, and you will describe one interesting feature of how you did the programming.

Here are the different stages of your work on this POW:

• You give your teacher a statement of who your partner is.

• You and your partner hand in a description of what you want your program to do.

• You and your partner make a presentation to the class, lasting three to four minutes. Your presentation should include

  ✓ a demonstration of your program running on the overhead calculator

  ✓ a description of one interesting feature of your program

• You hand in the written outline, plain-language program, and code.

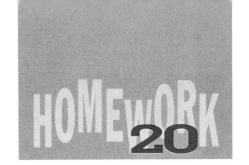

# "A Snack in the Middle" Revisited

You may recall from *Orchard Hideout* that Madie and Clyde sometimes spent their afternoons pruning their trees. Each afternoon, they would choose two trees that seemed most in need of pruning.

Pruning made them hungry, so they would set up a snack between the two trees they were working on. They knew they would both want to have snacks at various times during the afternoon, so they agreed to set up their snack at the midpoint of the segment connecting the two trees.

1. If they were working on the trees at $(24, 6)$ and $(30, 14)$, where should they set up the snack? Explain your answer.

2. If they were working on the trees at $(6, 2)$ and $(11, 9)$, where should they set up the snack? Explain your answer.

One afternoon, Clyde was daydreaming of his delicious snack, and he slipped from his ladder and cracked his kneecap. Madie graciously offered to do the pruning herself, but Clyde would not hear of it.

Madie also offered to keep the snacks at whatever tree Clyde was working on, but he wouldn't agree to that, either. Clyde finally agreed to have the snacks placed one-third of the way from himself to Madie, instead of halfway.

3. The next time they went out, Clyde was working on the tree at $(6, 9)$ and Madie was working on the tree at $(18, 15)$. According to their new agreement, where should they put the snack? Explain your answer.

# Fractional Snacks

You saw in *Homework 20: "A Snack in the Middle" Revisited* that Clyde had injured his knee. Because he was having trouble getting around, he and Madie decided to place their afternoon snack closer to Clyde than to Madie.

This activity continues with the lives of our busy pruners on the following day.

1. Unfortunately, Clyde felt even worse the next day. So he and Madie decided that the snacks would be only one-fourth of the way from Clyde to Madie. If Clyde worked on the tree at $(-2, 7)$ and Madie worked on the tree at $(14, 19)$, where should they put the snack?

2. Then Clyde began to feel a little better. So they increased the fraction so that the snack would be two-fifths of the way from Clyde to Madie. This time Clyde's position was $(6, 13)$ and Madie's was $(9, 1)$. Where should they put the snack?

3. As Clyde's condition varied, he and Madie kept changing the fraction that they used in deciding where to place the snack. Describe how to compute the coordinates of the snack if the given "fraction of the distance" is $r$.

# More Walking for Clyde

Clyde's knee is pretty well healed, but he needs to walk regularly to strengthen his leg muscles. Thus, Clyde and Madie have decided to place the snack so that Clyde actually has to walk past Madie to get to it.

For this assignment, assume that Clyde is at (10, 12) and that Madie is at (16, 2). The snack will still be on the straight line that connects their two positions.

1. Suppose Clyde and Madie decide to make the distance from Madie to the snack equal to half of her distance from Clyde. Where should they put the snack?

2. Suppose Clyde and Madie decide to make the distance from Madie to the snack equal to twice her distance from Clyde. Where should they put the snack?

3. In general, if the distance from Madie to the snack is $t$ times the distance from Madie to Clyde, where should they put the snack?

# Monorail Delivery

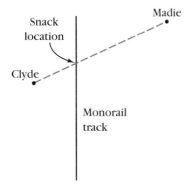

Snack location

Clyde

Madie

Monorail track

When Clyde recovered from his accident, his next project was to help Madie build a monorail in the orchard. (A monorail is a train that runs along a single track.)

Madie and Clyde planned to use the monorail to help them transport the apples they grew to a central location for shipping to market.

The first monorail they built ran along the line $x = 12$, and the train ran along this track in both directions. Clyde and Madie realized that they could also use the monorail to bring themselves fresh snacks when they were out in the orchard pruning trees. The monorail would drop off their snacks at the point where the line that joined their locations crossed the track. (They arranged to work on opposite sides of the track, and they had stopped worrying about who would be closer to the snack.)

1. If Clyde is working on the tree at $(3, 7)$ and Madie is working on the tree at $(30, 19)$, where should the monorail drop off the snack? Make a sketch of the situation and explain your answer.

2. If Clyde is working on the tree at $(-5, 28)$ and Madie is working on the tree at $(18, -14)$, where should the monorail drop off the snack? Make a sketch of the situation and explain your answer.

3. Generalize your work from Questions 1 and 2. If Clyde is working on the tree at $(a, b)$ and Madie is working on the tree at $(c, d)$, where should the monorail drop off the snack?

# Another Mystery

This assignment shows another plain-language program for the calculator. Your job is to figure out what it does and then create programming code for it.

*Note:* The order of operations for matrix arithmetic is the same as the order of operations for number arithmetic.

## PROGRAM: ANOTHER

Setup program

Clear the screen

Let A be the matrix $\begin{bmatrix} 1 & 1 \\ 4 & 1 \\ 2 & 4 \end{bmatrix}$

Let B be the matrix $\begin{bmatrix} 6 & -1 \\ 6 & -1 \\ 6 & -1 \end{bmatrix}$

Let C be the matrix $\begin{bmatrix} \cos 180 & \sin 180 \\ -\sin 180 & \cos 180 \end{bmatrix}$

For W from 1 to 4

- Draw a line from $(a_{11}, a_{12})$ to $(a_{21}, a_{22})$
- Draw a line from $(a_{11}, a_{12})$ to $(a_{31}, a_{32})$
- Draw a line from $(a_{21}, a_{22})$ to $(a_{31}, a_{32})$
- Replace A by the matrix $B + A \cdot C$

End the W loop

1. Make a careful drawing on graph paper of what the calculator screen will show after someone executes the program ANOTHER.

2. Create programming code for your calculator that will accomplish what this plain-language program describes.

# A Return to the Third Dimension

In the Year 3 unit *Meadows or Malls?*, you worked with the three-dimensional coordinate system to understand and solve linear programming problems. This activity will help you review ideas about that coordinate system.

**1.** Imagine a cube in the three-dimensional coordinate system, placed in a position that you choose. You may want to use yarn or a small cube, together with a cardboard version of the coordinate system, to create a model of the situation.

  **a.** Write down the coordinates of the eight vertices of your cube.

  **b.** A cube has six faces. Give the equations of the six planes that contain the faces of your cube.

  **c.** Draw a sketch of your cube in the three-dimensional coordinate system.

**2.** Write the equations of several pairs of planes that are parallel to each other.

**3.** Write the equations of a pair of planes that are neither parallel nor perpendicular to each other. Sketch your two planes.

# Where's Madie?

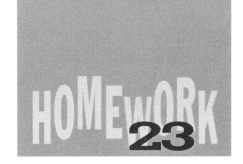

One day as he was pruning away, Clyde thought of something he wanted to ask Madie. He thought he'd take a break and walk over to see her.

He didn't remember where she was working, but he knew where his snack was on the line between them. He also remembered Madie saying she would have to walk twice as far for her snack that day as he had to.

**1.** If Clyde was at $(2, 6)$ and the snack was at $(12, 1)$, where was Madie?

**2.** Next, suppose that you don't know the exact coordinates of either Clyde's tree or the snack, but assume that the monorail still runs along the line $x = 12$. Create general instructions for finding the coordinates of the tree where Madie is working, and verify that your instructions work for the situation in Question 1.

**3.** Let Clyde's coordinates be $(a, b)$ and the snack's coordinates be $(12, c)$. Write a formula for the coordinates of Madie's tree.

# And Fred Brings the Lunch

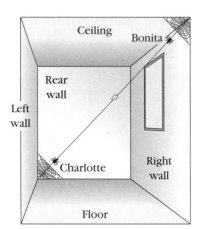

Once there were two spiders, Bonita and Charlotte. They liked to spin webs at opposite corners of a room. Bonita liked heights, and she always went to one of the corners of the ceiling.

Charlotte did not care for heights, and she always went for a corner of the floor. To give the proper artistic balance to the room, she went to the corner diagonally opposite from Bonita.

The spiders' webs were connected by a single thread. As they worked on their webs, they got hungry. So they had their associate, Fred the fly, bring in lunch each day. The spiders wanted their lunch partway between them along the connecting thread.

Fred did not glide up or down threads as the spiders did. He simply flew places. So Bonita and Charlotte mapped out a coordinate system to tell him where to fly. They designated the rear, left corner of the floor, where Charlotte usually hung out, as $(0, 0, 0)$.

Bonita was in the front, right corner of the ceiling. The spiders set up the system so that the coordinates for her position, $(a, b, c)$, worked this way.

- The first coordinate, $a$, represented how many feet to the right Bonita was from Charlotte.

- The second coordinate, $b$, represented how many feet up Bonita was from Charlotte.

- The third coordinate, $c$, represented how many feet forward Bonita was from Charlotte.

*Continued on next page*

1. One day, the spiders were in a room that was 11 feet wide, 13 feet tall, and 24 feet long. If Charlotte was at $(0, 0, 0)$ and Bonita was at the opposite corner at $(11, 13, 24)$, and they wanted lunch halfway between them, where should Fred bring lunch?

2. After she'd gotten used to this room, Charlotte got adventurous and built a web slightly out from her corner, at $(2, 1, 4)$. Bonita also left her corner, building her web at $(9, 12, 20)$. The connecting thread still went in a straight line between Bonita's web and Charlotte's, and they still wanted lunch halfway between them. Where should Fred make his delivery?

3. Charlotte suddenly decided that with her distaste for heights, she should not have to go halfway up. She and Bonita compromised, agreeing that Charlotte would go one-third of the way up the thread from her position while Bonita would come two-thirds of the way down. Based on Bonita's and Charlotte's positions in Question 2, where should Fred go?

4. Using the positions from Question 2 again, where should Fred go if the lunch is to be placed two-fifths of the way from Charlotte to Bonita?

5. Charlotte and Bonita are tired of all this mental activity, figuring out what to tell Fred. Could you provide a formula?

   Assume that Charlotte is at $(x_1, y_1, z_1)$, that Bonita is at $(x_2, y_2, z_2)$, and that $r$ is a fraction, so that they want lunch "$r$ of the way" along the thread from Charlotte to Bonita. Create a formula in terms of these variables that states where Fred should bring lunch.

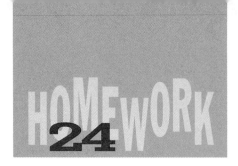

# Flipping Points

You have learned about translations and rotations, and developed formulas to find the new coordinates after one of these geometric transformations has been applied to a point.

Translations and rotations are two important examples of a special kind of transformation called an **isometry.** An isometry is a way of moving all the points in the plane (or in 3-space) so that the size and shape of objects are unchanged. The word *isometry* means "same measure," which means that the distance between two points doesn't change when the points are moved.

There is a third basic category of isometry called a **reflection.** (Reflections are also known as *flips*.) A reflection in the plane is defined by giving a **line of reflection.** The reflection then moves each point $P$ to the point $Q$ so that the line of reflection becomes the perpendicular bisector of the segment connecting $P$ and $Q$. In other words, $Q$ is chosen so that $\overline{PQ}$ is perpendicular to the line of reflection and the line of reflection intersects $\overline{PQ}$ at its midpoint. Point $Q$ is called the reflection of $P$ across the line of reflection.

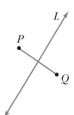

For example, in the diagram at the left, $L$ is the line of reflection, point $Q$ is the reflection of point $P$ across $L$, and $L$ is the perpendicular bisector of $\overline{PQ}$. Thus, the reflection of a point is the "mirror image" of the original point through the line of reflection.

*Continued on next page*

The diagram below shows a triangle in the first quadrant and its reflection using the $y$-axis as the line of reflection.

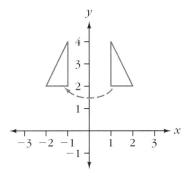

For instance, the reflection of the point $(1, 2)$ is the point $(-1, 2)$, and the line of reflection (the $y$-axis) is a line of symmetry between the original triangle and its reflection.

**1.** Using the diagram, give the coordinates for each of the other two vertices of the original triangle (in the first quadrant) and give the vertices of each of their reflections (in the second quadrant).

**2.** Generalize the result of Question 1. That is, if $(a, b)$ is an arbitrary point, what are the coordinates of its reflection through the $y$-axis?

**3.** Find a way to represent this transformation using a matrix.

# Where's Bonita?

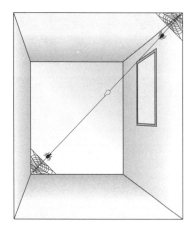

Fred generally got his instructions from Charlotte, and so he knew what her coordinates were. Of course, he also knew where he was putting the lunch. But after a while, he started wondering where Bonita was.

1. For example, one day, when Charlotte was at $(1, 3, 2)$, she told Fred that the lunch should be at $(5, 8, 9)$ and that this was halfway to Bonita. Where was Bonita?

2. On another occasion, when Charlotte would only go one-third of the way toward Bonita to get lunch, Charlotte told Fred to put the lunch at $(4, 4, 7)$. Charlotte herself was at $(2, 1, 1)$. Where was Bonita?

3. Fred's brain was really taxed one day when Charlotte told him to put the lunch at $(3, 6, 7)$, and explained that this would be two-fifths of the way to Bonita. Charlotte was at $(1, 2, 2)$ when she said this. Where was Bonita?

# Lunch in the Window

The two spiders are still spinning away, but Bonita has developed claustrophobia and prefers to work outside. So the spiders found a room where one of the windows is kept open. Charlotte works inside (which she prefers), while Bonita does her spinning outside.

The thread connecting them goes through the open window, and Charlotte and Bonita will have their lunch right where the thread passes through the opening of the window. Therefore, they need to figure out the coordinates of the point where the thread passes through the open window.

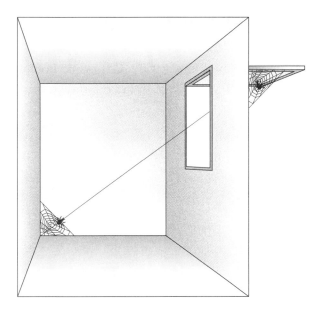

*Continued on next page*

Charlotte and Bonita are using the same coordinate system as before, with the origin at the rear, left corner of the floor. The first coordinate gives distance to the right, the second gives distance up, and the third gives distance toward the front. The window is in the wall on the right side of the room, and the room is 14 feet wide from left to right.

By the way, the spiders' associate Fred mysteriously disappeared after the last lunch. His son, Fred Jr., is now assisting them.

1. Before you get started on the lunch problems, find the equation of the plane that contains the window.

2. Suppose that Charlotte is at $(4, 2, 2)$ and Bonita is at $(24, 20, 8)$. Where should Fred Jr. bring their lunch? Explain your reasoning carefully.

3. Now suppose Charlotte is at $(10, 0, 4)$ and Bonita is at $(26, 16, 8)$. Where should Fred Jr. drop off lunch? Again, explain your reasoning.

4. This time Charlotte is at $(7, 0, 4)$, while Bonita is still at $(26, 16, 8)$. Give Fred Jr. directions about where to put lunch.

5. Generalize your results, based on the coordinates $(x_1, y_1, z_1)$ for Charlotte and $(x_2, y_2, z_2)$ for Bonita.

# Further Flips

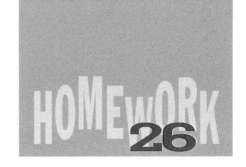

In *Homework 24: Flipping Points*, you looked at the isometry of reflecting figures through the *y*-axis, as shown in the first diagram here. But any line can be used as the line of reflection. In this assignment, you will consider some other cases.

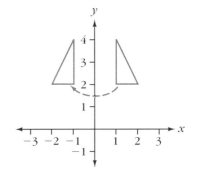

1. Start with the same original triangle, but this time use the line $y = x$ as the line of reflection, as shown in the next diagram. Find the coordinates of the vertices of both the original triangle and the reflected triangle.

2. Generalize Question 1 by finding the image of an arbitrary point $(a, b)$ under the reflection through the line $y = x$.

3. Express this reflection in terms of matrices. That is, find a matrix process that will turn the vector $\begin{bmatrix} a & b \end{bmatrix}$ into the corresponding image vector under the reflection.

4. Now repeat Questions 1 through 3 using the same original triangle and using the line $x = 6$ as the line of reflection. (*Suggestion:* Draw the diagram.)

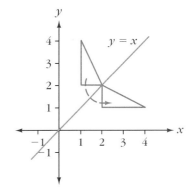

# Cube on a Screen

As part of the unit problem, you need to figure out how to draw a cube, which is three-dimensional, on the calculator screen, which is two-dimensional. Such a drawing is called a **projection.**

This activity should help you get some insight into how this can be done. You should work with a partner on this activity. You and your partner will need a cube, a sheet of clear plastic, and three pens of different colors. You can think of the plastic as representing the calculator screen. It should be set up vertically like a plane parallel to the *xy*-plane.

In Part I, partner A will hold the cube and screen while partner B makes three different sketches of the cube, as described in Questions 1, 2, and 3. In Question 4, the two partners will compare the three sketches.

The partners will switch roles in Part II, and partner A will make two sketches, as described in Questions 5 and 6. In Question 7, the two partners will again compare the sketches.

## Part I: Changing the Viewpoint, Moving the Cube

1. To begin with, partner A should take the cube and the screen, and place them in some fixed position, with the screen held vertically between the cube and partner B. Partner B need not be directly in front of the cube.

*Continued on next page*

Without moving her head, partner B should look at one corner of the cube and place a dot on the screen where her line of vision crosses the screen. (Partner B may want to imagine a laser beam from her eye to the corner of the cube. Place the dot where the beam would burn a hole in the screen.)

Partner B should continue like this, without moving, imagining her line of sight tracing all the edges of the cube, and marking on the screen where her line of vision would cross the screen as the cube is traced. The result should be a two-dimensional drawing—a projection—of the three-dimensional cube.

**2.** When the drawing from Question 1 is complete, partner B should move so that she is in a different position compared to the cube. *The cube and screen should be left in the same position as in Question 1.*

Partner B should now do a tracing of the cube from this new position, using the same "laser" method as in Question 1, but with a pen of a different color.

*Continued on next page*

3. Next, partner A should move the cube closer to the screen. *Partner B should stay in the same position as in Question 2.* Partner B should make a third sketch of the cube, again using the "laser" method, but with the third pen.

4. The two partners should compare the drawings from Questions 1 through 3. How are they different? Has the drawing merely moved, or has it actually changed?

## Part II: Rotating the Cube

Now the partners should switch roles, with partner A doing the drawing and partner B holding the cube. Hold the screen so that a clean portion of it is between partner A and the cube.

5. Partner A should make an initial sketch of the cube, as described in Question 1.

6. Partner A and the screen should stay in the same position while partner B moves the cube through a partial rotation (such as 45° or 90°) around the "*z*-axis." That is, imagine a line perpendicular to the screen, and have the cube do a partial rotation around this axis, turning as it goes around the axis as in the central unit problem.

   Partner A should do a sketch of the cube with the cube in its new position, using a pen of a different color from that used in Question 5.

7. The two partners should then compare the drawings from Questions 5 and 6. How are they the same, and how are they different? Has the drawing merely turned, or has it actually changed?

# Spiders and Cubes

You've recently completed a series of problems involving the eating habits of the spiders Bonita and Charlotte.

- *And Fred Brings the Lunch*

- *Homework 25: Where's Bonita?*

- *Lunch in the Window*

But the unit is about programming a graphing calculator to draw a turning cube. What do lunch arrangements for spiders have to do with the unit problem? Your task in this assignment is to figure out and explain this connection.

# Find Those Corners!

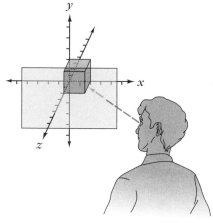

Let's fix a 2-by-2-by-2 cube in a three-dimensional coordinate system. For convenience, we'll place it snugly in the corner where the coordinate planes meet, so that three of the cube's faces are against the coordinate planes, with one vertex of the cube at $(0, 0, 0)$ and the diagonally opposite vertex at $(2, 2, 2)$.

**1.** Find the coordinates of the other six corners.

**2.** Imagine that the plane $z = 5$ is a screen. Your teacher will give you a viewpoint. Write down the coordinates of this viewpoint.

Using the plane $z = 5$ as the screen and the viewpoint you are given, determine the coordinates where each of the vertices of the cube will be projected on the screen.

**3.** Plot the projections of the vertices you found in Question 2 on a large piece of graph paper, thinking of the piece of graph paper as the plane $z = 5$. Put an appropriate scale on the axes.

Label the projections for the vertices $(2, 2, 2)$, $(0, 0, 0)$, and so on, and connect them to draw the cube. Use solid lines for the edges that are visible and dotted lines for the edges that are hidden by the rest of the cube.

*Comment:* If your drawing doesn't look something like a cube, you will need to revise your work.

# An Animated Outline

In this assignment, you and your partner will complete the outline for your animation project, *POW 5: An Animated POW*. You will turn it in tomorrow, but you should keep a copy so you can continue your work.

The next stage after this assignment will be to write the program itself, beginning with a plain-language program. Remember to keep written copies of all your work on the program. This will reduce the risk of losing valuable work. It may also be easier to find errors in your written copy than on the calculator.

Plan to have your program entered well before your presentation day. Usually, "debugging" your program takes more time than writing the first draft.

# Mirrors in Space

You've looked at coordinate and matrix representations in two dimensions for each of the three basic types of isometries: *translations, rotations,* and *reflections.*

In this assignment, you will explore reflections in 3-space. In this setting, we use a **plane of reflection,** which is analogous to a *line* of reflection in two dimensions. The reflection of a point $P$ through a plane $m$ is the point $Q$ that makes $m$ the perpendicular bisector of $\overline{PQ}$. In other words, $\overline{PQ}$ is perpendicular to $m$, and $m$ intersects the segment at the midpoint of the segment. The plane $m$ will be a plane of symmetry between any set of points and the set of their reflections through $m$.

**1. a.** Begin with the point $(4, 6, 2)$, and imagine reflecting that point using the *yz*-plane as the plane of reflection. (The *yz*-plane is the same as the plane $x = 0$.) Determine where the point $(4, 6, 2)$ should end up.

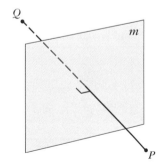

**b.** Now generalize your work from Question 1a, using the point $(x, y, z)$. That is, find the coordinates of the point you would get if you reflected the point $(x, y, z)$ through the *yz*-plane.

**2.** Find a matrix $A$ that will do the work of Question 1b for you. That is, find a matrix $A$ so that the matrix product $[x \ y \ z] A$ gives the coordinates of the reflection of the point $(x, y, z)$ in the *yz*-plane.

# Where Are We Now?

This is a good time to reflect on the unit. Your tasks in this assignment are to describe the unit goal, to summarize what has happened in the unit so far, and to indicate what you think remains to be done.

1. Describe what your expectations were early in the unit. That is, what did you think the unit would be about? What mathematics did you think you would be learning?

2. What have turned out to be the key mathematical ideas of the unit? How do they relate to the unit problem?

3. What ideas or procedures do you think you still need to learn in order to solve the unit problem?

# Rotating in Three Dimensions

*Joel Picazo uses coordinates and matrices to rotate in three dimensions.*

You are finally ready for the cube! You need only combine what you know about rotations in two dimensions with what you know in general about three dimensions to create matrices for rotating in three dimensions. Then you will be turning the cube!

# Follow That Point!

1. Consider the point $(2, 3, -5)$, and imagine that this point is rotated $20°$ counterclockwise around the $z$-axis. Where does this point end up?

2. Now suppose you have a segment connecting $(2, 3, -5)$ and $(5, 2, 6)$, and you rotate that segment $20°$ counterclockwise around the $z$-axis. What is the result of this rotation?

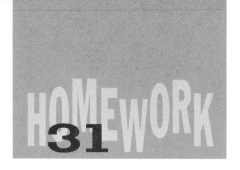

# One Turn of a Cube

Imagine placing a cube in 3-space. For simplicity, choose a placement for which the faces of the cube are parallel to the coordinate planes.

**1.** Write down the coordinates in 3-space for the eight vertices of your cube.

**2.** Imagine that the cube has been rotated 30° counterclockwise around the $z$-axis. Choose one face of the cube, and find the new coordinates of the vertices on that face. (Round off the coordinates to the nearest tenth.)

**3.** Make two sketches, one showing your cube in its original position in 3-space and another showing its position after rotation.

# Rotation Matrix in Three Dimensions

You have seen that, if a point $(x, y, z)$ is rotated counterclockwise around the $z$-axis, through an angle of $30°$, its new coordinates are

$$(x \cos 30° - y \sin 30°, x \sin 30° + y \cos 30°, z)$$

**1.** Find a rotation matrix for this transformation. That is, find a matrix $B$ so that

$[x \; y \; z] B =$
$$[x \cos 30° - y \sin 30° \quad x \sin 30° + y \cos 30° \quad z]$$

**2.** What should the rotation matrix be if the rotation is around the $x$-axis? The $y$-axis?

# The Turning Cube Outline

Writing animation programs is a very complicated task, and the unit problem is no exception. You have had to learn many ideas about mathematics and programming to develop a program for the turning cube, and you now have all the necessary pieces.

Most programmers find it helpful to write an outline for a program before developing the code. Your task in this assignment is to look over your work for the unit, and develop an outline for a program to turn the cube. You need not give line-by-line details. Instead, give the general structure of how the program should be organized.

# Beginning Portfolio Selection

Now that you have turned the cube, you can understand the different items on the outline you saw at the beginning of the unit. That outline probably looked something like this.

**1.** Draw a picture on the graphing calculator.

**2.** Create the appearance of motion.

**3.** Change the position of an object located in a two-dimensional coordinate system.

**4.** Create a two-dimensional drawing of a three-dimensional object.

**5.** Change the position of an object located in a three-dimensional coordinate system.

Choose three of the items from this outline. For each item, choose one assignment that was important in developing that item. Explain how that assignment helped you understand the given item and how that item fit into the overall development of the unit.

You will work with the remaining two items in *Homework 35: Continued Portfolio Selection*.

# An Animated POW

*Leah Allen and Lou Allen Wheeler work together to create their own animation to present to their classmates.*

Now that you have turned the cube, you are ready to create an interesting animation of your own. Over the next several days, you will put together your work on *POW 5: An Animated POW,* present it, and see the animations your classmates have created.

# "An Animated POW" Write-up

You and your partner should now have almost completed your work on *POW 5: An Animated POW*.

Your homework tonight is to complete your work on this POW. This has several parts.

**1.** Complete the program.

**2.** Prepare your written copy of the program.

**3.** Develop a presentation for the class, lasting three to four minutes. Your presentation should include

   • A demonstration of the program

   • A description of one interesting feature of the program

# Continued Portfolio Selection

In this assignment, you continue the work on your portfolio that you began in *Homework 33: Beginning Portfolio Selection*. In that assignment, you looked at the different stages in the outline you saw at the beginning of the unit:

**1.** Draw a picture on the graphing calculator.

**2.** Create the appearance of motion.

**3.** Change the position of an object located in a two-dimensional coordinate system.

**4.** Create a two-dimensional drawing of a three-dimensional object.

**5.** Change the position of an object located in a three-dimensional coordinate system.

In the earlier assignment, you selected three of the items from this outline. In tonight's assignment, you should work with the remaining two items. As before, for each of these items, choose one assignment that was important in developing that item, explain how the assignment helped you understand the item, and explain how the item fit into the overall development of the unit.

# As the Cube Turns Portfolio

Now that *As the Cube Turns* is completed, it is time to put together your portfolio for the unit. Compiling this portfolio has three parts.

• Writing a cover letter in which you summarize the unit

• Choosing papers to include from your work in this unit

• Discussing your personal growth during the unit

## Cover Letter for *As the Cube Turns*

Look back over *As the Cube Turns* and describe the central problem of the unit and the main mathematical ideas. This description should give an overview of how the key ideas were developed in this unit and how they were used to solve the central problem.

*Continued on next page*

## Selecting Papers from *As the Cube Turns*

Your portfolio for *As the Cube Turns* should contain these items.

* *Homework 17: How Did We Get Here?*

* *Homework 27: Spiders and Cubes*

* *Homework 33: Beginning Portfolio Selection* and *Homework 35: Continued Portfolio Selection*

  Include your own work on the activities from the unit that you selected in these assignments.

* A Problem of the Week

  Select one of the first two POWs you completed during this unit (*"A Sticky Gum Problem" Revisited* or *A Wider Windshield Wiper, Please*).

* Your work on *POW 5: An Animated Project*

  Include both *Homework 28: An Animated Outline* and *Homework 34: "An Animated POW" Write-up.*

## Personal Growth

Your cover letter for *As the Cube Turns* describes how the unit develops. As part of your portfolio, write about your own personal development during this unit. Because this is the first unit with a significant focus on programming, you may want to address this issue.

> *How have you grown in your understanding of the task of writing and interpreting programs?*

You should include here any other thoughts you might like to share with a reader of your portfolio.

# Appendix

# Supplemental Problems

The supplemental problems for *As the Cube Turns* continue the unit's areas of emphasis—programming, trigonometry, matrices, and transformational geometry—although other topics appear as well. Here are some examples.

- *Loopy Arithmetic* and *Let the Calculator Do It!* give additional work on writing programs.

- *Sum Tangents* and *Half a Sine* look at the development of other trigonometric formulas.

- *Bugs in Trees* shows a new application for matrices.

- *The General Isometry* is a challenging activity about combining isometries.

PROBLEM

# Loopy Arithmetic

## The Basic For/End Loop

For/End loops can be used in programs to do a variety of repetitive tasks, including arithmetic.

By combining this type of loop with a display of results on the screen, you can get your graphing calculator to show you the work it's doing.

For example, the screen for this plain-language program will show the calculator counting from 20 to 100.

> For A from 20 to 100
>> • Display the number A on the screen
> End the A loop

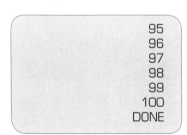

Well, actually, you won't see most of the counting happen, because the numbers will whiz by on your screen. But when the program is finished running, it will look something like the screen shown at the left.

## Beyond Counting

Your graphing calculator can do more challenging tasks than counting, though. Here are two programs for you to write.

1. Write a program using a loop to compute factorials (without using an explicit factorial command). Your program should ask the user for an input and then give the factorial of that number.

   *Important:* The challenge of this program is writing it without using the calculator's factorial instruction.

*Continued on next page*

**2.** You may be familiar with the Fibonacci sequence of numbers, which begins like this:

$$1, 1, 2, 3, 5, 8, 13, 21, 34, \ldots$$

In this sequence, each term is obtained by adding the two previous terms. For example, the term 34 comes from the sum $13 + 21$.

Your task in this problem is to write a program using a loop to compute and display the first 40 Fibonacci numbers.

# Sum Tangents

The sine and cosine functions are not the only ones for which there are angle sum formulas. The tangent function has this angle sum formula:

$$\tan (A + B) = \frac{\tan A + \tan B}{1 - \tan A \tan B}$$

Your task in this problem is to show how to prove this formula. One useful fact in proving this is the relationship $\tan \theta = \frac{\sin \theta}{\cos \theta}$.

**1.** **a.** Use the right-triangle definitions of the sine, cosine, and tangent functions to prove the relationship $\tan \theta = \frac{\sin \theta}{\cos \theta}$ for acute angles.

   **b.** Explain why this relationship holds for all angles.

**2.** Use the relationship $\tan \theta = \frac{\sin \theta}{\cos \theta}$ and the angle sum formulas for sine and cosine to prove the angle sum formula for the tangent function.

**3.** Develop an angle sum formula for the cotangent function similar to that for the tangent function. Here are two possible approaches.

   **a.** Apply the fact that $\cot \theta$ can be defined as $\frac{1}{\tan \theta}$ directly to the tangent-of-a-sum formula.

   **b.** Combine the fact that $\cot \theta$ is equal to $\frac{\cos \theta}{\sin \theta}$ with the angle sum formulas for sine and cosine.

# Moving to the Second Quadrant

In *The Sine of a Sum*, you proved this sine-of-a-sum formula:

$$\sin(A + B) = \sin A \cos B + \cos A \sin B$$

Unfortunately, the proof suggested in that activity depends on a diagram that requires $A$ and $B$ to be acute angles. So the proof in *The Sine of a Sum* does not apply in all cases.

Fortunately, the formula does hold for all angles. In this activity, you need to prove that it holds when $A$ is in the second quadrant (and $B$ is still in the first quadrant).

The basic idea is to express $A$ as $90°$ more than some first-quadrant angle. To use this idea, you need to develop formulas connecting the sine and cosine of a second-quadrant angle with the sine and cosine of the first-quadrant angle that is $90°$ less.

1. The first step is to find a formula for $\sin(\theta + 90°)$ in terms of either $\sin \theta$ or $\cos \theta$.

    **a.** Pick a value for $\theta$ and find $\sin(\theta + 90°)$. Then find $\sin \theta$ and $\cos \theta$, and write a general formula based on what you find.

    **b.** Verify your formula from Question 1a using other values for $\theta$.

*Continued on next page*

**c.** Explain why your formula from Question 1a holds for all values of $\theta$, in these ways:

- Using the graph from *Homework 14: Oh, Say What You Can See*

- Using the Ferris wheel model

- Using the general definition of the sine function in terms of coordinates

**2.** Develop and justify similar formulas for each of these expressions:

**a.** $\cos (\theta + 90°)$

**b.** $\sin (\theta - 90°)$

**c.** $\cos (\theta - 90°)$

**3.** Use your results from Questions 1 and 2 to find a formula for $\sin (A + B)$ for the case in which $A$ is in the second quadrant but $B$ is in the first quadrant.

*Hints:* Write $A$ as $x + 90°$ and show that $\sin (A + B)$ is equal to $\sin [(x + B) + 90°]$. Then apply the formula from Question 1 to express $\sin [(x + B) + 90°]$ as a trigonometric function of $x + B$. Next, use the appropriate function-of-a-sum formula to express this function of $x + B$ in terms of the sine and cosine of $x$ and $B$. Finally, get back to $A$ by using the fact that $x$ is $A - 90°$ and applying appropriate formulas from Question 2.

# Adding 180°

In *Moving to the Second Quadrant*, you developed and explained formulas for the expressions $\sin(\theta + 90°)$ and $\cos(\theta + 90°)$ in terms of either $\sin\theta$ or $\cos\theta$. This activity is similar, except that you will be adding 180° to $\theta$ instead of adding 90°.

**1.** Find a formula for $\sin(\theta + 180°)$ in terms of either $\sin\theta$ or $\cos\theta$, using these steps.

   **a.** Pick a value for $\theta$ and find $\sin(\theta + 180°)$. Then find $\sin\theta$ and $\cos\theta$, and write a general formula based on what you find.

   **b.** Verify your formula from Question 1a using other values for $\theta$.

   **c.** Explain why your formula from Question 1a holds for all values of $\theta$, in at least one of these ways:

     • Using the graph from *Homework 14: Oh, Say What You Can See*

     • Using the Ferris wheel model

     • Using the general definition of the sine function in terms of coordinates

**2.** Develop a similar formula for $\cos(\theta + 180°)$ and justify your result.

**3.** Explain how to use your answers to Questions 1 and 2 to get formulas for $\sin(\theta - 180°)$ and $\cos(\theta - 180°)$. That is, show how to develop formulas in which you subtract 180° instead of adding 180°.

# Sums for All Quadrants

In *The Sine of a Sum*, you showed that if $A$ and $B$ are first-quadrant angles, then $\sin(A + B)$ is equal to $\sin A \cos B + \cos A \sin B$. In *Moving to the Second Quadrant,* you showed that this formula works when one of the angles is in the second quadrant and the other is in the first quadrant.

Your task in this activity is to prove this formula for other cases.

**1.** Prove the formula for the case in which both $A$ and $B$ are second-quadrant angles.

   *Hint:* Adapt the method used in *Moving to the Second Quadrant* by writing $A$ as $x + 90°$ and writing $B$ as $y + 90°$. You will also need a formula for $\sin(\theta + 180°)$ in terms of either $\sin\theta$ or $\cos\theta$.

**2.** Prove the formula for all other cases, considering the possible combinations of quadrants for $A$ and $B$. Use the periodicity of the sine and cosine functions, and express angles in various quadrants in terms of appropriate first-quadrant angles.

   *Suggestion:* Begin by listing the cases you need to consider, and think about how to avoid duplication. For instance, if you do the case in which $A$ is in the third quadrant and $B$ is in the second quadrant, you do not have to also do the case in which these quadrants are reversed.

# Bugs in Trees

Matrices are basically a shorthand for representing certain numerical information, and matrix operations are a convenient way to describe certain arithmetic processes.

In this unit, matrices have been used as a way of doing the arithmetic involved in geometrical transformations, such as translations and rotations. In *Meadows or Malls?* (in Year 3), you used matrices to represent systems of linear equations.

This problem will illustrate another context in which matrices can provide a useful way to describe patterns of arithmetic operations.

## The Situation

A pair of trees, tree A and tree B, are side by side. Some bugs have infested the trees, and the bugs are moving back and forth. A researcher watches the activities of the bugs, recording their movements once per hour, and reaches these conclusions:

- If a bug is in tree A at a particular observation, there is a 70% chance that it will still be in tree A at the next observation and only a 30% chance that it will be in tree B at the next observation.

- If a bug is in tree B at a particular observation, there is a 60% chance that it will be in tree A at the next observation and only a 40% chance that it will still be in tree B at the next observation.

*Continued on next page*

*Comment:* In studying sequences of coin flips, you learned that each flip is independent of the previous flips. In other words, the probability of getting heads or tails on a given flip does not depend on what was flipped in the past. In the situation here, the position of a bug at a given observation is analogous to the outcome of a given coin flip. But unlike the coin situation, a bug's position at a given observation is not independent of where it was before. Specifically (according to this researcher, at least), the position of a bug at a given observation depends (in a probabilistic way) on where it was at the preceding observation.

A situation in which each trial depends probabilistically on the preceding trial is called a *Markov chain.* The theory of Markov chains derives its name from the Russian probabilist A. A. Markov (1856–1922), who did pioneering work in this field.

## Some Sample Questions

1. Suppose that in a certain observation, there are 110 bugs in tree A and 90 bugs in tree B. If the movement of the bugs follows the researcher's analysis, how many will be in each tree at the next observation?

2. Suppose the trees become infested with many thousands of bugs. At a given observation, 25% of the bugs are in tree A and 75% are in tree B. If these bugs continue to move according to the researcher's analysis, what fraction of them will be in each tree at the next observation?

*Continued on next page*

## The Matrices

The researcher's probabilities can be put into this matrix:

$$\begin{bmatrix} .7 & .3 \\ .6 & .4 \end{bmatrix}$$

This is called a *transition matrix,* because it describes how the bug's position might change from one observation to the next.

The results of a particular observation can be put into a row matrix. For example, in Question 1, the information obtained can be represented by the row vector [110 90].

**3.** Show why the arithmetic you did in Question 1 can be represented in matrix form by the product

$$[110 \quad 90] \begin{bmatrix} .7 & .3 \\ .6 & .4 \end{bmatrix}$$

**4.** Show how to represent the arithmetic of Question 2 as the product of a row vector and a matrix.

## The Hours Go By

For the rest of this assignment, continue to assume that the researcher's analysis holds. Start with the situation from Question 2 and suppose that you make an observation every hour. Treat the initial situation as hour 0 and your result from Question 2 as hour 1.

**5.** Find the percentage of bugs in each tree at hour 2. (Remember that a bug's position at hour 2 depends on where it was at hour 1, but not on where it was at hour 0.)

*Continued on next page*

**6.** Develop a matrix expression for the distribution of the bugs at hour $n$.

**7.** What will happen in the long run? Will there ever come a time when the bugs are all in tree A? Explain your answers.

Adapted with permission from the *Mathematics Teacher*, © May 1998, by the National Council of Teachers of Mathematics.

# Half a Sine

You have found formulas that allow you to find the sine and cosine of the sum and the difference of two angles in terms of the sines and cosines of the two angles themselves. You also found formulas for double angles in *Homework 18: Doubles and Differences*.

Your task in this problem is somewhat the opposite, namely, to find formulas for the sine and cosine of *half* of a given angle in terms of the sine and cosine of the angle itself.

In other words, you want to find formulas that look like this:

$$\sin \frac{A}{2} = \ldots$$

$$\cos \frac{A}{2} = \ldots$$

In each case, the right side of the equation can involve any trigonometric functions using the angle $A$ itself.

*Hint:* Start by thinking of $A$ as being twice $\frac{A}{2}$, and use the double-angle formula to write $\cos A$ in terms of $\sin \frac{A}{2}$ and $\cos \frac{A}{2}$. Then use the Pythagorean identity, $\sin^2 \theta + \cos^2 \theta = 1$, to get $\cos A$ in terms of only $\sin \frac{A}{2}$ or only $\cos \frac{A}{2}$, and work from that to get $\sin \frac{A}{2}$ and $\cos \frac{A}{2}$ in terms of $\cos A$.

# SUPPLEMENTAL
## PROBLEM

# The General Isometry

Mathematicians often use the word *transformation* to indicate a function in which the domain and range are sets of points. If we use the letter *f* to represent a specific transformation, then *f*(*X*) represents the point to which *X* is moved.

An isometry is a special type of geometric transformation—one in which the distance between two points remains unchanged. In other words, if *f* is an isometry and *A* and *B* are any two points, then the distance from *f*(*A*) to *f*(*B*) must be equal to the distance from *A* to *B*.

You've also seen that there are three fundamental types of isometries of the plane: translations, rotations, and reflections. In this activity, you should suppose that *ABC* is a triangle and that *f* is an isometry of the plane. Your task in this activity is to show, as described in Questions 1 through 3, that *f* can be created by combining the three basic types of isometries.

1. Suppose *RST* is a triangle that is congruent to *ABC*, with *AB* = *RS*, *BC* = *ST*, and *AC* = *RT*. (*Reminder:* The notation *XY* means the distance from *X* to *Y*.)

   Show that one of these two statements must be true.

   • There is a translation *g*, a rotation *h*, and a reflection *k* for which *R* = *k*(*h*(*g*(*A*))), *S* = *k*(*h*(*g*(*B*))), and *T* = *k*(*h*(*g*(*C*))).

*Continued on next page*

- There is a translation $g$ and a rotation $h$ for which
  $R = h(g(A))$, $S = h(g(B))$, and $T = h(g(C))$.

*Hint:* First show that there is a translation $g$ for which
$g(A) = R$. Then show that there is a rotation $h$ around
$R$ for which $h(g(B)) = S$. Finally, decide if a reflection
through the line $RS$ is needed.

**2.** Suppose $RST$ is a triangle, and suppose that points $X$
and $Y$ satisfy these three conditions:

- $RX = RY$

- $SX = SY$

- $TX = TY$

Show that $X$ and $Y$ are actually the same point. (*Hint:*
Show that if $X$ and $Y$ were different points, then
$R$, $S$, and $T$ would all be on the perpendicular
bisector of $\overline{XY}$.)

**3.** Use your results from Questions 1 and 2 to prove that
one of these two statements must be true.

- There is a translation $g$, a rotation $h$, and a
  reflection $k$ such that $f(X) = k(h(g(X)))$ for every
  point $X$.

- There is a translation $g$ and a rotation $h$ such that
  $f(X) = h(g(X))$ for every point $X$.

In other words, show that $f$ is either a combination of
a translation, a rotation, and a reflection or a
combination of only a translation and a rotation.

# SUPPLEMENTAL
## PROBLEM

# Perspective on Geometry

One of the key tasks in this unit is deciding how to represent a three-dimensional object—the cube—on the two-dimensional calculator screen.

Artists use the general term *perspective* to describe the various methods they use to create this type of representation. Your task in this assignment is to do some research on the history of perspective in art.

Your report should describe different schemes of perspective and explain the geometric principles behind them. You may want to include examples of famous works of art showing different methods or create your own drawings illustrating how the same object might be drawn using different methods.

*"Venice: A Regatta on the Grand Canal" by the Italian painter Canaletto (1697–1768).*

# Let the Calculator Do It!

In *Find Those Corners!* you projected the vertices of a cube on the plane $z = 5$. You probably found that computing the projections for each vertex was a lot of work.

In this assignment, you will write a program for your calculator (or a computer, if you and your teacher prefer) to do the work.

Your program should ask the user for the vertex of the cube or for any point that the user wants projected. It should also ask the user for the viewpoint. Your program should then tell the user the projection of the given point, using the given viewpoint, on the plane $z = 5$.

# DAYS 1–7
## On Your Own

# DAY 8 and Beyond
## An Independent Learning Project

# On Your Own

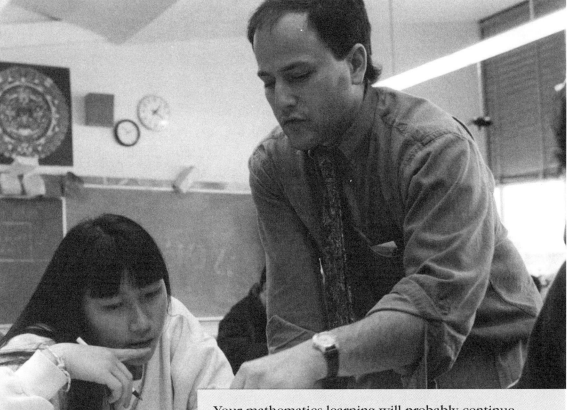

*Katrina Chan and IMP teacher Dean Orfanedes share their views about the difference between memorizing a formula and really understanding it.*

Your mathematics learning will probably continue beyond high school. Whether you go on to college or enter the work force directly, you will encounter situations in which you need to learn mathematics that you have not encountered before.

You may no longer have the same level of teacher and peer support that you had in high school, so you need to develop the ability to learn on your own. In this unit, you will investigate some resources and methods for independent learning.

# Knowing What You Know

*This bronze cast of "The Thinker" by Auguste Rodin is displayed at the Rodin Museum in Paris, France.*

1. Individually, write down examples of mathematics topics that used to be difficult for you but that you really understand now.

2. As a group, share the topics you listed in Question 1, perhaps adding items to your own list from what your fellow group members share. Are there any topics that everyone feels were once difficult but that they now understand?

3. As a group, discuss what it means to "know something" in mathematics. For example, does reading a definition of a concept ensure that you know what it means? What more could be needed? Keep a record of your group's ideas on this issue.

4. Imagine that you have finished high school and are in some new work or classroom situation. Suppose someone expects you to know something that you have not learned before.

   As a group, make a list of ways you might be able to learn whatever it is that you need to know. Be as specific as possible. For example:

   • If you say "ask someone," discuss who you actually know whom you could ask or how you would find a good person to ask.

   • If you say "look it up," discuss where or how you would begin your search.

   • If you say "work on it," discuss what this might entail.

5. Brainstorm with your group some topics that you would like to know more about.

# Which Weights Weigh What?

Do you remember the economical king with the different kinds of scales? (You first met him in Year 1 in *POW 14: Eight Bags of Gold* and *POW 15: Twelve Bags of Gold*, and he reappeared in Year 3 in *POW 14: And a Fortune, Too!*) He has now decided that an old-fashioned balance scale is what he wants. But he wants to be able to use it as efficiently as possible (of course).

In the king's country, it is customary to pay for food by weight, but the king doesn't trust the merchants' scales. He insists on using his balance scale to verify their claims.

He has decided that he only needs to verify the weights of packages that weigh whole numbers of ounces. He wants to be able to verify weights starting from 1 ounce and including all possibilities up to some still-undecided value. (He's the king, so he can make rules like that.) But he's concerned that in order to weigh different amounts, he might need a large set of standard weights—a 1-ounce weight, a 2-ounce weight, a 3-ounce weight, and so on.

## Method 1: Combining Weights on One Side

One of the king's advisors points out that the situation is not so bad. For example, the king doesn't need a 3-ounce weight, because he can verify the weight of a 3-ounce package by balancing it against a combination of a 1-ounce and a 2-ounce weight, as shown here.

*Continued on next page*

The king is relieved to hear this, but he still needs to decide what weights to buy. No specific set of weights will cover all possibilities, so the choice seems to depend on *how many* weights he is willing to buy.

Of course, if he buys only one weight, it will need to be a 1-ounce weight. Unfortunately, that will only allow him to verify the weight of a 1-ounce package.

Suppose the king is willing to buy two weights. Exactly which weights should he buy in order to verify the weight of as heavy a package as possible (and still include all whole-number possibilities of lesser weight)? And what if he buys three weights? Or four? The king isn't sure what to do.

## Method 2: Using Weights on Both Sides

Another advisor suggests that perhaps the king can omit both the 2-ounce weight and the 3-ounce weight. For example, to verify a merchant's claim that a package weighs 3 ounces, the king can put the package together with a 1-ounce weight on one side of the balance scale and put a 4-ounce weight on the other side, as shown here. If the two sides balance, then the king will know that the package really does weigh 3 ounces. (But the King will need something other than the 1-ounce and 4-ounce weights to check a 2-ounce package.)

This method seems to provide more options, and so the king may be able to weigh more possibilities for a given number of weights. As with the first method, if the king buys only one weight, it will need to be a 1-ounce weight. But that will only allow him to verify the weight of a 1-ounce package.

*Continued on next page*

Interactive Mathematics Program

Suppose the king is willing to buy two weights. Which weights should he buy? And what if he buys three weights? Or four? Again, he isn't sure what to do.

## Your Task: Consider Each Method

First consider Method 1, in which the weights must all go on one side of the balance scale and the package on the other side. Start with the specific cases of two weights, three weights, and four weights, and tell the king which weights he should choose in each case and what package weights his choice will allow him to verify. Then look for a general procedure that tells him what weights to choose and what package weights he will be able to verify.

Next, consider Method 2, which allows the king to put weights on both sides of the balance scale. (In Method 2, he can still put the weights all on one side if he chooses.) Again, start with specific cases of two weights, three weights, and four weights, and tell the king which weights he should choose in each case and what package weights his choice will allow him to verify. Then look for a general procedure that tells him what weights to choose and what package weights he will be able to verify.

## Write-up

Your write-up should contain these components:

**1.** *Problem Statement*

**2.** *Process*

**3.** *Solution:* For each method, include a clear explanation of why the weights you choose are the best. State how high your choice of weights will allow the king to go, and explain this result. Include a general solution if you can.

**4.** *Evaluation*

**5.** *Self-assessment*

# Ask Someone!

## Part I: A Future Problem

Imagine that you are in a college mathematics class and you come across this question on your homework assignment:

**Solve this equation by factoring:**

$$x^3 + 5x^2 - 6x = 0$$

Although you have learned something about factoring, you may not recall how to answer this particular question. "What should I do about this?" you wonder.

For this assignment, you should ask someone. (You can do this in person, by phone, or on-line.) You may need to ask

*Continued on next page*

more than one person before you find someone who can help. After you've gotten help, do the two things below.

1. State and explain the answer to the homework problem.

2. Describe what you learned about how to get information about mathematics from people.

## Part II: A Measurement Problem

The next problem is related to *POW 6: Which Weights Weigh What?* First read the problem, and then answer Questions 3 and 4.

> *Suppose you are camping and have a pancake recipe that calls for exactly 10 ounces of milk. Unfortunately, you brought only 8-ounce and 6-ounce cups. How can you use these two types of cups to measure out exactly 10 ounces? What other amounts could you measure out exactly?*

3. Answer the specific questions in the problem.

4. Discuss how this problem is mathematically similar to the POW and how it is different.

# Radian Measure

Again, imagine that you're at college in your new math class. Suddenly, you hear the professor saying, "Consider this angle of $\frac{\pi}{2}$ radians. . . ."

"Whoa!" you say. "A *radian*. What is that? I've seen it on my calculator, but what is it?"

Don't panic—you can find out. As a group, begin by finding the topic of radians in one of the textbooks your teacher has available, reading the appropriate material, and working on some of the problems. Then do each of these tasks.

1. In your own words, explain what a radian is.

2. Solve some of the problems in the textbook, and write out your solutions. You may want to use both the radian and degree settings on your calculator.

3. State some questions you have about radians that the textbook did not address fully or at all.

4. Describe what you've learned about the process of using a textbook to find out about a new topic.

# The Law of Sines

This assignment contains an example of a lesson in the style of a traditional textbook. In Part I, you will read the material, including Exercises 1 through 6. In Part II, you will do the exercises and then answer one additional question.

## Part I: The Reading

### The Law of Sines

We will now look at a general triangle $ABC$ and study the relationship between the angles in the triangle—$\alpha$ ("alpha"), $\beta$ ("beta"), and $\gamma$ ("gamma")—and the sides opposite them—$a, b, c$.

**Theorem (The Law of Sines). In the general triangle $ABC$ shown here, the following equations hold:**

$$\frac{\sin \alpha}{a} = \frac{\sin \beta}{b} = \frac{\sin \gamma}{c}$$

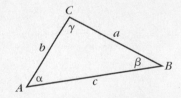

**Proof:** We show that $\frac{\sin \alpha}{a} = \frac{\sin \beta}{b}$ in the case where angles $\alpha$ and $\beta$ are both acute. The proof for the case in which one of these angles is not acute is Exercise 6, and the proof that $\frac{\sin \beta}{b} = \frac{\sin \gamma}{c}$ is left to the reader.

Drop a perpendicular $\overline{CD}$ from vertex $C$ to the line containing vertex $A$ and vertex $B$. Because $\alpha$ and $\beta$ are acute, $D$ lies between $A$ and $B$ as shown here.

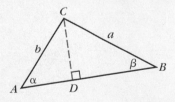

In the right triangles $ADC$ and $BDC$, we have

$$\sin \alpha = \frac{CD}{b} \text{ and } \sin \beta = \frac{CD}{a}$$

so

$$b \sin \alpha = CD \text{ and } a \sin \beta = CD$$

Thus, we have

$$b \sin \alpha = a \sin \beta$$

Dividing both sides by $ab$ gives

$$\frac{\sin \alpha}{a} = \frac{\sin \beta}{b}$$

as desired, which concludes the proof.

**Given two angles and a side**

Note that the law of sines can be written as

$$\frac{a}{\sin \alpha} = \frac{b}{\sin \beta} = \frac{c}{\sin \gamma}$$

If two angles of triangle $ABC$ are given, then the third angle can be found by using the law

$$\alpha + \beta + \gamma = 180°$$

So if two of the angles are known, then all three denominators in the fractions $\frac{a}{\sin \alpha}$, $\frac{b}{\sin \beta}$, and $\frac{c}{\sin \gamma}$ can be found using a calculator. If any one of the sides $a$, $b$, or $c$ is also known, then the equations

$$\frac{a}{\sin \alpha} = \frac{b}{\sin \beta} = \frac{c}{\sin \gamma}$$

can be solved for the remaining two sides of the triangle. Therefore:

**If we know any two angles and one side of a triangle, then we can find the third angle, and we can use the law of sines to solve the triangle.**

**Example:** In triangle $ABC$, suppose $\alpha = 40°$, $\beta = 75°$, and $a = 70$. Solve for $\gamma$, $b$, and $c$.

**Solution:** $\gamma = 180° - \alpha - \beta = 180° - 40° - 75° = 65°$. By the law of sines,

$$\frac{a}{\sin 40°} = \frac{b}{\sin 75°} = \frac{c}{\sin 65°}$$

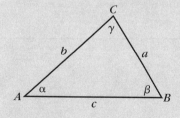

*Continued on next page*

Because $a = 70$, we have

$$b = \frac{a \sin 75^\circ}{\sin 40^\circ} = \frac{70 \sin 75^\circ}{\sin 40^\circ} \approx 105.2$$

and

$$c = \frac{a \sin 65^\circ}{\sin 40^\circ} = \frac{70 \sin 65^\circ}{\sin 40^\circ} \approx 98.7$$

**Exercises:** In Exercises 1 through 4, use the law of sines to solve triangle $ABC$. Round off angles and lengths to the nearest tenth.

**1.** $a = 30$, $\beta = 50^\circ$, $\gamma = 35^\circ$

**2.** $b = 15$, $\alpha = 120^\circ$, $\gamma = 30^\circ$

**3.** $b = 21$, $\beta = 35^\circ$, $\gamma = 25^\circ$

**4.** $c = 72.4$, $\alpha = 52.3^\circ$, $\beta = 45.7^\circ$

**5.** A surveyor measures the distance between points $A$ and $B$ along one side of a river and finds that the points are 256 meters apart. Point $C$ on the opposite bank serves as the third vertex of a triangle. The surveyor finds that angle $CAB$ is 61° and that angle $CBA$ is 55°.

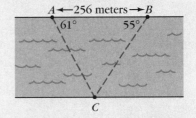

   **a.** Find the distance between $A$ and $C$.

   **b.** Find the distance between $B$ and $C$.

   **c.** How wide is the river?

**6.** (Extra Credit) Adjust the proof of the law of sines to take care of the case in which angle $\alpha$ is obtuse.

## Part II: Your Assignment

**1.** Do Exercises 1 through 5 from Part I.

**2.** In your own words, explain what you think the law of sines is and why it is useful.

**3.** (Challenge) Do Exercise 6.

# The Ellipse

Like *Homework 2: The Law of Sines*, this assignment contains a lesson in the style of a traditional textbook. In Part I, you will read the material, including Exercises 1 through 4. In Part II, you will do the exercises and then answer some additional questions.

## Part I: The Reading

### The Ellipse

The **ellipse** is one of several shapes, called **conic sections,** that one can get by taking the intersection of a plane with a cone.

By changing the angle of the plane, one gets other conic sections, including circles, parabolas, and hyperbolas. The accompanying diagram shows a case in which the intersection is an ellipse.

All the conic sections can be represented by quadratic equations in two variables. For example, a circle of radius 15 whose center is at the origin is represented by the equation $x^2 + y^2 = 225$.

As we will see, merely a change in coefficients gives the equation of an ellipse. For example, the ellipse shown in Figure 1 is represented by the equation $9x^2 + 25y^2 = 225$.

An ellipse can be defined geometrically as follows:

> **An ellipse is the set of all points the sum of whose distances from two fixed points is a given positive constant.**

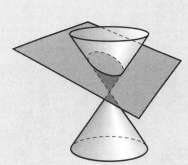

**Figure 1**

The two fixed points are called the **foci** (plural of "focus"). The midpoint of the line segment connecting the foci is called the **center** of the ellipse.

*Continued on next page*

In order to obtain an ellipse with the simplest possible equation, we place the ellipse so that the foci are on one of the coordinate axes and the center is at the origin.

For example, suppose we place the foci on the $x$-axis at $(c, 0)$ and $(-c, 0)$. The ellipse will meet the $x$-axis in two points called the **vertices** (plural of "vertex"). We will label the vertices as $(a, 0)$ and $(-a, 0)$. (If the foci are on the $y$-axis, then so are the vertices.)

Our ellipse also meets the $y$-axis in two points, which we will label as $(0, b)$ and $(0, -b)$. The four points $(a, 0)$, $(-a, 0)$, $(0, b)$, and $(0, -b)$ are called **critical points** or **extreme points.**

This situation is shown in Figure 2. The point $(x, y)$ is a general point on the ellipse, and $d_1$ and $d_2$ are the distances from this point to the two foci.

The line segment connecting the vertices, $(a, 0)$ and $(-a, 0)$, is called the **major axis,** and the line segment connecting the other two critical points, $(0, b)$ and $(0, -b)$, is called the **minor axis.**

For the special case in which the point $(x, y)$ is at the vertex $(a, 0)$, we have $d_1 = a - c$ and $d_2 = a - (-c)$, so $d_1 + d_2 = 2a$. Because the sum $d_1 + d_2$ is a constant on the ellipse, we have $d_1 + d_2 = 2a$ for every point on the ellipse.

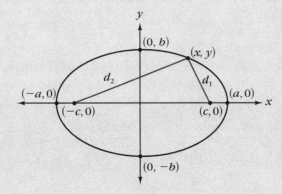

**Figure 2**

Continued on next page

Figure 3 shows the special case in which the point $(x, y)$ is at $(0, b)$. In this case, $d_1$ and $d_2$ are equal. Because their sum is $2a$, each is equal to $a$. Thus, $a$ is the hypotenuse of a right triangle whose legs are $b$ and $c$. By the Pythagorean theorem, we have $a^2 = b^2 + c^2$.

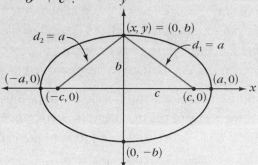

**Figure 3**

The condition $a^2 = b^2 + c^2$ shows that $a^2 > b^2$, so the major axis must be longer than the minor axis.

Going back to the general point $(x, y)$ on the ellipse in Figure 2, we can see that the distance formula gives $d_1 = \sqrt{(x - c)^2 + y^2}$ and $d_2 = \sqrt{(x + c)^2 + y^2}$. Substituting these expressions into the equation $d_1 + d_2 = 2a$ and simplifying (using the fact that $a^2 = b^2 + c^2$) gives the equation

$$\frac{x^2}{a^2} + \frac{y^2}{b^2} = 1$$

for the ellipse. (The complicated algebraic details are omitted.)

For example, the case $a = 5$ and $b = 3$ gives the equation $\frac{x^2}{25} + \frac{y^2}{9} = 1$. This is equivalent to the equation $9x^2 + 25y^2 = 225$, whose graph was shown in Figure 1. You can easily verify that the vertices $(5, 0)$ and $(-5, 0)$ and the points $(0, 3)$ and $(0, -3)$ all fit this equation. You can also use the equation $a^2 = b^2 + c^2$ to see that the foci of this ellipse are at $(4, 0)$ and $(-4, 0)$.

*Continued on next page*

Similar reasoning shows that if the foci are on the $y$-axis, at $(0, c)$ and $(0, -c)$, and the ellipse has vertices $(0, a)$ and $(0, -a)$, then the equation is $\frac{y^2}{a^2} + \frac{x^2}{b^2} = 1$, where the relationship $a^2 = b^2 + c^2$ still holds.

The relative size of the coefficients of $x^2$ and $y^2$ will tell you which axis contains the foci.

**Example:** Consider the equation $100x^2 + 36y^2 = 3600$. Putting this in the form used earlier, we get $\frac{x^2}{6^2} + \frac{y^2}{10^2} = 1$. Because the denominator associated with the $y^2$ term is larger, the foci are on the $y$-axis.

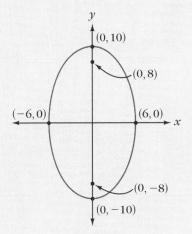

We have $a = 10$ and $b = 6$, so the vertices are located at $(0, 10)$ and $(0, -10)$, and the other critical points are at $(6, 0)$ and $(-6, 0)$. The major axis has length 20, and the minor axis has length 12.

The equation $a^2 = b^2 + c^2$ gives $c^2 = 64$, so $c = 8$. Therefore, the foci are at $(0, 8)$ and $(0, -8)$.

The graph is shown in Figure 4.

**Figure 4**

**Exercises:** For Exercises 1 through 4, do these four things.

    **a.** Find the coordinates of the critical points, and identify which are the vertices.

    **b.** Find the lengths of the major and minor axes.

    **c.** Find the coordinates of the foci.

    **d.** Sketch the ellipse.

  **1.** $16x^2 + 25y^2 = 400$

  **2.** $289x^2 + 225y^2 = 65{,}025$

  **3.** $25x^2 + 169y^2 = 4225$

  **4.** $144x^2 + 169y^2 = 24{,}336$

*Continued on next page*

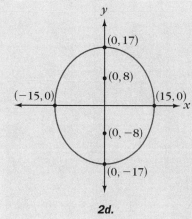

**2d.**

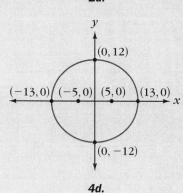

**4d.**

**Answers to even-numbered exercises:**

**2. a.** Vertices are $(0, 17)$ and $(0, -17)$; other critical points are $(15, 0)$ and $(-15, 0)$

**b.** Length of major axis = 34; length of minor axis = 30

**c.** Foci are $(0, 8)$ and $(0, -8)$

**d.** See graph at left.

**4. a.** Vertices are $(13, 0)$ and $(-13, 0)$; other critical points are $(0, 12)$ and $(0, -12)$

**b.** Length of major axis = 26; length of minor axis = 24

**c.** Foci are $(5, 0)$ and $(-5, 0)$

**d.** See graph at left.

## Part II: Your Assignment

**1.** Do Exercises 1 through 4 from Part I, including explanations of how you got your answers.

**2.** Discuss whether the inclusion of answers for Exercises 2 and 4 was helpful to you, and if so, how it was helpful.

**3.** Based on the geometric definition of an ellipse, why is a circle a special type of ellipse?

**4.** Compare your experience with this assignment to your experience with *Homework 2: The Law of Sines*.

# Now Let's Prove It!

Over the course of several units, you have gained increasing insight into quadratic functions and quadratic equations. You have gotten numerical approximations to the solutions to quadratic equations using graphs, and you have studied the graphs of quadratic functions using ideas such as vertices and lines of symmetry.

In *High Dive,* you saw that there is a general expression that allows you to get the exact solution to *any* quadratic equation. In fact, this general expression, called the *quadratic formula,* even allows you to work with a quadratic equation in which the coefficients are themselves variables, by expressing the solutions in terms of those coefficients. Here is a summary of the quadratic formula.

$$\text{If } ax^2 + bx + c = 0 \text{ and } a \neq 0,$$

$$\text{then}$$

$$x = \frac{-b \pm \sqrt{b^2 - 4ac}}{2a}$$

Your task in this activity is to work with your group to explain the quadratic formula as fully as you can. You may use any resources you wish, including textbooks and other people.

In particular, you should find a proof that the formula works for every quadratic equation. Write out each step of your proof, and explain in your own words what is happening from one line to the next. Also include any ideas on how someone might have come up with the formula in the first place.

# What to Know When

Over the course of your mathematics education, you've probably seen quite a few formulas of various kinds. For example, the equation $a^2 + b^2 = c^2$ (from the Pythagorean theorem) and the formula for the chi-square distribution are general principles that can be used in many situations.

You probably understand different principles at different levels. For example, although you have used the formula for the chi-square distribution (in the Year 2 unit *Is There Really a Difference?*), you may not know where the formula comes from or why it works.

The Pythagorean theorem, on the other hand, is something that you have used in many situations. You have seen a proof of this theorem, and you have used the equation $a^2 + b^2 = c^2$ to develop other formulas.

1. Reflect on your experiences with mathematical formulas, and write an essay about them in terms of these kinds of questions.

   • When is it important to really understand a formula, and when is it enough simply to be able to use it?

   • When is it worthwhile to memorize a formula?

   • Which should come first—the proof or the examples?

   • When and why is it important to understand the proof of a general principle?

*Continued on next page*

Interactive Mathematics Program

**2.** Pick two topics that seemed difficult to you at first but that you now feel you know quite well.

   **a.** For each topic, describe what it means to "know" that topic. What exactly do you know, and what can you do with regard to that topic?

   **b.** For each topic, describe what you did to understand it. Be as specific as possible.

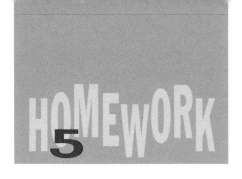

# A Fractional Situation

Once again, your task is to read the material in Part I and then answer the questions in Part II.

## Part I: The Reading

### Simplifying Algebraic Fractions

It is often helpful in your work if you replace a complex expression by a simpler equivalent expression. One important aspect of this process is the simplification (or "reduction") of fractions. Simplifying fractions involving algebraic expressions works much like simplifying fractions.

For example, to simplify the fraction $\frac{6}{10}$, you might write it as $\frac{3 \cdot 2}{5 \cdot 2}$ and then "cancel" the factors of 2 in the numerator and denominator. The process is often written like this:

$$\frac{6}{10} = \frac{3 \cdot \cancel{2}}{5 \cdot \cancel{2}} = \frac{3}{5}$$

More formally, instead of "canceling," you can write $\frac{3 \cdot 2}{5 \cdot 2}$ as $\frac{3}{5} \cdot \frac{2}{2}$, and use the fact that $\frac{2}{2}$ is equal to 1.

Similarly, suppose you have the algebraic fraction $\frac{12xy}{20x}$. You can simplify this by finding a common factor in the numerator and denominator, and then "canceling." You can write the process like this:

$$\frac{12xy}{20x} = \frac{3y \cdot \cancel{4x}}{5 \cdot \cancel{4x}} = \frac{3y}{5}$$

The more formal explanation of cancellation applies here as well. That is, you can write the expression as the product $\frac{3y}{5} \cdot \frac{4x}{4x}$ and use the fact that $\frac{4x}{4x}$ is equal to 1. Thus, if the numerator and the denominator of a fraction have a common nonzero factor, these factors

*Continued on next page*

will "cancel each other" because any nonzero number divided by itself is 1 and any number times 1 is that number.

Symbolically, the general principle can be described using this sequence of equations:

$$\frac{a \cdot c}{b \cdot c} = \frac{a}{b} \cdot \frac{c}{c} = \frac{a}{b} \cdot 1 = \frac{a}{b}$$

To apply this principle, you may need to factor the numerator or denominator. For example, the fraction $\frac{x^2 + 4x}{x^2 + 5x + 4}$ can be simplified by writing the numerator as $x(x + 4)$ and the denominator as $(x + 1)(x + 4)$. The fraction $\frac{x(x + 4)}{(x + 1)(x + 4)}$ can then be simplified to $\frac{x}{x + 1}$.

**Exercises:** Simplify each of these expressions.

1. $\dfrac{(x + 5)(y - 3)}{25(x + 5)}$

2. $\dfrac{(c + 7)^2(d - 1)}{(c + 7)(d - 1)}$

3. $\dfrac{t^2 + 3t - 18}{t - 3}$

4. $\dfrac{r^3 + r}{4r^2 + 4}$

**Answers to odd-numbered exercises:**

1. $\dfrac{y - 3}{25} \ (x \neq -5)$

3. $t + 6 \ (t \neq 3)$

# Part II: Your Assignment

1. Do Exercises 1 through 4 from Part I, including explanations of how you got your answers.

2. Explain why the answer given for Exercise 1 says "$x \neq -5$" and the answer given for Exercise 3 says "$t \neq 3$." Do you need to include a similar condition for Exercise 2? What about for Exercise 4? Why or why not?

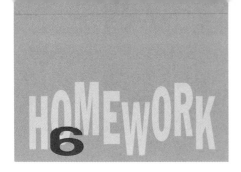

# HOMEWORK 6

# Complex Numbers

You know that the product of two negative numbers is positive, so the square of a negative number cannot be negative. Similarly, the square of a positive number cannot be negative, and certainly the square of zero is not negative.

In summary, this means that no real number has a negative square. (Real numbers are the numbers represented on the ordinary number line, whether negative, positive, or zero. The set of real numbers includes integers, fractions, and irrational numbers.)

In particular, the number $-1$ has no real-number square root. Another way to state this is to say that the equation $x^2 + 1 = 0$ has no solution using real numbers.

To remedy the situation of having such a simple equation with no solution, mathematicians have devised a larger number system. While this may seem like pulling a rabbit out of a hat, it is not that different from the creation of the

*Carl Friedrich Gauss (1777–1855) is considered one of the greatest mathematicians of all time. He made major contributions in many areas of both mathematics and physics, including pioneering work with complex numbers.*

*Continued on next page*

system of negative numbers, which allows us to solve an equation like $x + 1 = 0$, which has no whole-number solution.

In this assignment, you will read a passage that might be used to introduce this expanded number system, and then, as in earlier assignments, you will answer questions based on the reading.

# Part I: The Reading

## The Complex Number System

Mathematicians recognize that there is no real number whose square is $-1$, so they have created a number system in which the equation $x^2 = -1$ has a solution. This enlarged number system, called the **complex numbers,** begins by assuming that $\sqrt{-1}$ exists. This number is represented by the symbol $i$. In other words, by definition, we have $i^2 = -1$.

The complete system of complex numbers consists of formal sums that have the form $a + bi$, where $a$ and $b$ are real numbers. For example, $3 + 2i$, $\sqrt{2} + (-4)i$, and $(-5) + 3i$ are all complex numbers. Sums like these cannot be simplified further. In other words, there is no way to write the sum of 3 and $2i$ as a "single number."

For a complex number $a + bi$, we refer to $a$ as the **real part** and $bi$ as the **imaginary part.** Complex numbers for which $a = 0$ are called **pure imaginary.** A pure imaginary number $0 + bi$ is usually written simply as $bi$. The number $i$ itself is the pure imaginary number $0 + 1i$.

Two complex numbers are considered to be equal if their real and imaginary parts are the same. That is, we make this definition:

$a + bi = c + di$ if and only if $a = c$ and $b = d$

*Continued on next page*

A complex number of the form $a + 0 \cdot i$ is considered to be the same as the real number $a$.

## Arithmetic of Complex Numbers

Rules for doing arithmetic with two complex numbers are based on the commutative, associative, and distributive properties and the basic fact that $i^2 = -1$. For example, $[3 + 2i] + [(-5) + 3i]$ is equal to $3 + (-5) + 2i + 3i$, and we can then combine terms to get $-2 + 5i$.

More formally, we define the **sum** of two complex numbers this way:

$$(a + bi) + (c + di) = (a + c) + (b + d)i$$

Similarly, we define the **difference** of two complex numbers this way:

$$(a + bi) - (c + di) = (a - c) + (b - d)i$$

Multiplication of complex numbers is more complicated, but the principle is the same. The distributive property gives this:

$$(a + bi)(c + di) = ac + adi + bic + bidi$$

Commutativity of multiplication and addition, combining terms, and the fact that $i^2 = -1$ leads us to define the **product** of two complex numbers this way:

$$(a + bi)(c + di) = (ac - bd) + (ad + bc)i$$

We omit discussion of division of complex numbers for now.

**Example:** Find the sum, difference, and product of the complex numbers $5 - 2i$ and $-4 + 7i$.

*Continued on next page*

**Solution:** We have these results.

For the sum:

$$(5 - 2i) + (-4 + 7i) = (5 - 4) + (-2 + 7)i = 1 + 5i$$

For the difference:

$$(5 - 2i) - (-4 + 7i) = [5 - (-4)] + (-2 - 7)i = 9 - 9i$$

For the product:

$$(5 - 2i)(-4 + 7i) = 5(-4) + 5 \cdot 7i + (-2i)(-4) + (-2i)(7i)$$

$$= -20 + 35i + 8i - 14i^2$$

$$= -6 + 43i$$

**Exercises:** Find the sum, difference, and product for each of these pairs of complex numbers.

1. $3 + 2i$ and $1 - 4i$

2. $\frac{1}{2} + 3i$ and $4 + \frac{1}{3}i$

3. $2 + i$ and $2 - i$

4. $3i$ and $2 - i$

# Part II: Your Assignment

1. Do Exercises 1 through 4 from Part I, and show how you got your answers.

2. Discuss the connection between complex numbers and the quadratic formula.

# What Kind of Learning?

Mathematics education is changing. Some of the changes are in response to reports issued in the late 1980s about what society needs and how students learn.

One of these reports was entitled *Everybody Counts: A Report to the Nation on the Future of Mathematics Education*.

The next paragraph is taken from this report.

> In reality, no one can *teach* mathematics. Effective teachers are those who can stimulate students to *learn* mathematics. Education research offers compelling evidence that students learn mathematics well only when they *construct* their own mathematical understanding. To understand what they learn, they must enact for themselves verbs that permeate the mathematics curriculum: "examine," "represent," "transform," "solve," "apply," "prove," "communicate." This happens most readily when students work in groups, engage in discussion, make presentations, and in other ways take charge of their own learning.

This "myth" and "reality" appear alongside the paragraph just quoted.

> **Myth:** Students learn by remembering what they are taught.

*Continued on next page*

**Reality:** Students construct meaning as they learn mathematics. They use what they are taught to modify their prior beliefs and behavior, not simply to record and store what they are told. It is students' acts of construction and invention that build their mathematical power and enable them to solve problems they have never seen before.

## Your Assignment

Write an essay on what you think about the ideas expressed in the excerpts above and how they relate to your own experience learning and doing mathematics.

*Everybody Counts,* National Research Council, National Academy Press 1989. Excerpts are from pages 58–59.

# An Independent Learning Project

*Erika Cohen prepares to present to her classmates the mathematics topic she investigated.*

The balance of this unit is set aside for you and your group to investigate a mathematical topic together. You will select the topic, locate textbooks or other resources to provide information about the topic, learn what you can, and then make a report to the class.

# *Know How* Project

To conclude this unit, you will learn about some mathematics topic. You will then make a presentation to the class, summarizing what you have learned. You will have about 15 minutes for your presentation.

In addition to this presentation to the class, you will turn in a written report containing these components:

• A summary of the important ideas you learned about your topic

• A set of problems that are related to your topic, together with your solutions to these problems

• A description of the process you went through to collect the information

• A bibliography of books you used, as well as a list of any other sources (including people!)

• A discussion of how your experiences in this unit helped you with your learning and your gathering of information

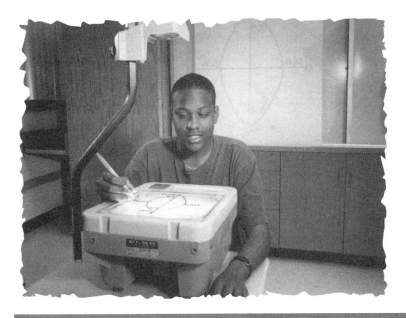

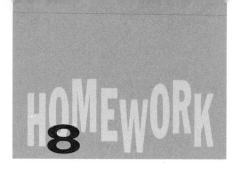

# *Know How* Portfolio

Now that *Know How* is completed, it is time to put together your portfolio for the unit. Compiling this portfolio has these three parts:

• Writing a cover letter for the unit

• Choosing papers to include from your work in this unit

• Discussing your personal growth in this unit

## Cover Letter for *Know How*

One of the goals of *Know How* was for you to get some insight into ways of learning mathematics. Discuss how the unit helped you in that respect, and select one or two assignments in which you learned something valuable about your own learning process.

*Continued on next page*

## Selecting Papers from *Know How*

Your portfolio for *Know How* should contain these items:

• *Homework 4: What to Know When*

• *POW 6: Which Weights Weigh What?*

• Your individual report from *"Know How" Project*

• The activities that you selected in connection with your cover letter

## Personal Growth

Your cover letter for *Know How* describes how the unit helped you learn about learning mathematics. As part of your portfolio, write about your own personal development during this unit. You may want to address this question:

> *How do you feel you will be able to apply what you have learned about learning after you leave high school?*

You should include here any other thoughts you might like to share with a reader of your portfolio.

# Appendix

# Supplemental Problems

This short unit has only four supplemental problems, on two main topics.

- *Derivative of the Sine* and *Sine Derivative on the Ferris Wheel* both concern the way the use of radian measure affects the derivative of the sine function.

- *The Ellipse Equation* and *Moving the Ellipse* continue the work with ellipses.

# Derivative of the Sine

In *High Dive*, you saw that the trigonometric functions can be defined for any angle in a way that is consistent with the right-triangle definitions for acute angles. In the activity *Radian Measure* (in this unit), you learned about a method of measuring angles called *radians*.

It turns out that using radian measures, rather than degrees, to measure angles leads to simpler formulas for derivatives of trigonometric functions. In particular, if angles are measured in radians, then the derivative of the sine function is the cosine function.

In symbolic form, we can express the idea this way:

If $f(x) = \sin x$, with $x$ in radians,
then $f'(x) = \cos x$.

**1.** Find a proof in a calculus textbook of this statement about the derivative of the sine function.

*Continued on next page*

**2.** Read the proof and then restate it in your own words, filling in the details as best you can.

**3.** Identify the part of the proof in which you need the fact that the angle is measured in radians.

**4.** Now consider working with the sine function using angles measured in *degrees.* In other words, consider the function $g(x) = \sin x$, where $x$ is measured in degrees. (Make the necessary adjustment on your calculator.)

   **a.** Pick five angles and use a numerical approach to get an approximation for the derivative of the sine function for those angles. In other words, find $g'(x)$ using those angles as the values for $x$.

   **b.** Put your results from Question 4a into an In-Out table, in which the *In* is the angle and the *Out* is the derivative for $g$ at that angle.

   **c.** Make a graph from your table.

   **d.** Find a formula for your table. (*Suggestion:* You may want to find additional rows for your table and use a pattern of *In* values from different quadrants.)

# Sine Derivative on the Ferris Wheel

In the supplemental activity *Derivative of the Sine*, you were told that if angles are measured in radians, then the derivative of the sine function is the cosine function. This statement can be proved using the relationship between the trigonometric functions and motion on the Ferris wheel.

The next several sections provide an explanation of why the derivative of the sine function is the cosine function. Read the explanation (through "Putting It Together") and then do "The Assignment" at the end.

## Sines and Ferris Wheels

As you saw in *High Dive*, the height of a rider on a Ferris wheel involves the sine of the angle through which the rider has turned. To make the function describing this height as simple as possible, we will use a Ferris wheel that has a radius of 1 foot. Also, because we want to use radian measure, we will assume that the Ferris wheel has a constant angular velocity of 1 radian per second, so that its period is $2\pi$ seconds.

If, as in *High Dive*, the rider starts from the 3 o'clock position and goes counterclockwise, then the rider's height after $t$ seconds, relative to the center of the Ferris wheel, is given by the equation $h(t) = \sin t$.

*Continued on next page*

## Instantaneous Rate of Change in Height

As you have seen, *instantaneous rate of change* can be expressed by using the derivative. Therefore, in this case, the instantaneous rate of change in the rider's height, at a given instant $t = X$, is given by $h'(X)$.

## Vertical Component of Overall Velocity

The circumference of this Ferris wheel is $2\pi$ feet, and a complete turn takes $2\pi$ seconds. Thus, the rider is moving at a constant overall speed of 1 foot per second.

At each instant, the rider's velocity can be thought of as having a vertical component and a horizontal component. The vertical component of velocity measures the rate at which the rider's height is changing.

In *High Dive*, you saw that the vertical component can be found by multiplying the overall speed by the cosine of the angle through which the Ferris wheel has turned. After $X$ seconds, the rider has moved through an angle of $X$ radians. Because the overall speed is 1 foot per second, this means that the vertical component of the rider's speed at $t = X$ is equal to $\cos X$, as illustrated in the diagram. (Note that although there are two segments

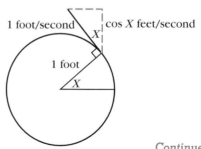

*Continued on next page*

labeled "1" in this diagram, the radius segment is a length—1 *foot*—while the segment tangent to the circle represents velocity, and is given as 1 *foot per second*.)

## Putting It Together

If you compare these two methods—derivative of the height function and vertical component of overall velocity—you get two different expressions for the rate at which the rider's height is changing at $t = X$.

• One approach says this rate is $h'(X)$.

• The other approach says this rate is $\cos X$.

Putting the two approaches together proves this formula:

$$h'(X) = \cos X$$

## The Assignment

Go back through the reading and restate the ideas in your own words, filling in details and explanations that you think might help to clarify the ideas. In particular, answer each of these questions.

• Why does the function $h(t) = \sin t$ describe the rider's height?

• Why is the overall velocity multiplied by $\cos X$ to get the vertical component?

• Why does "instantaneous rate of change in height" mean the same thing as "vertical component of overall velocity"?

# The Ellipse Equation

In *Homework 3: The Ellipse,* you saw that an ellipse is the set of all points the sum of whose distances from two fixed points is a given positive constant. Those two points are called the *foci* of the ellipse.

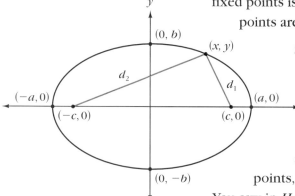

Suppose the ellipse is in "standard position," with its center at the origin and its foci on the $x$-axis at $(c, 0)$ and $(-c, 0)$.

The ellipse meets the $x$-axis in two points, which we will label as $(a, 0)$ and $(-a, 0)$, and it meets the $y$-axis in two points, which we will label as $(0, b)$ and $(0, -b)$.

You saw in *Homework 3: The Ellipse* that the numbers $a$, $b$, and $c$ satisfy the condition $a^2 = b^2 + c^2$.

If $(x, y)$ represents a general point on the ellipse, then the distances from $(x, y)$ to the foci are given by the equations

$$d_1 = \sqrt{(x - c)^2 + y^2}$$

and

$$d_2 = \sqrt{(x + c)^2 + y^2}$$

For the special case in which $(x, y) = (a, 0)$, the sum of the distances to the foci is $2a$. Therefore, the equation of the ellipse is $d_1 + d_2 = 2a$.

Based on this information, show that the equation of the ellipse can be simplified to

$$\frac{x^2}{a^2} + \frac{y^2}{b^2} = 1$$

# Moving the Ellipse

In *Homework 3: The Ellipse,* you considered an ellipse whose center is at the origin and whose critical points are at $(a, 0), (-a, 0), (0, b),$ and $(0, -b)$.

The equation for this ellipse is

$$\frac{x^2}{a^2} + \frac{y^2}{b^2} = 1$$

This ellipse is shown in the accompanying diagram.

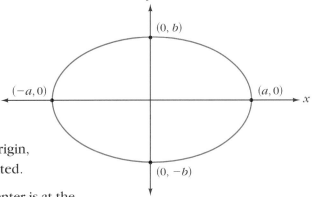

If the center of the ellipse is not at the origin, then the equation is a bit more complicated.

Suppose an ellipse is located so that its center is at the point $(h, k)$. Suppose also that its major axis is horizontal, with length $2a,$ and that its minor axis is vertical, with length $2b$. In other words, this ellipse has the same shape as the ellipse with equation $\frac{x^2}{a^2} + \frac{y^2}{b^2} = 1,$ but it has been translated $h$ units to the right and $k$ units up. (If $h$ or $k$ is negative, then the ellipse has been translated left or down.)

1. Find the equation of this translated ellipse, and find the coordinates of its foci and critical points.

2. How is this equation similar to the equation of a circle with center at $(h, k)$?

# The World of Functions

# DAYS 1-3

# The What and Why of Functions

*Nicole Hartley looks back at the role functions played in a Year 3 IMP unit.*

This unit gives you the opportunity to look back over your past work in mathematics and examine the roles played by functions. In this unit, you will pull together ideas about functions that you studied previously, and you will learn new ways of thinking about functions.

You begin the unit by recalling what you know about functions and then trying to make sense of some data on stopping distances.

# Brake!

A good driver should know how far the car will go when he or she hits the brakes. The table shown here gives a certain car's stopping distance as a function of the car's speed at the time the driver hits the brakes. (Here, "stopping distance" means the distance a car travels from the moment the driver actually begins applying the brakes until the car stops.)

| Speed (in miles per hour) | Stopping distance (to the nearest tenth of a foot) |
| --- | --- |
| 20 | 22.2 |
| 25 | 34.7 |
| 30 | 50.0 |
| 35 | 68.0 |
| 40 | 88.8 |
| 45 | 112.4 |
| 50 | 138.8 |

Based on this table, figure out as much as you can about how stopping distance is affected by speed. Your work should include these elements.

• A graph of the data set, with appropriate scales and labels for the axes

• A verbal description of any patterns you see in the data set

• A prediction of what the stopping distance would be for a speed of 70 miles per hour, with an explanation of how you made your prediction

Table is based on data from the California Driver Handbook.

# Story Sketches

This assignment presents several situations, each described in fairly general terms. In each case, you are asked to draw a "story sketch" of what the graph might look like or give a possible table of values. (This is similar to assignments in the Year 1 unit *The Overland Trail*, although some of the situations here are more complex than those in earlier assignments.)

If no particular numbers are provided in a given problem, make the situations more specific by making specific numerical assumptions so you can use scales on the axes of your graphs. In each problem, explain any assumptions you make in developing your graph sketch or table.

1. Students are putting on a show. Sketch a graph showing their overall profit as a function of the number of tickets they sell.

2. You ride down in the elevator from the top floor of a 20-story building without making a stop. Sketch a graph showing your height off the ground as a function of the time you have spent on the elevator since it began moving.

3. You have invested $1000 in a savings account that pays 4 percent interest per year. Sketch a graph showing the amount of money in the account as a function of the time elapsed since you made the investment.

4. A colony of bacteria is beginning to grow in someone's lung. Starting with a specific number of bacteria, chart their growth in a table of values over time, and then make a graph.

5. Make up a situation of your own about some function, and draw that function's graph.

# One Mile at a Time

You may have noticed that many highways have signs along the side of the road that list your mileage from some place behind you. This POW concerns a situation involving these mileposts.

## The Situation

You are driving down a highway and notice a milepost showing a distance that is a two-digit number. Exactly one hour later, you notice a milepost that shows the same two digits as the first, but in the opposite order.

Then, exactly one hour after seeing the second milepost, you notice a third one that shows a three-digit number. The middle digit on this sign is 0. The other two digits are the same as those on the first milepost and are in the same order as on that first milepost.

## Your Task

The basic question for the situation is, "How fast have you been traveling?" This question has a simple numerical answer that you may be able to find by guess-and-check. (Assume that you have been traveling at the same speed throughout your trip.)

Your task is to go beyond finding the answer, by expressing the situation in algebraic terms and proving, using algebra, that your solution to the problem is correct. (*Hint:* Recall that a number like 386 can be written as $3 \cdot 100 + 8 \cdot 10 + 6$ and apply this idea to express an arbitrary two- or three-digit number in terms of its digits.)

*Continued on next page*

# Write-up

**1.** *Process*

**2.** *Solution:* Answer the question and give a complete explanation of how you can be sure that your answer is correct. Your explanation is the most important part of this POW.

**3.** *Evaluation*

**4.** *Self-assessment*

# Story Sketches II

As in *Homework 1: Story Sketches,* your task here is to develop a "story sketch" that shows the general shape of a graph for the given situation. Again, explain the assumptions you make in developing each sketch. Be sure to provide scales for each axis.

1. Someone is riding on a Ferris wheel. Sketch a graph of that person's height above the ground over time.

2. The amount of sunlight in a day changes throughout the year. Sketch the number of hours of sunlight in a day as a function of the time of year.

3. A certain radioactive material loses half the carbon it contains every 20 years. Sketch a graph showing the amount of carbon left as a function of time.

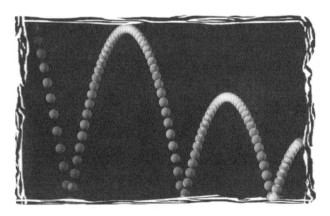

4. A ball is dropped off the roof of a building. It hits the ground, bounces up, goes back down, bounces up again, and so on. Each time it bounces, it loses some of its height. Make a table showing how high it goes on each bounce. (*Note:* This is different from a table showing the height of the ball over time.)

5. Make up a situation whose graph has the same general shape as one of the graphs for Questions 1 through 4. Make your situation as different as possible from the previous situation.

# What Good Are Functions?

You have met many functions in connection with the solution of unit problems. The purpose of this assignment is for you to recall some ways in which functions were helpful to you.

Select a unit you studied previously and a specific function from that unit. Then do three things.

• Describe the problem context in which the function was used, and explain what the input and output for the function represent in terms of the problem context.

• Describe how the function was helpful to you in solving the central unit problem or some other problem in the unit.

• If possible, tell what family the function is from. (You need not give the exact formula for the function.)

If time permits, do the same things for some other units.

# More Families

As you have seen, functions from the same family have several things in common.

- Their graphs are similar.

- Their equations can be put into similar forms.

- The real-world situations that relate to them have common properties.

The two problems in this assignment continue your work with families of functions.

1. An object is dropped from a cliff. As the object falls, its height off the ground is a function of how long it has been falling.

    a. Make a sketch of the graph of the function, listing any assumptions needed.

    b. Give a name to the function family involved.

    c. Describe the general algebraic form for functions in the family.

2. A sporting-goods company packages the balls it produces in cube-shaped boxes. The volume of a cube is a function of the length of its sides.

    a. Make a sketch of the graph of the function, listing any assumptions needed.

    b. Give a name to the function family involved.

    c. Describe the general algebraic form for functions in the family.

# DAYS
# 4-9

# Tables

*Amleshni Prasad, David Granados, and Jessica Espino look for patterns in tables to identify different families of functions.*

You have seen that one way of representing a function is with a table. In the next several days, you will figure out how to tell which family certain tables belong to, and you will prove some of the properties of tables that you discover for these families.

# Linear Tables

One way to look at a function is through its table of values. In this activity, you will look specifically at tables of *linear* functions—functions described by an equation of the form $y = ax + b$.

In particular, you will explore the relationship between patterns in the tables of linear functions and other aspects of these functions, especially their algebraic form. In subsequent activities, you will do similar investigations for other families of functions.

1. Start with the specific function $f(x) = 4x + 7$.

   a. Create an In-Out table for $f$ using equally spaced inputs.

   b. Look for a pattern in the *Out* values.

2. Next, consider other specific linear functions.

   a. Examine the table of each function using equally spaced inputs, and look for patterns. Use a variety of "equal spacings" from one example to the next.

   b. Formulate a general statement of a pattern that holds in the tables of *all* linear functions.

3. Use the algebraic form $y = ax + b$ for linear functions to prove your results from Question 2.

4. Explain why the patterns you found in Question 2 make sense in terms of the graphs of linear functions.

5. Create a real-world situation that is described by a linear function. Explain why the pattern from Question 1 makes sense in terms of that situation.

# Story Sketches III

This assignment provides some more real-world situations for which you will sketch graphs or make tables. As before, explain any assumptions you need to make about the situations in order to make your graphs or table.

You may also choose to assign numerical values to certain parts of the problems if that will clarify your work. Include scales on the axes for your graphs.

1. You are driving due north on the highway. Ahead, but off to the east of the road, you see a tall tower. Sketch a graph and make a table showing your distance from the tower as a function of time as you continue north.

2. You're preparing a turkey for a family dinner. You turn on the oven and set it at 325°. Sketch a graph or make a table of the temperature in the oven as a function of time as the day goes on.

3. Each morning, you write down the time at which the sun rises. Make a table or sketch a graph showing how this might vary over the course of the year.

# Quadratic Tables

You have seen that the In-Out tables for linear functions all have a special property and that this property can be proved in terms of the algebraic form of linear functions.

In this activity, you will look for a similar property in the tables for functions in the quadratic family. (In subsequent activities, you'll examine whether this new property can be proved in terms of the algebraic form of functions in that family.)

1. Start by choosing a specific quadratic function. Create an In-Out table for that function using equally spaced inputs, and then look for patterns. Be sure to consider both positive and negative inputs.

2. Continue with other functions in that family, looking for some type of pattern that holds for the tables of *all* quadratic functions. Consider tables in which the difference between inputs is a value other than 1, and also consider quadratic functions in which the coefficient of $x^2$ is a value other than 1.

3. Examine how the pattern you found in Questions 1 and 2 varies from one quadratic function to another. State your observations in as general a way as you can.

# Back to the Basics

The family of linear functions is a basic part of the world of functions. This assignment presents four different real-world situations in which someone might consider using a linear model.

In each of Questions 1 through 4, use a table, a graph, or an algebraic expression to explain how to solve the problem using the assumption of linearity. If a problem is impossible to solve, explain why, and describe how it can be changed so it can be solved. In Question 5, you will consider the appropriateness of the linear model in each case.

**1.** Ms. Jackson is buying scientific calculators for her math class. She told the principal that a classroom set of 30 calculators would cost $388.50. The principal wants to know the cost of purchasing calculators for the entire school. How much would it cost to buy 300 calculators?

**2.** A hiker is climbing steadily up a mountain. If he reaches an altitude of 3000 feet at 3 p.m., what will his altitude be at 6 p.m.?

*Continued on next page*

**3.** Peter and Cynthia each rented a car for the day from the Rent-the-Best car rental agency. Rent-the-Best charges a daily minimum rate plus a per-mile charge. Peter drove 200 miles and paid $41. Cynthia drove 250 miles and paid $45.

If your budget allows $50 for car rental for the day, how many miles can you afford to drive if you use Rent-the-Best?

**4.** Bertha is spending $75 a day on her vacation. Day 6 finds her lying on a Caribbean beach with $784 left to spend. Her plans have her returning home on Day 10. How much money will she have left then?

**5.** For each of the situations in Questions 1 through 4, answer these two questions.

**a.** What clues tell you that the problem, *as written*, represents a linear situation?

**b.** Does the problem describe a situation that would be linear *in real life?*

# Quadratic Tables by Algebra

The purpose of this assignment is to prove algebraically that a specific quadratic function has constant second differences, at least for the case in which the inputs differ by 1. Question 1 examines the function numerically, and Question 2 represents the general proof.

**1.** Consider the function $f(x) = x^2 + 2x + 3$.

   **a.** Complete the In-Out table shown here.

   **b.** Find the differences between successive outputs in the table, and then find the second differences.

| $x$ | $f(x)$ |
|-----|--------|
| 7   |        |
| 8   |        |
| 9   |        |
| 10  |        |

**2.** Consider the same function as in Question 1. But now, suppose that the first input in the table is represented by the variable $w$ and that subsequent inputs are expressed in terms of $w$, as shown in the next table.

   **a.** Complete the table.

   **b.** Find the differences between successive outputs in the table, and then find the second differences.

   **c.** Describe the connection between your answers to Question 2b and your answers to Question 1b.

   **d.** Explain why your results for this question prove that the function $f$ has constant second differences.

| $x$ | $f(x)$ |
|-------|--------|
| $w$   |        |
| $w + 1$ |        |
| $w + 2$ |        |
| $w + 3$ |        |

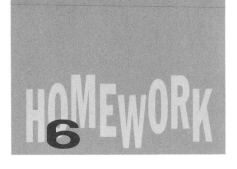

# A General Quadratic

In *Quadratic Tables by Algebra,* you looked at part of an In-Out table for the function *f* defined by the specific equation $f(x) = x^2 + 2x + 3$. Now consider a general quadratic function, given by the equation $g(x) = ax^2 + bx + c$.

1. First, consider a table using the same numerical inputs you used in *Quadratic Tables by Algebra,* as shown here, but using the general quadratic function *g*.

   **a.** Complete the In-Out table.

   **b.** Find the differences between successive outputs in the table, and then find the second differences.

| x | g(x) |
|---|------|
| 7 | |
| 8 | |
| 9 | |
| 10 | |

2. Now use *w, w* + 1, and so on, as the inputs, as shown in the next table.

   **a.** Complete the In-Out table (still using the general quadratic function *g*).

   **b.** Find the differences between successive outputs in the table, and then find the second differences.

| x | g(x) |
|---|------|
| w | |
| w + 1 | |
| w + 2 | |
| w + 3 | |

3. Describe in specific terms how your answers to Questions 1 and 2 here relate to your answers to Questions 1 and 2 of *Quadratic Tables by Algebra.*

# Exponential Tables

You have seen that In-Out tables for linear and quadratic functions have special properties. You have also seen that those properties can be proved in terms of the algebraic form of functions in those families.

In this activity, you will look for properties of tables for the *exponential* family of functions and explain those properties in terms of the algebraic form of functions in that family.

For linear and quadratic functions, you found patterns by subtracting consecutive outputs. Here, you can find two patterns: one by subtracting consecutive outputs and another by dividing consecutive outputs.

1. First look for patterns by *dividing* consecutive outputs.

    a. Start by choosing a specific exponential function. Create an In-Out table for that function using equally spaced inputs and look for patterns in the *ratios* of consecutive outputs.

    b. Continue with other exponential functions, looking for some type of pattern that holds in the tables of *all* exponential functions.

2. Explain your results from Question 1 in terms of the type of formula used to express exponential functions. Give as general a proof of your results as you can.

*Continued on next page*

**3.** Now look for a second pattern in the table by *subtracting* consecutive outputs.

**a.** As in Question 1, start by choosing a specific exponential function. Create an In-Out table for that function using equally spaced inputs, but now look for patterns in the *differences* of consecutive outputs.

**b.** Continue with other exponential functions, looking for some type of pattern that holds in the tables of *all* exponential functions.

# A Cubic Pattern

You have looked at patterns for the tables of functions in both the family of linear functions and the family of quadratic functions. Differences and second differences for the outputs of these tables played important roles in those patterns.

Now consider the family of cubic functions, which is the set of functions defined by equations of the form $f(x) = ax^3 + bx^2 + cx + d$. Specifically, consider the simplest function in this family, which is given by the equation $f(x) = x^3$.

1. Make an In-Out table for this function (using equally spaced inputs).

2. Find and state clearly a pattern in your table.

3. Use algebra to prove that pattern for the case in which the inputs differ by 1.

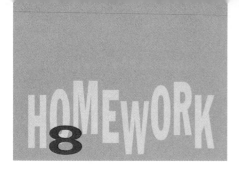

# Mystery Tables

The table shown here actually represents In-Out tables for six different "mystery" functions, called *f, g, h, F, G,* and *H*. All six In-Out tables use the same set of *x*-values. To get the In-Out table for a given function, combine the first column of the table with the column for that particular function. For instance, the table shows that $G(-2) = -8$.

For each function, do two things.

• Decide what family the function belongs to.

• Find an algebraic expression for the specific function.

As you work on each function, keep notes on what you tried and what led you to the next step. This will serve as your detective's notebook as you track down each function.

| $x$ | $f(x)$ | $g(x)$ | $h(x)$ | $F(x)$ | $G(x)$ | $H(x)$ |
|---|---|---|---|---|---|---|
| $-5$ | 26 | 35 | 27 | 0.015625 | $-230$ | 96 |
| $-4$ | 17 | 24 | 22 | 0.03125 | $-112$ | 48 |
| $-3$ | 10 | 15 | 17 | 0.0625 | $-42$ | 24 |
| $-2$ | 5 | 8 | 12 | 0.125 | $-8$ | 12 |
| $-1$ | 2 | 3 | 7 | 0.25 | 2 | 6 |
| 0 | 1 | 0 | 2 | 0.5 | 0 | 3 |
| 1 | 2 | $-1$ | $-3$ | 1 | $-2$ | 1.5 |
| 2 | 5 | 0 | $-8$ | 2 | 8 | 0.75 |
| 3 | 10 | 3 | $-13$ | 4 | 42 | 0.375 |
| 4 | 17 | 8 | $-18$ | 8 | 112 | 0.1875 |
| 5 | 26 | 15 | $-23$ | 16 | 230 | 0.09375 |

# A Spin on Transitivity

Betty, Al, and Carlos are playing games with the three spinners shown here. The game is played by having each participant in a given game spin his or her spinner. The player with the highest number is the winner. (Because the numbers on the spinners are all different, there are never any ties.)

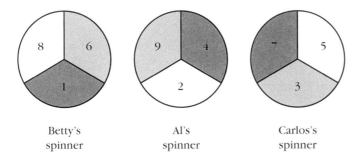

Betty's
spinner

Al's
spinner

Carlos's
spinner

Each spinner is divided into three equal parts, so each numerical result on a given spinner is equally likely. (*Note:* The size of the winning number is not important. For instance, if Al spins 2 and Carlos spins 3, Betty can win with either 6 or 8. In either case, she is simply credited with a win.)

## Part I: Comparing the Spinners

The first stage of your POW involves investigating the outcomes of each of the possible *two-person* competitions in this game.

1. Suppose that Betty plays directly against Al (without Carlos participating). What percentage of the time will Betty win? What percentage of the time will Al win? Explain your answers.

*Continued on next page*

2. Next, suppose that Betty plays directly against Carlos (without Al participating). What percentage of the time will Betty win? What percentage of the time will Carlos win? Explain your answers.

3. Finally, suppose that Al plays directly against Carlos (without Betty participating). What percentage of the time will Al win? What percentage of the time will Carlos win? Explain your answers.

If you did your work carefully, you should have gotten a rather strange combination of results. It turns out that Al beats Betty most of the time, so we can say that Al's spinner is better than Betty's. Similarly, Betty's spinner is better than Carlos's (because Betty beats Carlos most of the time), and Carlos's spinner is better than Al's (because Carlos beats Al most of the time).

*Note:* If you didn't get these outcomes, you should go back and reexamine your work. Keep in mind, though, that for Questions 1 through 3, you need to give the percentage of the time each player wins, not simply say who wins most of the time.

## Transitive Relationships

Why are these results strange? The answer is this: You might expect that because Al's spinner is better than Betty's and Betty's spinner is better than Carlos's, then surely Al's spinner will be better than Carlos's. But, in fact, it isn't.

Many forms of comparison do work the way you'd expect. For example, consider the idea of one person being taller than another. If person A is taller than person B, and person B is taller than person C, then you can be sure that person A is taller than person C. We express this by saying that "being taller than" is a **transitive relationship.**

*Continued on next page*

The relationship "being greater than" (for real numbers) is also a transitive relationship. In other words, if $x > y$ and $y > z$, then you can be sure that $x > z$.

What you saw in Questions 1 through 3 is that for spinners, "being better than" is not transitive. We can describe the spinners in this problem as "a nontransitive set of spinners."

## Part II: Investigating Transitivity

The main task of your POW is to investigate some questions about nontransitive sets of spinners. Try to prove any conclusions you reach. Here are some questions to consider. If you get stuck on one question, try another, and feel free to investigate other questions about transitive spinners.

• Is there another nontransitive set of three spinners (different from the ones that Betty, Al, and Carlos are using), each divided into three parts, using each of the numbers 1 through 9 exactly once?

• Is there a nontransitive set of three spinners, each divided into two parts, using each of the numbers 1 through 6 exactly once?

• Is there a nontransitive set of three spinners, each divided into four parts, using each of the numbers 1 through 12 exactly once? If so, is there more than one such set of spinners?

• How do the answers to these questions change if you allow the same number to be used on more than one spinner (that is, if you make it possible for ties to occur)?

## Write-up

Your write-up should consist of your answers to Questions 1 through 3, with explanations, and any results you got for Part II (with proofs, if possible).

# *Brake!* Revisited

Let's now go back to the table you saw in *Brake!,* which shows the distance a car travels in terms of the speed of the car at the time the driver applies the brakes.

In this activity, you can apply what you have learned recently about tables.

Here's the data set again.

| Speed (in miles per hour) | Stopping distance (to the nearest tenth of a foot) |
| --- | --- |
| 20 | 22.2 |
| 25 | 34.7 |
| 30 | 50.0 |
| 35 | 68.0 |
| 40 | 88.8 |
| 45 | 112.4 |
| 50 | 138.8 |

1. This table can be approximated very closely by a function from one of the basic families. Which family do you think this function belongs to? Justify your answer.

2. Find the family member. That is, find a formula, $y = f(x)$, where $x$ stands for the speed of a car and $y$ is the approximate stopping distance. Once you have a formula, give a careful description of how you found it.

# Bigger Means Smaller

Questions 1 and 2 of this assignment involve fairly straightforward situations. As you work on them, think about what principles they illustrate. Question 3 asks you to discuss the connection between the two problems, and Question 4 asks you to create similar problems of your own.

1. A farmer decides to devote an acre of his land to corn. (One acre is equal to 43,560 square feet.) Assume that he decides to use a rectangular plot of land for the corn.

   **a.** If the width of the cornfield is 200 feet, what is the length (in feet)?

   **b.** How would the length have to change if the width were doubled? Tripled? Halved?

   **c.** Develop a formula for the length of a one-acre rectangular field in terms of its width.

2. Suppose you go on a 300-mile car trip.

   **a.** If your average speed is 50 miles per hour, how long will the trip take?

   **b.** How would the time of the trip be affected if your average speed were only half as big? What if you took a high-speed train that went twice as fast? Three times as fast?

   **c.** Develop a formula for the time of a 300-mile trip in terms of the average speed.

3. What is the mathematical connection between Questions 1 and 2?

4. Make up a situation and questions of your own that illustrate the same ideas used in Questions 1 and 2.

# Going to the Limit

*Mario Saccheri reflects on what asymptotes mean in the context of specific problems.*

In the next part of this unit, you will examine the fact that for some functions, certain numbers can't be used as inputs. You'll look at what this means in terms of the graphs of these functions when the inputs are near those "forbidden" values.

It turns out that this issue creates a real problem for graphing calculators. A related problem is the fact that for most functions, a graphing calculator can show only part of the graph. You'll be looking at what happens in the portion of the graph the calculator doesn't show.

# Don't Divide That!

In *Homework 9: Bigger Means Smaller*, the formulas you found probably involved fractions with a variable in the denominator. Such algebraic fractions raise some important questions.

- How do you evaluate an algebraic fraction when the denominator comes out to zero?

- What happens in the graphs of functions that have variables in the denominator?

In this activity, you look at these two issues.

## Part I: Why Can't You Divide by Zero?

Division by zero is said to be *undefined*. This seems strange to some people, who may reason like this: "You can divide by any other number, and zero is just a number, so why not divide by zero also?"

One answer comes from the relationship between multiplication and division. For instance, we know that $12 \div 3 = 4$ because $4 \cdot 3 = 12$.

Discuss with your group how allowing division by zero would contradict this relationship between multiplication and division.

## Part II: Graphs Involving Division by Zero

For each of the equations in Questions 1 and 2 on the next page, there is an $x$-value that makes the right side of the equation undefined, because the denominator is zero at that $x$-value. Because the expression on the right is undefined, there is no point on the graph for that $x$-value.

*Continued on next page*

For each equation, do three things.

- Find the value of $x$ that will make the denominator equal to zero.

- Sketch a graph of the function by hand, considering all four quadrants. You will probably need to plot quite a few points to get a good sketch. (*Note:* The graphs might do funny things right around the $x$-values where the functions are not defined, so be sure to check $x$-values that are very close to those $x$-values.)

- Graph the function on a graphing calculator, and compare the calculator graph with your sketch.

**1.** $y = \dfrac{1}{x}$

**2.** $y = \dfrac{10}{3 - x}$

# Difficult Denominators

You've seen that algebraic fractions create special complications for graphing.

For each of the functions in Questions 1 through 3, first make a table of values, especially including $x$-values very near the vertical asymptotes. Then make a graph based on your table. Give special attention to what happens to the graph near any vertical asymptotes. Plot each function on a separate set of axes.

As in *Don't Divide That!,* you will probably need to plot quite a few points to get a clear idea of what the graph looks like.

1. $y = \dfrac{1}{x + 5}$

2. $y = \dfrac{1}{(x - 2)^2}$

3. $y = \dfrac{25x}{x^2 - 25}$ (*Note:* There are two values of $x$ where this function is undefined.)

# Return of the Shadow

A bunch of young boys and girls were standing near a lamppost. Horace pointed to his little sister, Emily, and said, "My mom is twice as tall as Emily. If my mom were standing where Emily is, my mom's shadow would be twice as long as Emily's shadow."

Horace apparently thinks that shadow length is directly proportional to height. Investigate, using diagrams and geometrical ideas, whether this is true.

More specifically, consider the case of a lamppost that is 20 feet tall and a person who is standing 12 feet away from the lamppost. The length $\ell$ of that person's shadow will be a function of his or her height $h$.

Find an expression for $\ell$ as a function of $h$. In particular, find out whether $\ell$ is directly proportional to $h$.

# An Average Drive

Amparo took a trip on a warm, sunny day to her favorite spot overlooking the ocean. That spot was 100 miles from home. Amparo knew that in order to be home on time, she needed to average 50 miles per hour for her overall trip.

1. As Amparo reached her destination, she realized that she had made good time while still staying within the legal speed limit. She figured out that she had averaged 60 miles per hour on her trip there. What should Amparo's average speed be on the return trip so that her average speed for the round trip will be 50 miles per hour?

   (*Warning:* The answer is *not* 40 miles per hour!)

2. On another trip to the same spot, Amparo took a more leisurely pace. When she reached her destination, she realized she was late! She had averaged only 25 miles per hour getting there. What should Amparo's average speed be on the return trip so that her average speed for the round trip will be 50 miles per hour?

   (*Warning:* The answer is *not* 75 miles per hour!)

3. Amparo makes this round trip frequently, and her goal is to average 50 miles per hour for the round trip. However, her average speed for the trip to the ocean varies.

   Let $x$ be her average speed (in miles per hour) on the way to the ocean. Find an expression in terms of $x$ that tells Amparo what her average speed should be on the return trip in order for her average speed for the whole trip to be 50 miles per hour.

# Approaching Infinity

In *Homework 11: An Average Drive,* you examined the function defined by the equation $y = \frac{100x}{4x - 100}$ (or something equivalent) and saw that the graph of this equation has a **horizontal asymptote** at $y = 25$. That is, as $x$ gets very big, the $y$-value of the function gets closer and closer to 25.

The behavior of a function as $x$ gets very big is sometimes called its **end behavior.** Keep in mind that this term refers to both the positive and negative ends of the $x$-axis.

When $x$ is *increasing* arbitrarily (that is, going "far" in the *positive* direction), we say, "$x$ is approaching positive infinity," and we write $x \to +\infty$ (or simply $x \to \infty$) as shorthand for this. If the value of the function is getting arbitrarily close to some number as $x$ gets very large, we represent that number by the notation $\lim_{x \to \infty} f(x)$. This expression is read as "the limit of $f(x)$ as $x$ approaches infinity." For example, for very large values of $x$, the expression $\left(1 + \frac{1}{x}\right)^x$ gets close to the special number $e$, so $\lim_{x \to \infty} \left(1 + \frac{1}{x}\right)^x = e$.

As the value of $x$ moves toward the negative end of the $x$-axis, we say, "$x$ is approaching negative infinity," and write $x \to -\infty$. If the value of $f(x)$ is getting arbitrarily close to some number as $x$ gets "very large" in the negative direction, we represent that number by the notation $\lim_{x \to -\infty} f(x)$. If the same thing is happening whether $x \to \infty$ or $x \to -\infty$, we can write $|x| \to \infty$.

*Comment:* The phrase "getting arbitrarily close" is being used here in an intuitive way. This is actually a very deep concept, and the formal mathematical definition is quite technical.

# The End of the Function

You've seen that horizontal asymptotes are a particular type of end behavior. But what else can happen with end behavior? Keep in mind that a graph has two "ends": one end where $x$ is a large positive number and the other end where $x$ is a "large" negative number (that is, a negative number with a large absolute value).

1. Look at examples of polynomials of different degrees. In each case, try to figure out what happens to the $y$-value as $x$ increases in absolute value. (The result may depend on whether $x$ is positive or negative.) Take notes on your results and any general conjectures you make.

   A graphing calculator can help you to some extent, but the graph that a calculator shows can only give you part of the picture. Thus, you should come up with algebraic or numerical explanations for your conclusions about the end behavior of your examples.

2. Next, look at functions from other families: exponential functions, functions from the sine family, rational functions, and any other families you want to consider. Again, take notes on your results and any general conjectures that you make.

# Creating the Ending You Want

You have looked at specific functions and examined their end behavior. Your task in this assignment is to turn the process around.

1. Parts a through d describe functions with four different possible end behaviors. For each behavior, do three things.

   • Draw a graph of a function with that behavior.

   • Create an algebraic formula for a specific function that behaves in that way.

   • Explain how you know that your formula leads to the given end behavior.

   **a.** A function for which $y \to \infty$ (that is, $y$ becomes very large and positive) as $x \to \infty$ and for which $y \to -\infty$ (that is, becomes "large negative") as $x \to -\infty$.

   **b.** A function for which $y \to \infty$ both as $x \to \infty$ and as $x \to -\infty$.

   **c.** A function for which $y \to \infty$ as $x \to \infty$ and that has the $x$-axis as a horizontal asymptote as $x \to -\infty$.

   **d.** A function with the $x$-axis as a horizontal asymptote at both ends and with no vertical asymptotes.

2. List some other possible end behaviors. If possible, find formulas for functions with those behaviors.

---

# Who's Who?

*Tanisha Shafer and Gino Quinn work on the graphs and equations they used to fit specific criteria before presenting them to their class.*

You've gotten pretty good at finding which family certain functions belong to. Now you're going to learn ways of identifying a particular family member to suit a given situation and set of data.

# Families Have Many Different Members

One step in finding a function to fit a situation is deciding which family the function should be in. But even after you've identified the family, the problem is not completely solved. You still have to figure out which member of the family it is. That usually means determining the special numbers, often called *parameters,* that distinguish the desired function from its "relatives." The situations in Questions 1 and 2 will give you some experience doing this.

1. For a science experiment in biology, Binh is observing the growth of a bacteria colony. At 2 p.m., he estimates that there are 1000 bacteria. When he returns to check at 5 p.m., there are about 2200.

   a. If the bacteria continue to reproduce at this rate, how many will there be by midnight?

   b. Find a function that will tell you how many bacteria will be present at any given time.

*Continued on next page*

**2.** A helicopter is bringing supplies to an isolated town where housing has been destroyed by an earthquake. As the helicopter hovers at 200 feet above the ground, a crew member throws a pack of blankets downward with a certain force. Three seconds later, the blankets reach the ground. How high was the pack of blankets after two seconds?

*Reminder:* If an object has initial height $h_0$ and initial upward velocity $v_0$ at time $t = 0$, then its height off the ground (in feet) after $t$ seconds is given by the expression $h_0 + v_0 t - 16t^2$. An initial downward velocity is represented by using a negative value for $v_0$.

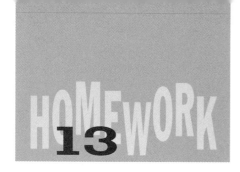

# Fitting Mia's Bird Houses Again

Do you remember Mia and her bird houses? They initially appeared in the Year 1 unit *The Pit and the Pendulum*. In that unit, you were told how many bird houses she and her friends had painted after one hour and after three hours. Your task was to predict how many they would paint in eight hours.

Mia and her friends reappeared in the Year 3 unit *Meadows or Malls?* in a problem that provided additional information. You had to explain why a linear function wouldn't fit the data.

Perhaps you don't remember the details, so here they are:

> Mia and her friends had spent the semester building bird houses, and now they were painting them. In one hour, they had painted two bird houses, and after three hours, they had painted six bird houses. After five hours, they had painted eight bird houses.

**1.** Plot this data set, using *number of hours* for the *x*-axis and *number of bird houses painted* for the *y*-axis.

**2.** Find a quadratic function that fits this data set. That is, find specific numbers for *a*, *b*, and *c* so that all three data points fit the equation $y = ax^2 + bx + c$. (*Hint:* What equation involving *a*, *b*, and *c* do you get from the fact that Mia and her friends built two bird houses in one hour? What does the other information tell you?)

**3.** Does it make sense to use a quadratic function to fit this data set? Are there any other function families that you think might better fit this situation and data set?

# Mystery Tables II

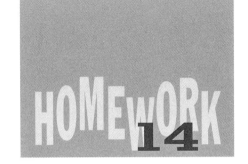

As in *Homework 8: Mystery Tables*, the tables here each combine In-Out tables for several different functions. Your task again is to find an algebraic formula for each function.

In this assignment, the table on the left represents functions *f*, *g*, and *h*, and uses one set of input values. The table on the right, for functions *F*, *G*, and *H*, uses a different set of input values.

| x | f(x) | g(x) | h(x) |
|---|------|------|------|
| −5 | −7 | 20 | −7 |
| −4 | −5 | 18 | −13 |
| −3 | −3 | 16 | −17 |
| −2 | −1 | 14 | −19 |
| −1 | 1 | 12 | −19 |
| 0 | 3 | 10 | −17 |
| 1 | 5 | 8 | −13 |
| 2 | 7 | 6 | −7 |
| 3 | 9 | 4 | 1 |
| 4 | 11 | 2 | 11 |
| 5 | 13 | 0 | 23 |

| x | F(x) | G(x) | H(x) |
|---|------|------|------|
| 0 | 0 | 0 | 2 |
| 15 | 0.26 | 0.5 | 2.26 |
| 30 | 0.50 | 0.87 | 2.50 |
| 45 | 0.71 | 1 | 2.71 |
| 60 | 0.87 | 0.87 | 2.87 |
| 75 | 0.97 | 0.5 | 2.97 |
| 90 | 1 | 0 | 3 |
| 105 | 0.97 | −0.5 | 2.97 |
| 120 | 0.87 | −0.87 | 2.87 |
| 135 | 0.71 | −1 | 2.71 |
| 150 | 0.50 | −0.87 | 2.50 |
| 165 | 0.26 | −0.5 | 2.26 |
| 180 | 0 | 0 | 2 |

For each of the six functions, do three things.

- Graph each function on its own pair of axes, with appropriate scales.

- Decide what family the function belongs to, and explain your reasoning.

- Find a specific algebraic expression for the function.

# What Will It Be Worth?

Imagine that you bought a house in 1990 for $100,000 and took out a thirty-year mortgage as part of the purchase process. (This means that you borrowed money to buy the house and will pay back the money over a thirty-year period.)

As part of your financial planning, you would like to make an educated guess about how much your house will be worth when the loan is paid off, in the year 2020. You know that the house was worth $50,000 in 1970.

**1.** First, assume that housing prices are increasing linearly over time. Based on this model, what is your prediction?

**2.** Next, assume that housing prices are increasing exponentially over time. Based on this model, what is your prediction?

**3.** Now pick a third model. That is, come up with some other possible way in which prices might be changing. Then give your prediction using this model, and explain your reasoning.

**4.** Which of the three models do you think makes the most sense, and why?

# And Now ...
# Back to Marcus
# Dunkalot

In the Year 1 unit *The Overland Trail*, you worked on a situation involving star basketball player Marcus Dunkalot. Here is the original problem.

> The general manager of the Slamajamas has a difficult decision to make.
>
> A key player, Marcus Dunkalot, suffered a sprained knee on March 20, about one month prior to the beginning of the playoffs, and was put on the disabled list.
>
> It is now just over two weeks later, April 6. The general manager needs to decide immediately whether or not to keep Marcus on the disabled list. If he keeps Marcus on the disabled list, it will be for the remainder of the regular season, which means that Marcus will be disqualified for the playoffs.
>
> Here are the advantages and disadvantages of each choice.
>
> • If he takes Marcus off the disabled list now, he can hope that Marcus will be well in time for the playoffs. But if Marcus is not ready in time, then the Slamajamas will have one less player available for the rest of the season, including the playoffs.

*Continued on next page*

- If he keeps Marcus on the disabled list, then he can sign another player (of lesser ability) to take his place. But then he gives up all hope of having Marcus for the playoffs.

The playoffs begin on April 18.

The original assignment included a report from the physical therapist, on which the general manager needed to base his immediate decision. You were asked to graph the data in the report and use your graph to help the coach decide. Here is the report.

---

# Professional Physical Therapy

Patient's name: Marcus Dunkalot

Sex: male     Height: 6'8"

Age: 24     Weight: 225 lbs

Diagnosis: sprained knee

Prescribed treatment: strengthen and stretch

3/20    Mr. Dunkalot was administered a Cybex strength test upon arrival. Quadriceps of the injured leg measured 55 foot-pounds in extension. Normal measurement for a player to return to play without reinjury is 250 foot-pounds.

3/25    Daily regimen is contributing to patient's progress. Cybex test measures 90 foot-pounds.

4/1    Some swelling earlier in the week. General reports of less pain. Cybex test measures 140 foot-pounds.

4/6    Less swelling. Range of motion has shown marked increase. Cybex test measures 185 foot-pounds.

---

Continued on next page

## Two Suggested Solutions

Two students working on this problem gave different advice to the coach. Both students designated March 20 as Day 1, so April 18 became Day 30. (March has 31 days.)

Student A said that the function $f$ given by the equation $f(x) = 40 + 8x$ approximated the data set well. So student A predicted that on April 18, Marcus would have 280 foot-pounds of strength and would be strong enough to play.

Student B said that the function $g$ given by the equation $g(x) = 55 + 6x$ approximated the data set well. So student B predicted that on April 18, Marcus would have only 235 foot-pounds of strength and would not be strong enough to play.

## Your Questions

1. Which student's function seems to you to fit the data set better, and why?

2. Do you have a function that you think fits the data set better than either of these? If so, what is it?

3. Develop a mathematical procedure by which you might judge when one function fits a data set better than another.

# A Tight Fit

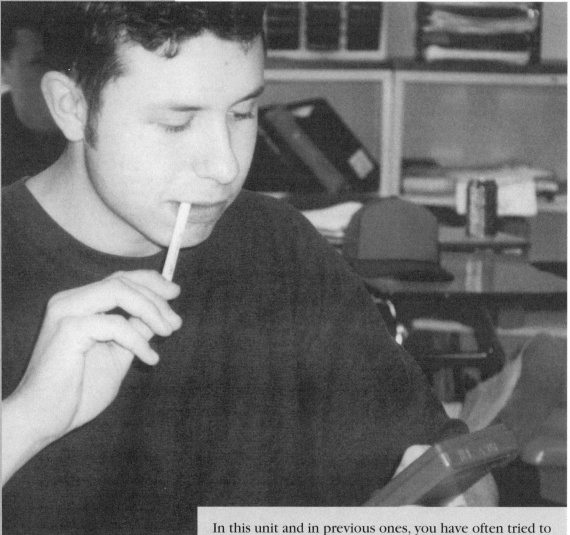

*Daniel Smith uses the graphing calculator's regression feature to further explore the meaning of "best fit."*

In this unit and in previous ones, you have often tried to find a function whose graph came very close to a given set of data points. Now you will examine the question of what "close" means.

# Let's Regress

Throughout various IMP units, you have been asked to do some curve-fitting. If you know the family of functions your data set belongs to, your graphing calculator can use a technique called *regression* to find the function of best fit for that family.

When you can solve problems that way, life is easy. In this activity, you apply regression on the calculator to two problems that may be familiar.

## Part I: The Hobby Shop

This problem is based on an assessment task from the Year 1 unit *The Pit and the Pendulum*.

> Steve works in a hobby shop. He was looking at the relationship between the length of certain models and the amount of paint they require.
>
> Here are some estimates he came up with.

| Length of model (in feet) | Amount of paint (in ounces) |
|:---:|:---:|
| 1 | 2 |
| 2 | 6 |
| 3 | 14 |
| 5 | 40 |

> Assuming that this pattern continues, estimate how much paint would be needed for a model that was 10 feet long. Explain your reasoning.

*Continued on next page*

You may have solved this problem previously by simply plotting the points, connecting them with a smooth graph, and then extending the graph. Your task now is to solve it using the regression feature of the graphing calculator.

**1.** Choose a regression model—that is, choose a function family to model the situation—and explain your choice.

**2.** Apply your regression model to the data items in the table, and give the resulting function.

## Part II: Growing Up

This graph shows the average height for boys age 0 to 6 in the United States around the middle of the twentieth century. (You may recall the graph from an assignment in the Year 3 unit *Small World, Isn't It?*)

**3.** Suppose you want to use regression with the information in this graph to predict the average height for a nine-year-old boy in the United States at the time.

**a.** Choose three different models for regression, and explain your choices.

**b.** Give the function and the prediction that you get for each model.

**c.** Discuss which model you think is best, and explain your reasoning.

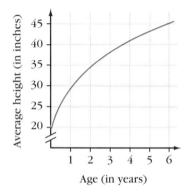

(Source: Department of Pediatrics, State University of Iowa, 1943)

# Midnight Express

**1.** The Midnight Express postal train moves along at a steady 70 miles per hour, passing through Nowheresville exactly at midnight, without even slowing down.

  **a.** Make a graph showing the train's distance from Nowheresville as a function of time. Use midnight as $t = 0$, and include both positive and negative values of $t$ in your graph. (For example, $t = -1$ will represent an hour before midnight, which is 11 p.m.)

  **b.** Write a rule for how to find the train's distance from Nowheresville as a function of $t$.

**2.** This table gives first-class postal rates for 1997.

| Weight | Cost |
|---|---|
| Up to 1 ounce | 32¢ |
| More than 1 ounce but no more than 2 ounces | 55¢ |
| More than 2 ounces but no more than 3 ounces | 78¢ |
| More than 3 ounces but no more than 4 ounces | 101¢ |

The rates continue like this, with each additional ounce costing another 23¢.

  **a.** Make a graph showing cost as a function of weight, up to a weight of 7 ounces.

  **b.** Write a rule for how to find the cost of mailing a letter that weighs $n$ ounces.

# In the Lead

**1.** Our favorite track star, Speedy, has a friend named Sporty who is also quite athletic. Although running isn't Sporty's best event, the two friends like to race against each other.

You may recall this information about Speedy from the Year 2 unit *Solve It!:*

> A sports analyst recently studied the film of a race in which Speedy competed. The analyst came up with the formula $m(t) = 0.1t^2 + 3t$ to describe the distance Speedy had run $t$ seconds after beginning the race.

The same analyst came up with the expression $0.095t^2 + 2.92t$ to describe the distance Sporty has run $t$ seconds after beginning a race.

**a.** After 10 seconds, how far ahead is Speedy?

**b.** Write a function that describes how far ahead Speedy is after $t$ seconds.

*Continued on next page*

**2.** On January 1, 1960, the population of Smallville was 30,000. Over the next decade, the population grew by 2 percent each year.

**a.** Write an expression for the population of Smallville $t$ years after January 1, 1960.

During the period from 1960 to 1970, electricity usage rose as well. In fact, the usage *per person* went up. The average electricity usage per person as of January 1, 1960, was 5 kilowatts per day. On January 1, 1970, the average use per person was 7 kilowatts per day.

**b.** Assume that the per person electricity usage grew *linearly* during this period. Based on this assumption, find an expression for the average daily usage per person at time $t$.

**c.** Use your answers to Questions 2a and 2b to find an expression for the *total* daily electricity usage in Smallville at time $t$.

# It's Off to College We Go

Your task in this POW is to investigate and compile information on the cost of going to college for four years. The planning and mathematics you do to complete this POW will serve you well whether you actually attend college or not.

Keep in mind that college expenses include more than simply tuition, fees, and the cost of books. They also include ordinary living costs such as food and housing.

Be very detailed and accurate in your plan. For instance, if you are going to get your own apartment, then use the classified section of a newspaper to get an idea of the cost. If you plan to live in a dormitory, find the cost of dormitory living at the college of your choice.

You might plan to get a part-time job during the school year or to earn a partial scholarship. You will need to research how much money that will bring in. If you plan to work summers, determine how much you can earn from summer employment.

It will probably be helpful to you for this POW to interview people who are now in college—there is nothing like experience. What bills are you going to have to pay? How much should you plan to spend on books? On recreation and entertainment?

*Continued on next page*

Also keep in mind that prices do not stay fixed from year to year. (You've studied the way inflation works in a variety of activities in previous units.) To be specific, plan on an annual 2.5 percent inflation rate. That is, once you find the cost for the first year, you should expect prices to rise by 2.5 percent each additional year.

## Write-up

Write a report of your work and conclusions. Include a list of expenses for each year, as well as an explanation of how you arrived at those figures.

# Back to Arithmetic

*Clifford Chiba and Lolo Villagomez listen carefully to a presentation on "Back to the Corral."*

You may have thought you were finished studying arithmetic a long time ago. Now you will return to that study, but not to the arithmetic of numbers. In the next segment of the unit, you will use arithmetic to create new functions from existing ones.

# The Arithmetic of Functions

We can do "arithmetic" with functions almost as easily as we do arithmetic with numbers or algebraic expressions. For example, if $f$ and $g$ are any two functions, we can define a new function, called $f + g$, by the equation

$$(f + g)(x) = f(x) + g(x)$$

Suppose the function $f$ is defined by the equation $f(x) = x^2 + 3x + 4$ and the function $g$ is defined by the equation $g(x) = 2x^2 - x + 1$. Then we have $(f + g)(x) = (x^2 + 3x + 4) + (2x^2 - x + 1)$. In other words, $f + g$ is the function defined by the equation $(f + g)(x) = 3x^2 + 2x + 5$.

We can define the functions $f - g$, $f \cdot g$, and $f \div g$ similarly. We can even create more complex combinations out of $f$ and $g$, such as defining $3f - g$ by the equation

$$(3f - g)(x) = 3(x^2 + 3x + 4) - (2x^2 - x + 1)$$

## Functions Defined by Tables

Arithmetic operations can also be defined when the original functions are given in terms of a table. In this case, the new functions are defined only for numbers that are in the domain for both functions.

For example, the next page shows In-Out tables for two functions $h$ and $k$.

*Continued on next page*

| $x$ | $h(x)$ |
|---|---|
| 1 | −4 |
| 2 | 5 |
| 3 | −8 |
| 5 | 2 |
| 8 | 2 |

| $x$ | $k(x)$ |
|---|---|
| 2 | 7 |
| 3 | −5 |
| 4 | 6 |
| 5 | 1 |
| 7 | −3 |

## Your Assignment

Use the information in the In-Out tables for $h$ and $k$ to make In-Out tables for each of these functions. Make the tables as complete as possible.

1. $h + k$

2. $h \cdot k$

3. $2h − k$

4. $h^2 + k^2$

5. $(h + 1)(k + 2)$

# The Arithmetic of Graphs

You've seen some problems in which the function you were looking for could be expressed by doing some arithmetic operation on simpler functions.

In this assignment, you will look at how this "arithmetic of functions" can turn into an "arithmetic of graphs." (*Suggestion:* You may want to use colored pencils so you can easily identify the graphs of different functions.)

**1.** Define two functions, $h$ and $k$, by the equations $h(x) = 2x - 1$ and $k(x) = x + 2$.

   **a.** On a single set of axes, draw the graphs of $h$ and $k$ between $x = -3$ and $x = 3$.

   **b.** Draw the graph of the function $h + k$ on the same set of axes.

   **c.** Use the cases $x = -3$, $x = -1$, and $x = 2$ to describe how points on the graph of $h + k$ can be found from the graphs of $h$ and $k$. Try to express the process in terms of the lengths of certain line segments.

**2.** The graphs of two functions, $f$ and $g$, are shown on the axes in this diagram.

Make a copy of this pair of graphs, and then, on the same set of axes, draw a graph for each of these combination functions.

   **a.** $f + g$

   **b.** $f - g$

   **c.** $2g$

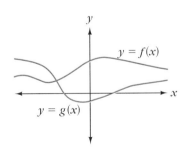

**3.** Why can't you use the graphs in Question 2 to get the graph of the product of the two functions, $f \cdot g$?

# Back to the Corral

You may remember rancher Gonzales and her corrals (from the Year 2 unit *Do Bees Build It Best?*). In that situation, she knew how much fencing she had, and her goal was to build the corral with the largest possible area using that amount of fencing.

Now she has a slightly different problem—she knows how much area she wants, and her goal is to minimize the amount of fencing. Specifically, she has two new horses and wants to build a corral for them with an area of 300 square feet. As before, she will need to decide on the exact shape of her corral.

1. Rancher Gonzales's initial plan is to build a rectangular corral. She needs to decide on the dimensions that will give an area of 300 square feet while using the least possible amount of fencing.

   a. Before working it out, make a guess as to what it will be.

   b. Demonstrate why your answer is correct.

2. Nephew Juan is back on the scene. Two years ago, he thought rectangles were boring, and he still does.

   This time he wants his aunt to build a corral in the shape of a rectangle with a semicircle on one end, as illustrated in the diagram. (The fence will only go around the outside. The dashed line is shown so you can identify the semicircle more clearly. There's no fencing needed where the dashed line is.)

   Determine what dimensions to use so that the whole corral has an area of 300 square feet and the amount of fencing is a minimum, and justify your answer.

# Name That Family!

In each of the situations in Questions 1 through 3, one variable is described as a function of another. For each function, do three things.

- Sketch a graph.

- State what family the function belongs to.

- Explain your reasoning, including any assumptions you make about the situation.

If you don't think the function fits exactly into any standard family you know, indicate what family you think comes closest.

1. A group of friends is weeding the garden. In this situation, the time needed to do the job is a function of the number of people doing the weeding.

2. A hot cup of coffee is placed on the table and forgotten. In this situation, the temperature of the coffee is a function of time. (*Note:* The rate at which the coffee temperature goes down is proportional to the difference between the temperature of the coffee and the temperature of the room.)

3. An ice cream store has a collection of cones, some larger and some smaller but all the same shape. Specifically, the ratio of the diameter at the top of a cone to the height of the cone is the same in all cases.

   In this situation, the amount of ice cream a cone holds is a function of its height. (Assume that cones are always filled level to the top, but no higher.)

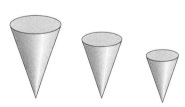

# Small World, Isn't It? Revisited

The rate of world population growth has varied over the centuries, which makes it difficult to get a good fit to all the data using an exponential function. But if you look at only some of the data, for a recent period, you might be able to get better results.

Consider these world population estimates, which are part of the data set you used in *Small World, Isn't It?*

| Year | Estimated population |
|------|---------------------|
| 1950 | 2,510,000,000 |
| 1970 | 3,680,000,000 |
| 1990 | 5,290,000,000 |

1. Using this table or a graph from the table, what would you estimate the population to be in the year 2050?

2. Find a general expression for predicting the world population in some arbitrary future year, based on this data set.

3. What population does your answer to Question 2 predict for the population in the year 2050? How does this compare with your estimate in Question 1?

# DAYS 21-26

# Composing Functions

**Patrick English works on graphing one of several functions to help him become facile with the composition of functions.**

You know that people compose music and poetry, but you may not have realized that they also compose functions. You will see in the next portion of this unit that an operation called *composition* provides an interesting way of creating new functions from existing ones.

What you learn about composition in the next several days will serve you well if you ever study calculus.

# Rumble, Grumble

When David is hungry, he gets grouchy. When he is not hungry, he stays in a good mood. In other words, David's mood is a function of his hunger level.

David's friend Karla usually has positive feelings toward him. When he is grouchy, however, Karla gets irritated with him. In other words, Karla's attitude toward David is a function of his mood.

Assume that David eats three meals a day, at normal times, so that his hunger level is a function of the time of day.

Sketch a graph of Karla's feelings toward David as a function of time over the course of two days.

# The Composition of Functions

You've seen in previous activities that you can combine functions using arithmetic operations. You can also create new functions from old ones by first applying one function and then applying another.

Given two functions, $f$ and $g$, we can combine them to create a new function called the **composition** of $f$ and $g$. This new function is written as $g \circ f$, and its output for the input $x$ is $g(f(x))$. Thus, $g \circ f$ is defined by the equation $(g \circ f)(x) = g(f(x))$. A new function created this way is called a **composite function.**

You can visualize the composition of functions using a "function machine" diagram like this, showing $x$ as the input for the function $f$ and showing the output $f(x)$ as the input for the function $g$.

$$x \rightarrow \boxed{f} \rightarrow f(x) \rightarrow \boxed{g} \rightarrow g(f(x))$$

The situations in Questions 1 and 2 illustrate the operation of composition.

1. Maria is working in order to save for college. This graph shows her earnings over a period of five weeks as a function of which week it is.

   Each week, Maria gives $50 of her earnings to her mother and saves half of the rest toward college, so the amount she saves is a function of her earnings.

   Draw a graph showing the amount Maria saves each week.

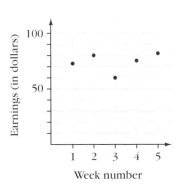

*Continued on next page*

**2.** Mario is also saving for college. He wants to earn enough money during his senior year of high school to put aside $500 for college expenses and still have another $500 to travel with friends across the country after graduation.

Mario decides to sell magazine subscriptions. Of course, he earns more if he sells more subscriptions, but it's better than that. He earns more *per subscription* if his sales go up. This chart explains how much he earns for each subscription.

| Subscription number | Earnings for each subscription |
|---------------------|--------------------------------|
| 1st through 10th | $5 each |
| 11th through 20th | $7.50 each |
| 21st through 30th | $10 each |
| 31st and beyond | $15 each |

For example, if Mario sells 7 subscriptions in a certain month, he gets $5 for each of them, for a total of $35 for that month. But if he sells 14 subscriptions in a given month, he gets $5 for each of the first 10, and then $7.50 for each of the next four, for a total of $80. And if he sells 23 subscriptions in one month, then he gets $5 for each of the first 10, $7.50 for each of the next 10, and $10 for each of the last 3, for a total of $155.

**a.** Make either a graph or a table of a magazine seller's earnings in a given month as a function of the number of subscriptions he sells that month. Include through at least 25 subscriptions.

*Continued on next page*

**b.** The school year is now over. The next table shows the number of subscriptions Mario sold each month as a function of which month it was.

| Month | Number sold |
|---|---|
| September | 7 |
| October | 15 |
| November | 9 |
| December | 32 |
| January | 8 |
| February | 13 |
| March | 23 |
| April | 18 |
| May | 36 |

Make a table showing Mario's earnings each month.

**c.** Determine if Mario will be able to take his cross-country trip.

# The Cost of Pollution

Once there was a peaceful river that emptied into a clear lake. The lake was filled with catfish, and a wonderful restaurant on the shore of the lake featured delicious catfish dinners.

Then a chemical company decided to build a plant on the shore of the river, upstream from the lake. Instead of disposing of its toxic waste in a responsible manner, the company dumped the waste right into the river. You've probably guessed the rest. The catfish began getting sick and dying.

*Continued on next page*

There are two functions involved in this situation. One function gives $c$, the number of catfish per acre, as a function of $w$, the number of gallons of toxic waste dumped per day. For this activity, you should suppose that $c = 50 - 5w$. We will write this function as $c = G(w)$, so $G$ is defined by the formula $G(w) = 50 - 5w$.

The second function expresses $p$, the price (in dollars) of a catfish dinner, as a function of $c$, the number of catfish per acre. For this activity, you should suppose that $p = 24 - 0.4c$. We will write this function as $p = H(c)$, so $H$ is defined by the formula $H(c) = 24 - 0.4c$.

**1.** Draw a function machine diagram showing how the variables $w$, $c$, and $p$ are related using the functions $G$ and $H$.

**2.** Write an equation expressing $p$ in terms of $w$, and represent this equation symbolically using composition notation.

**3.** What was the cost of a catfish dinner before the chemical company moved in?

**4.** Suppose you go to the restaurant and find that catfish dinners cost $12 apiece. How much waste is the chemical company dumping per day?

**5.** How much waste will the company have to dump per day in order for all of the catfish to be gone?

**6.** Make up your own situation using the composition of functions. (You might want to use an ecology theme.)

C Schaufele/ N Zumoff, EARTH ALGEBRA (adapted from page 45). ©1993 Addison Wesley Longman. Reprinted by permission of Addison Wesley Longman.

# Order Among the Functions

You learned a long time ago that for some numerical operations, you can interchange the numbers without changing the result. For example, the expressions $5 + 7$ and $7 + 5$ both give the sum 12. This fact is expressed by saying that addition is *commutative*.

You also know that for other operations, the order in which the numbers appear is very important. For instance, $12 - 8$ is not the same as $8 - 12$. In other words, subtraction is *noncommutative*.

In this assignment, you will consider several questions related to the commutativity or noncommutativity of the operation of composition of functions.

*Continued on next page*

1. Define functions $f$ and $g$ by the formulas $f(x) = x + 3$ and $g(x) = 7x$.

   a. Create separate function machine diagrams for both $f \circ g$ and $g \circ f$.

   b. Find a formula for the composite function $f \circ g$. That is, find an expression for $f(g(x))$.

   c. Find a formula for the composite function $g \circ f$.

   d. Is $f \circ g$ equal to $g \circ f$? In other words, do these two composite functions give the same output as each other for every possible input?

2. Your work on Question 1 should have shown that $f \circ g$ and $g \circ f$ are not the same function.

   a. Find a function $h$ for which the composite functions $h \circ f$ and $f \circ h$ are equal. (Find several choices for $h$ if you can.)

   b. Find a function $k$ for which the composite functions $k \circ g$ and $g \circ k$ are equal. (Find several choices for $k$ if you can.)

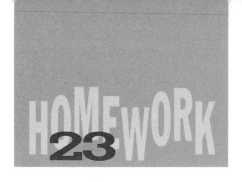

# Cozying Up to Composition

In Part I of this assignment, you are given several functions, and you need to find numerical values or algebraic expressions for various composite functions. In Part II, you will look at a familiar function and find two functions whose composition is that familiar function.

## Part I: Putting Functions Together

The functions $f$, $g$, $h$, and $k$ are defined by these equations.

- $f(x) = 3x^2 + 5$

- $g(x) = 2x - 7$

- $h(x) = 2^x$

- $k(x) = \sin x$

**1.** Find the numerical value of each of these expressions.

**a.** $(g \circ f)(4)$

**b.** $(f \circ g)(-2)$

**c.** $(h \circ f)(1)$

**d.** $(g \circ k)(90°)$

*Continued on next page*

**2.** Find an algebraic expression for each of these composite functions. Simplify the expressions if possible.

    **a.** $g \circ f$

    **b.** $f \circ g$

    **c.** $f \circ k$

    **d.** $h \circ g$

    **e.** $f \circ f$

    **f.** $g \circ g \circ g$

# Part II: Revisiting a Mess!

You may recall that in the Year 3 unit *Small World, Isn't It?*, pilot Linda Sue flew over an oil slick that was in the shape of a circle. When Linda Sue first flew over the circular oil slick, its radius was 70 meters. Later, she found that the radius of the circle was growing at the rate of 6 meters per hour.

**3.** Let $t$ represent the number of hours since Linda Sue first saw the oil slick and let $A(t)$ be the area of the oil slick after $t$ hours. Write an explicit equation for $A(t)$ in terms of $t$.

**4.** Define two specific functions whose composition is the area function $A(t)$ from Question 3.

# Taking Functions Apart

In Part I of *Homework 23: Cozying Up to Composition*, you put functions together to create more complex functions, using the operation of composition.

In this activity, you will do the opposite. That is, you will start with a complex function and find the simple functions that make it up.

Often, you can see how to do this by examining how you would compute a numerical output for the function. For example, consider the function defined by the equation $h(x) = (2x + 3)^3$. If you want to find $h(5)$, you can first compute $2 \cdot 5 + 3$, getting 13, and then find $13^3$. To express $h$ as the composition of two functions, you can define $g$ by the equation $g(x) = 2x + 3$ and $f$ by the equation $f(x) = x^3$ and then write $h$ as the composite function $f \circ g$. (*Comment:* This technique of "decomposing" a function is very useful in calculus.)

Each of the expressions in Questions 1 through 6 defines a function. Write each of these functions as the composition of two or more other functions. Give clear definitions for the functions you are using. (There may be more than one correct answer for some of these problems.)

**1.** $3x^2$

**2.** $\dfrac{1}{\sin x}$

**3.** $(3x^2 - 6)^5$

**4.** $\sqrt{x^2 + 2x - 4}$

**5.** $\ln (x^2 + 1)$

**6.** $3^{(x+2)} + 7$

# Fish, Ladders, and Bacteria

As you work on these problems, think about what they have in common.

**1.** In *The Cost of Pollution*, you were told that $c$, the number of catfish per acre, could be expressed in terms of $w$, the amount of waste dumped per day, by the equation $c = 50 - 5w$.

   **a.** If there are 20 catfish per acre, how much waste is being dumped per day?

   **b.** Develop a general expression for the amount of waste being dumped per day in terms of the number of catfish per acre.

**2.** A 12-foot ladder is leaned against a house, making an angle $\theta$ with the ground, so $h$, the height of the top of the ladder, is given by the equation $h = 12 \sin \theta$.

   **a.** If you want the top of the ladder to be 11 feet off the ground, what should you use for the angle between the ladder and the ground (to the nearest degree)?

   **b.** Develop a general expression for the angle between the ladder and the ground in terms of the height of the top of the ladder.

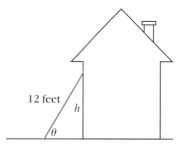

**3.** Suppose $b$, number of bacteria in a colony, starts at 50 and doubles every hour, so that after $t$ hours, the value of $b$ can be expressed by the equation $b = 50 \cdot 2^t$.

   **a.** How much time has gone by at the moment when the bacteria population reaches 1000? (You can give your answer to the nearest tenth of an hour.)

   **b.** Develop a general expression for the amount of time gone by in terms of the size of the bacteria population.

# Functions in Verse

The inverse of a function "undoes" the original function. For example, if $f$ is the function defined by the equation $f(x) = x - 8$, then its inverse function, written as $f^{-1}$, can be defined by the equation $f^{-1}(z) = z + 8$. (It's often helpful to use a different independent variable for the inverse function than was used for the original.) Similarly, if $k(t) = t^3$, then $k^{-1}(r) = \sqrt[3]{r}$.

This assignment looks at how the table of a function is related to the table of its inverse and how the graph of a function is related to the graph of its inverse.

1. Start with the function $k(t) = t^3$.

| $x$ | $k(x)$ |
|-----|--------|
| $-1$ | |
| $2$ | |
| $4$ | |
| $-3$ | |
| $5$ | |

    **a.** Complete the partial In-Out table for $k$ shown at the left.

    **b.** Make a partial In-Out table for $k^{-1}$, using the numbers you got in the *Out* column from Question 1a as the inputs for your table for $k^{-1}$.

2. Next, consider the function $f(x) = x - 8$.

    **a.** Make a partial In-Out table for $f$, using at least five different input values.

    **b.** Make a partial In-Out table for $f^{-1}$, using the numbers in the *Out* column from Question 2a as the inputs for your table for $f^{-1}$.

3. The table at the left is part of an In-Out table for some function $h$. Use this information to write a partial In-Out table for $h^{-1}$.

| $x$ | $h(x)$ |
|-----|--------|
| 3 | 7 |
| 5 | 9 |
| 7 | 6 |
| 9 | 15 |
| 11 | 13 |

*Continued on next page*

**4.** Based on Questions 1, 2, and 3, state a general principle about the relationship between the table of values for a function and the table of values for its inverse. Explain why your principle is true.

**5. a.** Sketch a graph for the function $k$ (from Question 1) using the same scale for both the $x$- and $y$-axes. Then sketch a graph of $k^{-1}$ on the same set of axes.

**b.** Sketch a graph for the function $f$ (from Question 2) using the same scale for both the $x$- and $y$-axes. Then sketch a graph of $f^{-1}$ on the same set of axes.

**c.** Plot the information you have from Question 3 for the function $h$, using the same scale for both the $x$- and $y$-axes. On the same set of axes, plot the points you know for the function $h^{-1}$.

**d.** The diagram at the right shows the graph of some function $g$. (Assume that the $x$- and $y$-axes use the same scale.) Copy this graph and then sketch the graph of $g^{-1}$ on the same set of axes.

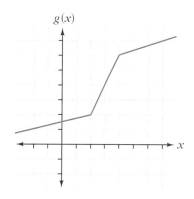

**e.** Based on Questions 5a through 5d, state a general principle about the relationship between the graph of a function and the graph of its inverse. Explain why your principle is true.

# Linear Functions in Verse

You have been examining functions and their inverses, and this assignment continues that work, focusing on the family of linear functions.

It's important to be aware, though, that not every function has an inverse. For example, the fact that $\sin 30° = \sin 150°$ means that the sine function cannot have a true inverse. [After all, $\sin^{-1}(0.5)$ cannot be equal to both 30° and 150°.]

And even when a function has an inverse, it isn't always possible to find an equation for the inverse from the equation of the function itself. For instance, it's possible to show that the function defined by the equation $y = x^7 + 5x^3 + 6x$ has an inverse, but there is no equation by which you can represent this inverse.

*Continued on next page*

Fortunately, many basic functions do have inverses. In particular, not only does every non-constant linear function have an inverse, but you can always find an equation describing the inverse. This assignment explores inverse functions for the family of linear functions, beginning with a specific example.

1. Suppose $f$ is the function defined by the equation $f(x) = 3x + 2$.

   a. Find a formula for the function $f^{-1}$.

   b. Make a partial In-Out table for the function $f$ by using $-2, -1, 0, 1,$ and $2$ as the *In* values and finding the corresponding *Out* values. Then check your answer to Question 1a by applying that inverse function to each *Out* value in your table. (If you don't get your *In* values as the results, you have made a mistake somewhere.)

2. Generalize your algebraic work from Question 1a. That is, suppose $f$ is the linear function defined by the equation $f(x) = ax + b$ with $a \neq 0$. Find an expression for $f^{-1}(w)$ in terms of $a$, $b$, and $w$.

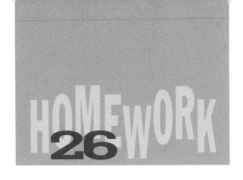

# An Inventory of Inverses

## Part I: Identity Elements

You are familiar with the concept of an identity element for arithmetic operations. For example, the number 1 is the identity element for the operation of multiplication, because $1 \cdot x = x \cdot 1 = x$, for any number $x$.

There is also an identity element for the operation of composition of functions. It is the function $I$, called the *identity function*, that is defined by the equation $I(x) = x$. The statement that $I$ is the identity element for composition means that $I \circ f = f$ and $f \circ I = f$ for every function $f$.

*Continued on next page*

**1.** The first part of this activity asks you to find identity elements for several other operations.

   **a.** Find a number that acts as the identity element for addition of numbers, and explain your reasoning.

   **b.** Find a 3-by-3 matrix that acts as the identity element for addition of 3-by-3 matrices, and explain your reasoning.

   **c.** Find a 2-by-2 matrix that acts as the identity for multiplication of 2-by-2 matrices, and explain your reasoning.

   **d.** Challenge: Define an operation * on people in the world like this.

   > If A and B are any two people, then A * B is the shorter of the two people. If A and B are identical in height, then A * B = A.

   Describe a person in the world who would be an identity element for this operation, and explain your reasoning.

## Part II: Inverses

Whenever an operation has an identity element, the next question to ask is whether individual elements have inverses. Intuitively, one element is the inverse of another if you get the identity element when you combine them using the given operation.

For example, the number $\frac{1}{5}$ is the inverse for 5 for the operation of multiplication because $\frac{1}{5} \cdot 5 = 1$ and $5 \cdot \frac{1}{5} = 1$ (and 1 is the identity element for multiplication).

Some functions have inverses under the operation of composition. Two functions $f$ and $g$ are inverses of each other if $f \circ g = I$ and $g \circ f = I$, where $I$ is the identity function.

*Continued on next page*

**2.** Consider the functions $f$ and $g$ defined by the equations $f(x) = 3x + 2$ and $g(x) = \frac{1}{3}(x - 2)$.

 **a.** Show the computation which demonstrates that $f \circ g = I$.

 **b.** Show the computation which demonstrates that $g \circ f = I$.

 **c.** Find an inverse (under composition) for the function $k$ defined by the equation $k(x) = 4x^3 - 5$. Show how you know that your answer is the inverse.

**3.** In Question 1, you found identity elements for several operations. Now consider the question of inverses for elements using those operations and their identity elements.

 **a.** Does every number have an inverse for addition? Explain your reasoning.

 **b.** Does every 3-by-3 matrix have an inverse under matrix addition? Explain your reasoning.

 **c.** Does every 2-by-2 matrix have an inverse under matrix multiplication? Explain your reasoning.

 **d.** Challenge: Consider the operation $*$ defined in Question 1d. Does every person have an inverse under this operation? Explain your reasoning.

# DAYS
## 27-28

# Transforming Functions

*Candice Davis prepares a poster to display the effects of having transformed a familiar function.*

First, you learned about individual functions, and then families of functions. Next, you did arithmetic with functions, and then composed them.

In the next portion of the unit, you will look at yet another way to work with functions—you can *transform* them. You will examine how transforming a function affects its different representations, in terms of symbols, tables, graphs, and real-world situations.

# Double Dose of Functions

You've looked at different ways to combine functions to get new functions, using arithmetic operations and composition. You've also looked at ways to use the graphs of the individual functions to get the graphs of such combinations.

In this assignment, rather than combining two or more functions at a time, you will look at specific ways to take a single function and alter it slightly. The functions created by these changes are called **transformations** of the original function. (There are other ways to transform functions besides those described here.)

Your task in this assignment is to examine how these alterations affect the graph. Knowing how transformations affect functions and graphs will help you take familiar graphs and adjust them to fit specific situations. (Although these questions ask about the *graphs* of functions, you may find it helpful to think about tables, rules, and real-world situations as well.)

In each of Questions 1 and 2, you begin with specific examples and then look for a general principle.

1. If $f$ is any function, we can define a related function $g$ by doubling the *output* for $f$. In other words, we define $g$ by the equation $g(x) = 2f(x)$. Your task here is to examine how the graph of $g$ is related to the graph of $f$. In each of parts a through c, graph the pair of functions on a single set of axes. (You may find it especially helpful to use tables as an aid to understanding what's happening.)

*Continued on next page*

**a.** Graph the functions defined by the equations $y = \sin x$ and $y = 2 \sin x$.

**b.** Graph the functions defined by the equations $y = x^2 + 2x - 7$ and $y = 2(x^2 + 2x - 7)$.

**c.** Pick another specific function for $f$ and graph the functions defined by the equations $y = f(x)$ and $y = 2f(x)$.

**d.** Based on your work in Questions 1a through 1c, describe the relationship between the graph of a function and the graph of the function with twice the output. Then explain why this relationship holds.

**2.** For a given function $f$, we can define another related function $h$ by doubling the *input* for $f$. In other words, we define $h$ by the equation $h(x) = f(2x)$. Examine how the graph of $h$ is related to the graph of $f$. (As in Question 1, graph each pair of functions on a single set of axes.)

**a.** Graph the functions defined by the equations $y = \sin x$ and $y = \sin (2x)$.

**b.** Graph the functions defined by the equations $y = x^2 + 3x - 7$ and $y = (2x)^2 + 3(2x) - 7$.

**c.** Pick another specific function for $f$ and graph the functions defined by the equations $y = f(x)$ and $y = f(2x)$.

**d.** Based on your work in Questions 2a through 2c, describe the relationship between the graph of a function and the graph of the function with twice the input. Then explain why this relationship holds.

# Slide That Function

In *Double Dose of Functions,* you investigated the effect on a graph of doubling either the output or the input of a function. In this assignment, you will investigate a different type of change to outputs and inputs.

You should look at the effect of two types of transformations.

- *Adding a fixed value to the output:* That is, if $b$ is some fixed number, how does the graph of the function $y = f(x) + b$ compare to the graph of the function $y = f(x)$?

- *Adding a fixed value to the input:* That is, if $c$ is some fixed number, how does the graph of the function $y = f(x + c)$ compare to the graph of the function $y = f(x)$?

Examine many examples, and be sure to include nonlinear functions. (For a linear function, it's hard to distinguish if you've moved the graph vertically or horizontally.) Also be sure to consider both positive and negative values for $b$ and $c$.

Write down the equations for each of the examples you consider along with rough but accurate sketches of their graphs. Summarize your results in a clear way, and explain why the conclusions you reach are correct.

# Transforming Graphs, Tables, and Situations

The activity *Double Dose of Functions* focused on the connection between the symbolic representation of a transformation and the effect of the transformation on the graph.

In this assignment, you will do another example involving graphs. But here, you will also examine how transformations are related to tables and the real-world contexts for functions.

1. This diagram shows the graph of the function defined by some equation $y = f(x)$.

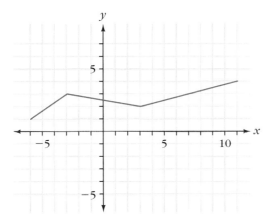

   Trace four copies of the graph. Then draw the graph of each of the equations in parts 1a through 1d, putting each new graph on the same axes as one of the copies of the original graph.

*Continued on next page*

(*Note:* Some of these functions have a different domain from the original function.)

**a.** $y = f(x) - 3$

**b.** $y = f(x + 2)$

**c.** $y = \frac{1}{2}f(x)$

**d.** $y = f(2x)$

| $x$ | $g(x)$ |
|-----|--------|
| $-2$ | 7 |
| $-1$ | 3 |
| 0 | 2 |
| 1 | 0 |
| 2 | $-3$ |
| 3 | $-2$ |
| 4 | 0 |
| 5 | 1 |
| 6 | 4 |

**2.** The table shown at the left goes with the function defined by the equation $y = g(x)$.

Use this table to create In-Out tables for each of the equations in Questions 2a through 2d. ( Your tables may have different inputs from the original table, but make your tables as complete as you can, based on the information you have about the function $g$.)

**a.** $y = g(x) + 2$

**b.** $y = g(x - 3)$

**c.** $y = 3g(x)$

**d.** $y = g\left(\frac{1}{2}x\right)$

**3.** Suppose the equation $y = h(x)$ gives the height in feet of a bouncing ball $x$ seconds after it was released. Questions 3a and 3b ask you how the function would have to be transformed if units different from feet or seconds were used.

**a.** Let $k(x)$ represent the height of the ball, *in inches, x* seconds after the ball is released. Write an equation connecting $k(x)$ to $h(x)$.

**b.** Let $j(x)$ be the height of the ball, in feet, $x$ *minutes* after it was released. Write an equation connecting $j(x)$ to $h(x)$.

# Back to the Beginning

*Ceanna Shira thoughtfully applies what she has learned about functions to the final problem of the unit.*

In the final activity of the unit, you go back to the opening problem of the unit and get the chance to apply some of the things you've learned. Well, it's not exactly the same as the opening problem. Instead, it's a more complicated (and more relevant) version of that problem.

# Better Braking

This final activity of the unit revisits the unit's opening problem. In that problem, *Brake!,* you looked at a data set showing how far a car goes from the time the driver hits the brakes. This stopping distance depended on the car's speed. But what really matters for safety is a little bit different.

Often, a driver needs to stop because she or he sees some danger ahead. But there is a delay between when the driver sees the danger and when the driver steps on the brakes. This delay is called *reaction time.* What really matters for safety is how far the car goes from when the driver sees the danger until the car stops.

This table gives that modified stopping distance.

| Speed (in miles per hour) | Stopping distance (to the nearest tenth of a foot) *including distance during reaction time* |
|:---:|:---:|
| 20 | 44.2 |
| 25 | 62.2 |
| 30 | 83.0 |
| 35 | 106.5 |
| 40 | 132.8 |
| 45 | 161.9 |
| 50 | 193.8 |

**1.** Explain what function family you think this table represents, and why. Your explanation should be in terms of both the table and the situation.

**2.** Find an algebraic rule that fits the table as well as possible. Be sure to test your rule on all the data items in the table.

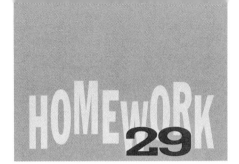
# Beginning Portfolio Selection

In your travels through *The World of Functions,* you looked at functions in four different ways.

- Using tables of values

- Using graphs

- Using formulas or algebraic expressions

- In terms of real-world situations

Because these four representations are simply different ways of viewing the same thing, these perspectives have strong connections to one another.

Pick three different assignments from *The World of Functions,* each of which helped you see a connection between two of these ways of viewing functions. (Each of the three assignments should look at the connection between a different pair of perspectives.) For each of the three assignments, do these things.

- State which two perspectives the assignment helped you connect.

- Describe how the assignment helped you make the connection.

- Describe in your own words what that connection is.

- Describe some other assignment you had in a mathematics class, this year or before, that made that same connection.

# The World of Functions Portfolio

Now that *The World of Functions* is completed, it is time to put together your portfolio for the unit. Compiling this portfolio has three parts.

- Writing a cover letter summarizing the unit

- Choosing papers to include from your work in this unit

- Discussing your personal mathematical growth in the unit

## Cover Letter for *The World of Functions*

For your cover letter for *The World of Functions,* focus on these two key ideas.

- The distinguishing characteristics of each of the family of functions you worked with, considered in terms of real-world situations, graphs, tables, and symbolic representations

- Methods of combining functions or transforming functions to create new ones

For each of these important aspects of the unit, choose an activity that illustrates that idea to include in your portfolio.

*Continued on next page*

# Selecting Papers from *The World of Functions*

Your portfolio from *The World of Functions* should contain these items.

• *Brake!*, *"Brake!" Revisited*, and *Better Braking*

Include a statement of how your understanding of the "braking" situation developed over the course of the unit.

• *Linear Tables*, *Quadratic Tables*, and *Exponential Tables*

Discuss how your understanding of the relationship between tables and algebraic representations grew through these three activities.

• Activities discussed in your cover letter

• *Homework 29: Beginning Portfolio Selection*

Include the activities from the unit that you selected in *Homework 29: Beginning Portfolio Selection*, along with your written work about those activities.

• A Problem of the Week

Select one of the three POWs you completed during this unit (*One Mile at a Time*, *A Spin on Transitivity*, or *It's Off to College We Go*).

## Personal Growth

Your cover letter for *The World of Functions* describes how the unit develops. As part of your portfolio, write about your own personal development during this unit. You may want to specifically address this issue.

> *How do you feel you have developed during this unit in terms of your ability to explore problems and prove conjectures in mathematics?*

You should include here any other thoughts you might like to share with a reader of your portfolio.

# Supplemental Problems

The supplemental problems for *The World of Functions* continue the exploration of properties of functions and how to use combinations of functions. Here are some examples.

- *Odd or Even?* looks at two algebraic properties of functions and asks how those properties are related to the graphs of functions.

- *Absolutely Functions* and *Graphing Power* give you an opportunity to work further with the families of absolute value functions and power functions.

- *Ferris Wheel on a Ramp* and *"Small World" Again!* involve combining functions to fit real-world situations.

# From Second Differences to Quadratics

In *Quadratic Tables,* you saw that if you make an In-Out table for a quadratic function using equally spaced inputs, then the second differences of the outputs are constant. In this activity, you will explore the converse of that statement.

Suppose that $f$ is a function. Suppose also that in any In-Out table for $f$ using consecutive integers as the inputs, the second differences of the outputs are constant. Prove that *for integers,* the function is quadratic.

*Hint:* Let $a$ represent $f(0)$, let $b$ represent the difference $f(1) - f(0)$, and let $h$ represent the constant second difference. [For instance, this second difference is the difference between $f(2) - f(1)$ and $f(1) - f(0)$.] Use these symbols to find expressions for $f(2), f(3), f(4)$, and so on, and then look for a generalization.

# SUPPLEMENTAL PROBLEM

# Real Domains

Any algebraic expression can be used to define a function. For example, the expression $2x + 3$ defines the function $f$ given by the equation $f(x) = 2x + 3$.

For some expressions, you can substitute any number for the variable. For instance, the expression $2x + 3$ makes sense no matter what value you substitute for $x$.

For other expressions, however, you need to be more careful. For example, consider the expression $\frac{1}{x^2 - 25}$. If $x$ is either 5 or $-5$, the denominator of this fraction is 0, so the fraction is not defined. Therefore, the numbers 5 and $-5$ cannot be used as the independent variable for the function $g$ defined by the equation $g(x) = \frac{1}{x^2 - 25}$. But any real number other than 5 or $-5$ can be used. (*Reminder:* The *real numbers* are the numbers represented on the number line. These include negative numbers, fractions, and irrational numbers, but do not include complex numbers.)

The set of number values for which an expression makes sense is the **domain** of the expression. That set is also the domain of the function *defined by* the expression. Thus, the domain of the function $g(x) = \frac{1}{x^2 - 25}$ is the set of all real numbers except 5 and $-5$.

Denominators are one source of limitations on the domain of a function. Square roots are another area of potential complication. For example, the expression $\sqrt{x - 3}$ only makes sense if $x \geq 3$. (*Note:* If you consider complex numbers, this expression has a larger domain. For this activity, you should only consider real numbers.)

*Continued on next page*

## Part I

Find the domain for each of these expressions. That is, find the set of real numbers for which each expression makes sense.

**1.** $\dfrac{x^2}{(x^2 + 1)(x + 3)}$

**2.** $\sqrt{x^2 - 16}$

**3.** $\sqrt{x^3 + 8}$

**4.** $\dfrac{1}{\sqrt{2x - 5}}$

**5.** $\dfrac{x^2 - 9}{x\sqrt{x^2 - 3x + 2}}$

## Part II

In Part I, you were given some expressions and had to find their domains. Part II works the other way. Here, you are given a domain, and your task is to create an expression whose domain is the given set.

**6.** Domain = the set of all real numbers less than or equal to 6

**7.** Domain = the set of all real numbers between $-2$ and 2 (including both $-2$ and 2)

**8.** Domain = the set of all real numbers between 1 and 4 (including both 1 and 4)

# Absolutely Functions

You've come across the concept of absolute value in a variety of contexts. Intuitively, the absolute value of a number is the "purely numerical" part of the number, without regard to sign.

The absolute value of a number $x$ is represented by the notation $|x|$. For example, $|4| = 4, |-7| = 7,$ and $|0| = 0$.

Notice that $|x|$ is sometimes the same as $x$ and sometimes the opposite of $x$. Formally, absolute value is defined like this.

$$|x| = \begin{cases} x \text{ if } x > 0 \\ 0 \text{ if } x = 0 \\ -x \text{ if } x < 0 \end{cases}$$

*Comment:* In the last part of this definition, "$-x$" is not a negative number; it represents the opposite of a number that is already negative.

Your main task in this activity is to investigate how absolute value affects functions and their graphs.

| $x$ | $f(x)$ |
|-----|--------|
| 3   | 7      |
| $-2$ | $-9$  |
| $-6$ | 11    |
| 8   | 0      |
| 0   | $-12$ |
| 1   | $-5$  |
| 7   | 2      |
| $-5$ | 8     |
| 11  | 7      |

1. Suppose that the table at the left comes from some function whose equation is $y = f(x)$.

   Based on this table, make a partial table for the function defined by the equation $y = |f(x)|$. Make your table as complete as possible.

*Continued on next page*

Interactive Mathematics Program

**2.** Sketch the graphs for each of these functions. Show the scales on both your horizontal and vertical axes. (Keep in mind that these functions may not be defined for all real numbers.)

   **a.** $g(x) = |\sin x|$

   **b.** $w(d) = \left|\dfrac{1}{d}\right|$

   **c.** $z(r) = |\log r|$

   **d.** $h(s) = \log |s|$

**3.** Suppose the graph at the right represents the function defined by the equation $y = k(x)$.

   Sketch the graph of the function defined by the equation $y = |k(x)|$.

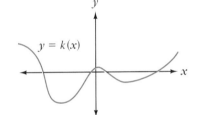

**4.** Now consider again the function $f$ whose table was given in Question 1.

   **a.** Graph the points that are given for $f$ in that table.

   **b.** Make an In-Out table for the function defined by the equation $y = f(|x|)$. Make your table as complete as possible with the information you have.

   **c.** Draw a set of axes identical to those you used in Question 4a, and graph the function $y = f(|x|)$ on this new set of axes.

**5.** Use the function $k$ whose graph is shown in Question 3, and make a graph for the function defined by the equation $y = k(|x|)$.

# SUPPLEMENTAL
## PROBLEM

# Odd or Even?

You know what *odd* and *even* mean when you're talking about integers. For example, $4, 26, 0,$ and $-10$ are all even integers, while $17, -1, 95,$ and $-513$ are all odd integers.

The same words, *odd* and *even,* are also used to define certain types of functions.

> A function *f* is an **even function** if it has the property that $f(x) = f(-x)$ for all values of $x$ in the domain of *f*.

> A function *f* is an **odd function** if it has the property that $f(-x) = -f(x)$ for all values of $x$ in the domain of *f*.

These definitions are rather abstract, so here's an example of each type.

> The function *g* defined by the equation $g(x) = x^2$ is an *even* function, because $g(x) = g(-x)$. For instance, $g(5) = g(-5)$, because both $g(5)$ and $g(-5)$ are equal to 25.

> The function *h* defined by the equation $h(x) = \sin x$ is an *odd* function, because $h(-x) = -h(x)$. For instance, $h(-30°) = -h(30°)$, because $\sin(-30°) = -0.5$ and $\sin 30° = 0.5$.

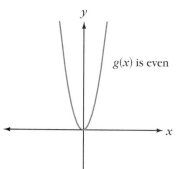

$g(x)$ is even

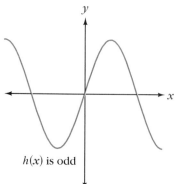

$h(x)$ is odd

*Continued on next page*

1. Find at least five more examples of even functions and at least five more examples of odd functions. Make your examples for each category as varied as you can.

2. Sketch the graphs of at least three functions in each category.

3. a. What general properties must the graph of an even function have?

   b. What general properties must the graph of an odd function have?

4. Give an example of a function that is neither even nor odd.

5. Think about the special case of functions of the form $k(x) = x^n$, for different whole-number values of $n$. What insights do these functions give you into the reason for the terms *odd function* and *even function*?

# SUPPLEMENTAL PROBLEM

# Graphing Power

In this assignment, you will explore the graphs for functions of the form $f(x) = ax^b$, where $a$ and $b$ are constants. These functions are called **power functions.** (In some contexts, it makes sense to use the term *power function* only when the exponent $b$ is a whole number, but for this activity, you should consider all values.)

For example, the functions $f$ and $g$ defined here are both power functions.

$$f(x) = x^3$$
$$g(x) = -2x^{0.5}$$

Begin by looking only at power functions in which the coefficient $a$ is equal to 1 and the exponent $b$ is positive. Keep in mind that $b$ does not have to be a whole number. Focus your attention especially on the part of the graph between $x = 0$ and $x = 1$.

That is, your first job is to answer this question.

1. How do the graphs of power functions of the form $y = x^b$ behave between $x = 0$ and $x = 1$ for different positive values of $b$?

Then consider these questions.

2. How do these graphs behave outside the set of values between $x = 0$ and $x = 1$?

3. How would the graph of a power function change if the coefficient $a$ were different from 1?

# Ferris Wheel on a Ramp

In *High Dive,* you explored height on a Ferris wheel for various radii and periods. But now there's a new complication.

The Ferris wheel itself has been placed on a ramp, as shown in this diagram, and the entire Ferris wheel gradually slides down the ramp as the Ferris wheel goes around. The ramp is 27 feet high at its upper end, and the base of the ramp extends 135 feet along the ground.

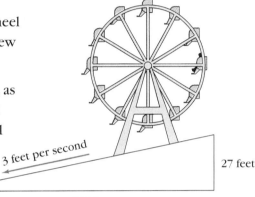

When the Ferris wheel starts sliding, its center is 45 feet above the ground. The entire Ferris wheel moves down the ramp so that its center travels 3 feet per second (in a direction parallel to the slant of the ramp itself). The Ferris wheel has a radius of 20 feet and a period of 12 seconds.

Suppose a rider is at the Ferris wheel's 3 o'clock position when the Ferris wheel starts sliding and that the Ferris wheel turns counterclockwise.

Find an expression for the rider's height off the ground after *t* seconds, and graph that expression from *t* = 0 to *t* = 24.

# SUPPLEMENTAL
## PROBLEM

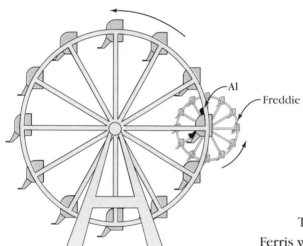

# Freddie on the Ferris Wheel

Al owns a miniature Ferris wheel, which runs on a battery. One day he brings this miniature Ferris wheel to the amusement park, along with his teddy bear, Freddie.

Of course, Freddie likes to ride in his own little seat, so Al puts Freddie in one of the seats of the miniature Ferris wheel.

Throughout the ride, Al holds the miniature Ferris wheel so that it's parallel to the big one and so that its center is at the same height as Al himself.

The two Ferris wheels start going simultaneously, with Al in his usual place, level with the center of the Ferris wheel. Freddie is also level with the center, as shown in the diagram. Both Ferris wheels turn counterclockwise.

The big Ferris wheel has a radius of 30 feet and a period of 20 seconds. The small Ferris wheel has a radius of 10 feet and a period of 10 seconds.

Find an expression for Freddie's height, relative to the center of the big Ferris wheel, after $t$ seconds. Then graph the function defined by this expression from $t = 0$ to $t = 40$.

# Over, and Over, and Over, and . . .

Functions can be composed with themselves as well as with different functions. For example, if $f$ is defined by the equation $f(x) = 3x + 2$, then we can form functions such as $f \circ f$ and even $f \circ f \circ f$.

For instance, $(f \circ f)(x)$ means $f(f(x))$, so $(f \circ f)(x) = f(3x + 2)$. This equals $3 \cdot (3x + 2) + 2$, which simplifies to $9x + 8$.

**1.** Verify that $(f \circ f \circ f)(x) = 27x + 26$.

We generally abbreviate $f \circ f$ as $f^2$, $f \circ f \circ f$ as $f^3$, and so on. (*Caution:* This notation can be misleading. For instance, $f^2$ could mean $f \cdot f$ rather than $f \circ f$, but the notation $f^2$ is generally used specifically for composition.)

The process of finding the repeated composition of a function with itself is called **iteration** or **iterating the function.**

Sometimes, interesting things happen with iteration. One thing to investigate is what happens if you start with a particular value for $x$—say, $x = c$—and then find $f(c)$, $f^2(c)$, $f^3(c)$, and so on.

*Continued on next page*

If $f(c) = c$, we say that $f$ has a **fixed point** at $x = c$ (or that *c is a fixed point for f* ). For example, the function $f$ defined by the equation $f(x) = 3x + 2$ has a fixed point at $x = -1$, because $f(-1) = -1$. For this function, if $c > -1$, $f^n(c)$ grows toward infinity as $n$ increases, while if $c < -1$, $f^n(c)$ grows toward negative infinity as $n$ increases.

**2.** Suppose $c$ is a fixed point for a function $g$. Explain why this guarantees that $g^n(c) = c$ for all positive integers $n$.

**3.** Suppose, as earlier, that $f$ is defined by the equation $f(x) = 3x + 2$. Find the numerical value of each of these expressions.

**a.** $f(2), f^2(2), f^3(2),$ and $f^4(2)$

**b.** $f(-3), f^2(-3), f^3(-3),$ and $f^4(-3)$

**4.** Consider the function $g$ defined by the equation $g(x) = x^2$.

**a.** Find out whether $g$ has any fixed points.

**b.** Describe what happens to $g^n(c)$ as $n$ increases, for values of $c$ other than the fixed points. ( What happens may be different for different values of $c$.)

**5.** Choose two other functions. For each of your functions, do two things.

**a.** Find the fixed points of your function (if any).

**b.** Describe what happens for various values of $x$, other than fixed points, as you keep iterating the function.

# Its Own Inverse

**1.** In *Homework 25: Linear Functions in Verse,*
$f$ was an arbitrary linear function, given by the
equation $f(x) = ax + b$ (with $a \neq 0$), and you
needed to find an expression for $f^{-1}(x)$.

Which linear functions are *their own* inverses? That
is, for what choices of $a$ and $b$ is $f$ equal to $f^{-1}$?
(*Note:* There are infinitely many possibilities.)

**2.** In *Functions in Verse,* you were asked to describe
the relationship between the graph of a function and
the graph of its inverse.

**a.** How could that relationship be used to help with
Question 1 of this assignment?

**b.** Can you find any *nonlinear* functions that are
equal to their own inverses?

SUPPLEMENTAL
PROBLEM

# A Hyperbolic Approach

In Question 1 of *Homework 4: Story Sketches III*, you considered this problem:

> You are driving due north on the highway. Ahead, but off to the east of the road, you see a tall tower. Sketch a graph and make a table showing your distance from the tower as a function of time as you continue north.

In this activity, you need to get more precise about the situation.

Suppose that the tower is 100 feet east of the road, that you are going 60 feet per second (roughly 40 miles per hour), and that at time $t = 0$, you are 1000 feet south of the point on the road that is due west of the tower.

1. Develop an equation that gives your distance $d$ from the tower as a function of $t$. (Express $d$ in feet and $t$ in seconds.)

2. Equations of the form $ay^2 - bx^2 = 1$, where $a$ and $b$ are positive numbers, give graphs that have a shape called a **hyperbola.** For example, the equation $y^2 - x^2 = 1$ has the graph shown here. Each of the two parts of the graph is called a **branch** of the hyperbola.

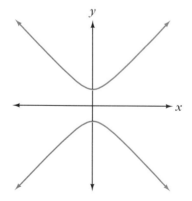

Explain, using ideas about transformations of functions, why the graph of your equation in Question 1 is a branch of a hyperbola.

# "Small World" Again!

Now that you've spent all this time learning about functions and how to put them together, you get one more opportunity to examine the population data set from *Small World, Isn't It?* Here's the data set.

| Year | Estimated population |
|------|---------------------|
| 1650 | 470,000,000 |
| 1750 | 694,000,000 |
| 1850 | 1,091,000,000 |
| 1900 | 1,570,000,000 |
| 1950 | 2,510,000,000 |
| 1960 | 3,030,000,000 |
| 1970 | 3,680,000,000 |
| 1980 | 4,480,000,000 |
| 1985 | 4,870,000,000 |
| 1990 | 5,290,000,000 |
| 1995 | 5,730,000,000 |

Use whatever techniques you can think of to find a function that fits this data set as well as possible, based on the least-squares method of evaluating approximations.

Write a report describing your work, your reasoning, your conclusions, and your final function.

Population data taken from *Information Please, 1996 Almanac,* 49th edition, Houghton-Mifflin, p. 133.

# The Pollster's Dilemma

# What's a Pollster to Think?

*Vanessa Fehl lists the principles underlying good polling practices.*

It's one thing to take a poll of potential voters. It's another thing to determine what the results of the poll really mean.

After looking at the central problem of this unit, you'll experiment to see how much variation can occur from one poll to another, even when the polls are taken from the same population.

# The Pollster's Dilemma

Many people in River City are tired of the corruption in their city government. Contracts are routinely awarded to relatives of people in power, and politicians routinely accept bribes for favors.

Coretta Collins is running for mayor of River City and has pledged to end the corruption.

Everyone working on Coretta's campaign is an unpaid volunteer. They are all learning about running a campaign while on the job. You are one of these volunteers, and you have been put in charge of handling all of Coretta's polls.

*Continued on next page*

Before you began, a poll was done of 500 eligible voters. It found that 53% of those polled intended to vote for Coretta. Of course, she wants to know whether she will win the election. You need to figure out what this poll means in terms of her chances of having a majority of the people vote for her.

There are 400,000 eligible voters in River City.

**1. a.** How many of the people polled indicated that they would vote for Coretta?

**b.** If different people had been selected for the poll, the results might have been different. How many "yes" votes (votes for Coretta) would have had to be replaced by "no" votes (votes for Coretta's opponent) for the result to be a tie?

**2.** Based on this poll, how secure should you and Coretta feel about her lead? That is, what significance can be attached to this result?

**3.** What information about the poll would you like to know so that you could trust it? Make a list of things that you would insist on for future polls in order to have confidence in their results.

# No Bias Allowed!

In everyday language, the word *bias* is often used to mean an unfair judgment, especially against a particular racial or ethnic group. But in statistics, the word does not carry this negative connotation. Rather, it refers to any built-in imbalance in the sampling process, which may occur without any malicious intent.

This means that a poll with a biased sample might not give correct information about the larger population, because it may slant the results in a certain direction, even if the pollster doesn't have that intention. In this assignment, you will look at ways in which bias might enter into the polling process for a particular situation.

Suppose a prom committee wants to know whether $75 per ticket is too much to charge. The committee decides to poll some students and use the results to help determine whether that price is too high.

1. **a.** Identify the overall population in this situation.

   **b.** What does the term "sample" refer to in this situation?

2. Explain what might be wrong with each of these methods of choosing a sample and how each might bias the results.

   **a.** Picking every tenth student who drives into the school parking lot

   **b.** Stopping a group of students coming out of school together and asking everyone in that group

   **c.** Picking one mathematics class at random and polling all the students in that class

3. Describe a specific plan for choosing a random sample of students in your high school. Then discuss the strengths and weaknesses of your plan.

# The King's Switches

Our favorite king has decided that he is tired of having his gold stolen. He is about to leave on a vacation, so he has installed an alarm system to prevent intruders from getting into his royal vault while he is gone.

The alarm system is activated and deactivated by the use of five switches. The only way to deactivate the system is to turn off all five switches.

You might think that a thief could simply turn off the switches, but that isn't so easy to do. The system is set up so that the switches can only be changed according to these rules.

- The switch on the left may be changed (turned on or off) no matter how the other switches are set.

- Any other switch may be changed only if the switch to its immediate left is on and all other switches to its left are off.

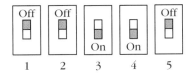

For example, if the switches are currently set as shown in the diagram, then you can change either switch 1 or switch 4, but you can't change switch 2, switch 3, or switch 5.

   **1.** When the king leaves for his vacation, all five switches are turned on. What is the minimum number of moves required to deactivate the king's alarm system?

Of course, this POW isn't only about the case of five switches, and it isn't only about getting a numerical answer. So here's more of the POW.

*Continued on next page*

---

Suppose you have $n$ switches, all turned on, and you want to turn them all off. Assume that you can only change a switch according to the rules in the king's alarm system.

**2.** Find the minimum number of moves required for the cases $n = 1, 2, 3$, and $4$, and prove your results. Also prove the result you found in Question 1 for the case $n = 5$.

**3.** Describe a pattern you see in your results or a procedure for finding new results based on results for smaller values of $n$. You might also make a guess about a general formula. You can get more data by considering cases where $n$ is more than 5 and then use this information either to make guesses or to test ideas.

**4.** Based on your pattern, procedure, or formula, find the number of moves that would be required for $n = 10$.

**5.** Try to *prove* that your pattern, procedure, or general formula works in all cases. (That's hard!)

## Write-up

In answering Questions 1 through 5, address these issues.

• The minimum number of moves required to deactivate the system for the specific cases you studied, including all cases up to $n = 5$

• Any ideas you have about a general pattern, procedure, or formula for describing the number of moves required, and an explanation of how to get the number of moves for $n = 10$

• Proofs, for each case up to $n = 5$, that your answer represents the minimum number of moves by which the system can be deactivated

Adapted from *MATHEMATICS: Problem Solving Through Recreational Mathematics*, by B. Averbach and O. Chein. Copyright © 1997 by B. Averbach and O. Chein. Used with permission.

# Sampling Seniors

In this activity, you will examine how well polls of different sizes reflect the reality of a population.

## The Scenario

The senior class at Bayside High is very lucky. They have two beautiful places where they can afford to hold their senior prom—Hamilton Hall and Cesar Chavez Center. The prom committee wants to poll the senior class to see which location members of the class prefer.

There are 150 seniors at Bayside High. Because Bayside seniors have such different schedules, it is both difficult and time-consuming to poll them all. Therefore, the committee must decide how many people they need to poll. They want to poll as few seniors as possible but still get a good idea of what the seniors truly want.

## Your Task

You will be simulating a Bayside High poll. (Actually, you will simulate many polls.) To set up the simulation, use 150 objects to represent the 150 students. The objects should be identical except for color.

*Continued on next page*

Although the prom committee doesn't know this, 60% of the students favor Cesar Chavez Center and the remaining 40% favor Hamilton Hall. Thus, use 90 objects of one color to represent the students who favor Cesar Chavez Center and 60 objects of another color to represent the students who favor Hamilton Hall. Then put the 150 objects in a bag and mix them up.

1. **a.** Choose a sample size. Then, without looking into the bag, pick that many objects from your bag and record the number of votes for Cesar Chavez Center. When you are done, return all the objects to the bag.

   **b.** Repeat the sampling process of Question 1a again and again, using the same sample size, until you have done a total of 20 polls. Be sure to record the result each time and to return the objects to the bag when you have finished each poll.

2. **a.** Make a frequency bar graph of the results of your 20 polls.

   **b.** Determine how many of your polls showed a majority favoring Cesar Chavez Center.

3. Repeat the steps of Questions 1 and 2 using a different sample size, doing another 20 polls. As time allows, continue with other sample sizes, again doing 20 polls for each size.

4. Based on your results, how small a group can the committee poll and still get a good idea of what the senior class prefers? Explain your answer.

# Pennant Fever Reflection

This assignment looks back at ideas from the Year 3 unit *Pennant Fever,* ideas that will also play an important part in this unit.

Recall that in *Pennant Fever,* the Good Guys baseball team had seven games remaining in their regular season. For each game they played, they had a probability of .62 of winning.

1. How is the polling process in *Sampling Seniors* like the sequence of games the Good Guys played in *Pennant Fever*? How is it different?

2. Find the probability of the Good Guys winning all seven of their remaining games, and explain your reasoning.

3. Find the probability of the Good Guys winning exactly six of their seven remaining games. (*Reminder:* There is more than one way to win six games and lose one.)

4. Find the probability of the Good Guys winning four and losing three of their seven remaining games.

# Throw Back the Little Ones

## Part I: With and Without Replacement

In *Sampling Seniors,* you completed each poll before returning the objects to the bag. This process is called **sampling without replacement.**

Another type of sampling involves picking the objects from the bag one at a time and returning each object to the bag (and mixing the objects) before picking the next object in the sample. This approach is called **sampling with replacement.**

In this assignment, you will investigate each process using two different population sizes.

1. Imagine a bag of 12 marbles of which 10 are red and 2 are blue.

    a. First suppose that marbles are pulled out of the bag one at a time and not put back in. (This is *sampling without replacement.*) If the first eight marbles pulled from the bag are red, what is the probability that the ninth marble pulled out will be red?

    b. Imagine that the same 12 marbles are back in the bag. Again, marbles are pulled out of the bag, but this time, suppose that after each marble is selected, it is returned to the bag and mixed in with the other marbles. (This is *sampling with replacement.*) If the first eight marbles pulled from the bag are red, what is the probability that the ninth marble pulled out will be red?

    c. Compare your results from Questions 1a and 1b.

*Continued on next page*

**2.** Now imagine a bag of 12,000 marbles, of which 10,000 are red and 2000 are blue.

**a.** As in Question 1a, suppose you use sampling without replacement, keeping marbles out after they are selected. If the first eight marbles pulled from the bag are red, what is the probability that the ninth marble pulled out will be red?

**b.** As in Question 1b, suppose you use sampling with replacement, returning each marble to the bag after it is selected. If the first eight marbles pulled from the bag are red, what is the probability that the ninth marble pulled out will be red?

**c.** Compare your results from Questions 2a and 2b.

**3.** How does population size affect the distinction between sampling without replacement and sampling with replacement?

*Continued on next page*

## Part II: Cones and Bowls

Part II of this assignment continues the review of ideas from *Pennant Fever*. You may recall the ice cream adventures of Jonathan and his sister Johanna. Jonathan likes to eat his ice cream out of a bowl, so it doesn't matter to him what order the flavors are in. For Jonathan, a bowl with a scoop of strawberry, a scoop of pistachio, and a scoop of butter pecan is the same as a bowl with a scoop of pistachio, a scoop of butter pecan, and a scoop of strawberry.

Johanna, on the other hand, eats her ice cream in cones, which means she first eats the flavor that's on top, then the next flavor, and so on. Therefore, it makes a big difference to Johanna what order the flavors are in.

4. If the ice cream store has 20 flavors, and Johanna is choosing a three-scoop cone (with three different flavors), how many different cones must she consider? Explain your answer.

5. At the same store, Jonathan is choosing a three-scoop bowl (again, with three different flavors). How many different bowls must he consider? Explain your answer.

6. Explain the relationship between the answers to Questions 4 and 5.

7. Repeat Questions 4 through 6 using four-scoop cones and bowls.

# DAYS
## 4-5

# Polls and
# *Pennant Fever*

*Erik Manzelli finds it useful to apply ideas he gained from the Year 3 unit "Pennant Fever" in order to determine theoretical probabilities in this unit.*

Now that you've done some experiments with polls, it's time to look at the theory. When you take a poll of a specific size from a specific population, what's the theoretical probability of getting each possible specific result?

Based on the ideas in Part I of *Homework 3: Throw Back the Little Ones,* you will be using the simplifying assumption that polling can be viewed as sampling with replacement. That assumption will allow you to apply ideas from the Year 3 unit *Pennant Fever* to find the probabilities.

# The Theory of Three-Person Polls

Imagine that you are conducting polls on behalf of a certain candidate in a two-candidate race. You will ask people whether they are going to vote for your candidate. You should assume that participants each give an honest answer of either "yes" or "no." (There are no undecided voters.)

The outcome—that is, the number of "yes" answers you get—will depend on how opinions are divided in the overall population and, of course, on the size of your poll. For polls of a given size, each possible outcome has a specific theoretical probability of occurring.

*Continued on next page*

In this activity, you will consider the case of 3-person polls from a specific overall population and find the theoretical probability distribution for the possible outcomes. That is, imagine that you are taking many separate polls and that you question three people in each poll.

Begin by making this assumption.

• The overall population is 60% in favor of your candidate.

This figure of 60% (or .6) is referred to as the **true proportion.**

For simplicity, you should make these two additional assumptions.

• Each voter polled is picked at random from the total voting population.

• The overall population is big enough compared to the sample size that you can treat the problem as if it involves sampling with replacement.

These three assumptions can be combined into one.

> **Every voter picked has a probability of .6 of being in favor of your candidate.**

Answer the questions based on this combined assumption.

**1.** List the possible outcomes for the number of "yes" votes in such a poll.

**2.** Find the probability of each possible outcome.

**3.** Make a probability bar graph showing your results.

# Graphs of the Theory

In *The Theory of Three-Person Polls,* you examined what happens if a 3-person poll is taken from a population that is 60% in favor of a given candidate. In Questions 1 through 3 of this assignment, you'll consider what happens as the true proportion changes. Question 4 asks you to think about the effect of changing the sample size. (You should continue to use a sampling-with-replacement model to find the probabilities.)

1. Suppose the true proportion, which we usually call *p,* is .55. That is, suppose that 55% of the overall population is in favor of a given candidate. The fraction of votes in favor of the candidate in a specific poll is called the **sample proportion.** We often use the symbol $\hat{p}$ for the sample proportion. (This symbol is read as "*p* hat.")

   Make a probability bar graph showing the probability of getting each possible value of $\hat{p}$ for a 3-person poll.

2. Now make a probability bar graph for the case in which the true proportion is 70%, and compare this graph with the graph from Question 1.

*Continued on next page*

**3.** Generalize your work from Questions 1 and 2. That is, assume the true proportion is $p$, and find the probability for each possible sample proportion for a 3-person poll. (Your probabilities will be expressions in terms of $p$. You do not need to make a probability bar graph for this general case.)

**4.** In Question 1, you made a probability bar graph for a *3-person* poll (using a true proportion of 55%). How do you think the graph would change if the sample size were increased (keeping the same true proportion of 55% for the overall population)?

# The Theory of Polls

In *The Theory of Three-Person Polls*, you found the theoretical probability for each possible outcome of a 3-person poll. As the person in charge of polls for Coretta Collins, you need to study the theory of polling more fully in order to better understand the reliability of polls.

For larger polls, there are more possible outcomes, each with a theoretical probability. The main focus of this activity is on how the probabilities change as the poll size changes.

For the sake of making comparisons, you should assume throughout this activity that the true proportion is .6; that is, assume that 60% of the population favors the candidate.

*Continued on next page*

Once a poll is taken, the pollster can compute the sample proportion, which is the fraction of those polled who favor the candidate. For the case of a 3-person poll, the theoretical distribution for the sample proportion is shown in the accompanying graph. Notice that roughly 35% of such polls (.064 + .288) would show that the candidate is trailing, even though the candidate has the support of 60% of the overall population.

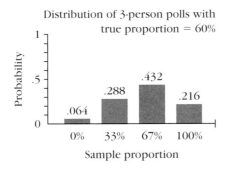

Distribution of 3-person polls with true proportion = 60%

1. Consider the case of a 5-person poll. The number of voters in the poll who support the candidate could be 0, 1, 2, 3, 4, or 5, so the sample proportion could be 0%, 20%, 40%, 60%, 80%, or 100%.

   a. Find the probability of each of these possible results. (*Reminder:* Assume that the true proportion is .60.)

   b. Make a probability bar graph of your results.

   c. What percentage of 5-person polls correctly show the candidate leading?

2. Now consider the case of a 9-person poll.

   a. Find the probability of each possible outcome.

   b. Make a probability bar graph of your results.

   c. What percentage of 9-person polls correctly show the candidate leading?

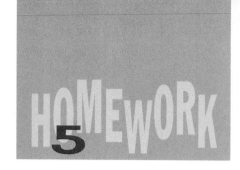

# HOMEWORK 5

# Civics in Action

The senior civics class is about to put some theory into practice by conducting the election of the senior class president. Clarence is one of two candidates running for this office.

There are 60 members of the senior class. Although nobody knows it yet (except you), 50 of these 60 students intend to vote for Clarence.

The editor of the class newspaper, Clarissa, plans to take an exit poll (a poll of people as they leave the voting booth) so she can publish a prediction before the votes are officially counted. She intends only to predict the winner, not to predict how many votes the winner will get.

*Continued on next page*

Clarissa has an important physics test coming up and needs to study for it. Therefore, although she will pick students randomly from a list and get their votes in an anonymous way, she probably won't bother actually to ask many students how they voted.

1. Suppose Clarissa asks only one person and uses that person's vote to make her prediction. What is the probability that she will get a result that correctly predicts the winner?

2. Suppose Clarissa polls three people.

    a. Make a probability bar graph for the possible outcomes of this 3-person poll.

    b. What is the probability that her poll will correctly predict the winner? In other words, what is the probability that the poll will show a majority supporting Clarence?

3. Pick at least one more poll size (greater than 3) and make a probability bar graph for the possible outcomes. Also find the probability that a poll of that size would correctly predict the winner of the election.

4. If it were up to you, what is the least number of people you would be satisfied to poll (assuming you didn't know the actual number of students in favor of Clarence)? Give some reasons for your answer.

# DAYS
# 6-10

# Normal Distributions Revisited

*Nikki King and Yaravi Anaya prepare the graphs they'll present to the class comparing normal curves with different means and standard deviations.*

Using the "sampling with replacement" model, you've seen two powerful facts about polling.

- Poll results follow a binomial distribution.

- For large polls, binomial distributions look a lot like normal distributions.

Because of these two facts, the normal distribution will play a key role throughout the rest of this unit. In the next portion of the unit, you'll review and extend what you learned in previous years about the normal distribution.

# The Central Limit Theorem

The **central limit theorem** is a powerful and general principle about statistics and probability. Although it applies to many situations, only one aspect of the theorem will be used in this unit. In a very succinct form, this special case says:

> **As *n* gets bigger and bigger, the probability distribution for an *n*-person poll looks more and more like a normal distribution.**

Explaining more fully what this principle means requires some discussion of both the distribution for *n*-person polls and the normal distribution.

## The *n*-person Poll and the Binomial Distribution

We need to start with this principle.

> **If *n* people are sampled from a population, and the size of the total population is much larger than *n*, then we can treat the poll as if it were a case involving sampling with replacement.**

According to this principle, polling people on how they will vote in a two-candidate election is similar to repeatedly flipping a coin (a not-necessarily balanced coin) or to playing a sequence of baseball games in which a team has a fixed chance of winning each game. For each person polled, there are two possible outcomes, which we might call "yes" and "no." The probabilities of these two outcomes are the same for every person polled.

*Continued on next page*

If $p$ represents the fraction of "yes" voters in the overall population (usually called the *true proportion*), then for each person polled, the probability of a "yes" vote is $p$ and the probability of a "no" vote is $1 - p$.

The number of "yes" votes in an $n$-person poll can be anywhere from zero through $n$. The probability distribution for the poll tells what the chances are of getting each of these results. Specifically:

> **The probability of getting exactly**
> **$r$ "yes" votes in an $n$-person poll**
> **is $_nC_r \cdot p^r \cdot (1 - p)^{n-r}$.**

This collection of probabilities, for the different values of $r$, is called the **binomial distribution.** This is a *discrete* distribution, and the set of possible outcomes is finite.

*Comment:* The binomial distribution is different for each choice of $n$ and $p$. In the general context, we often refer to $n$ as the number of "trials" and to $p$ as the probability of "success."

In comparing the binomial distribution to the normal distribution, we consider the *fraction* of "yes" votes in the sample, rather than the *number* of such votes. This fraction, usually called the *sample proportion*, is simply $\frac{r}{n}$. It is often expressed as a percentage, and it can be anywhere from 0% to 100%. (For any particular binomial distribution, the set of possible values within this range is finite. For instance, if $n = 4$, then the sample proportion must be one of these values: 0%, 25%, 50%, 75%, or 100%.)

## The Normal Distribution

The normal distribution is an example of a *continuous* distribution, because any numerical outcome is possible. Continuous distributions are described by giving the probability of getting a result within any interval, rather than by giving the probability of getting each particular result.

*Continued on next page*

The first diagram below shows an example of a normal curve. (The equation for this curve is discussed in the activity *Graphing Distributions*.) The probability of getting a result between *a* and *b* is equal to the area of the shaded region in the diagram, and the total area under the curve equals 1.

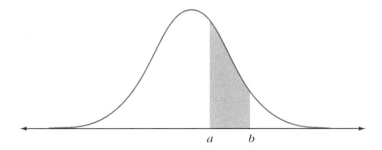

As with the binomial distribution, there are many different normal distributions. And like the binomial distribution, the normal distribution depends on two parameters. For the normal distribution, these two parameters are the *mean* and the *standard deviation*.

The *mean* gives the average result for the distribution, and the normal curve is symmetric about this value. The mean is often represented by the Greek letter $\mu$ ("mu"), and it can be positive, negative, or zero. The *standard deviation* tells how "spread out" the curve is. The standard deviation is generally represented by the Greek letter $\sigma$ ("sigma"), and it can be any positive number.

This diagram shows two normal curves with the same standard deviation but different means.

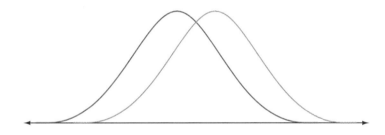

*Continued on next page*

This diagram shows two normal curves with the same mean but different standard deviations.

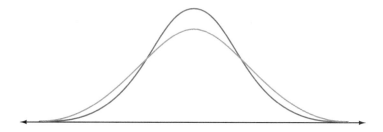

One useful aspect of the normal distribution is that the probability of getting a result within a given interval depends only on how the endpoints of the interval relate to the mean and standard deviation. For example, in the next diagram, the shaded area extends from one standard deviation below the mean to one standard deviation above the mean—that is, from $\mu - \sigma$ to $\mu + \sigma$. No matter what the values of $\mu$ and $\sigma$, this area is about 68% of the total area under the curve. Thus, if an experiment follows a normal distribution with mean $\mu$ and standard deviation $\sigma$, then in the long run, approximately 68% of all results from the experiment will fall between $\mu - \sigma$ and $\mu + \sigma$.

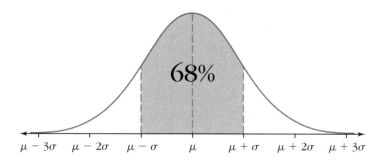

*Continued on next page*

In the next diagram, the shaded area includes all results within two standard deviations of the mean. This area is about 95% of the total. In other words, in the long run, approximately 95% of all results lie between $\mu - 2\sigma$ and $\mu + 2\sigma$. Again, this is true for every normal distribution.

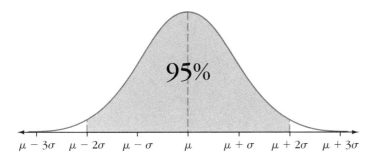

# The Central Limit Theorem

The central limit theorem tells what happens to the binomial distribution as $n$ gets larger. It states that the chance of getting a sample proportion within a certain interval is approximately the same as the chance of getting a result within the same interval for a certain normal distribution.

The values of $\mu$ (the mean) and $\sigma$ (the standard deviation) for the approximating normal distribution depend on $n$ (the poll size) and $p$ (the true proportion). Later in this unit, you will find formulas for $\mu$ and $\sigma$ in terms of $n$ and $p$.

For a fixed value of $p$, as $n$ gets bigger and bigger, the normal distribution becomes a better and better approximation for the binomial distribution. In fact, no matter how good an approximation you want, you can find a value of $n$ big enough to give an approximation that is that good.

# Deviations of Swinging

A group of students was trying to find out how long it took for 12 complete swings of a 30-foot pendulum. They repeatedly measured the time for 12 swings and got a variety of results. They determined that the mean of their results was 72 seconds and that the standard deviation was 1.5 seconds.

You should assume that measurements of the pendulum's period fit a normal distribution.

**1.** What percentage of future measurements should give results between 72 and 75 seconds?

**2.** What percentage of future measurements should give results greater than 73.5 seconds?

**3.** What percentage of future measurements should give results greater than 69 seconds?

# Means and More in Middletown

For each of Questions 1 through 3, assume that the situation involves a normal distribution. (Question 4 asks you to comment on these assumptions.)

In each case, make a sketch of a normal distribution, identifying and labeling the positions that are one and two standard deviations from the mean. Then use your sketches to help justify your answers.

1. An analysis of the cost of rental apartments in Middletown shows a mean price of $650 per month with a standard deviation of $150 per month. What are three conclusions you can draw from this information?

2. The Middletown Police Department gives a standardized test to potential captains. The mean score is 270 with a standard deviation of 15 points. A score of 300 points is required to pass. Approximately what percentage of those who take the test will pass?

3. The Middletown Track Club surveyed some of its members to get an idea of how they trained. The survey showed that they ran an average of 35 miles a week, with a standard deviation of 7 miles per week. Approximately what percentage of the runners in the club run less than 42 miles per week?

4. For each of Questions 1 through 3, discuss whether it's reasonable to assume that the situation involves a normal distribution.

# Graphing Distributions

The normal distribution is a very special set of probabilities for the possible outcomes of an experiment. In a normal distribution, any numerical result is possible, although not all results are equally likely. The probability of getting a result within a given interval is determined by a complex formula. Specifically, for a normal distribution with mean $\mu$ and standard deviation $\sigma$, the normal curve is the graph of this equation, in which $y$ is considered as a function of $x$.

$$y = \left( \frac{1}{\sigma\sqrt{2\pi}} \right) \cdot e^{-\frac{1}{2}\left(\frac{x-\mu}{\sigma}\right)^2}$$

The probability that a result is between $a$ and $b$ is the area under this curve between the vertical lines $x = a$ and $x = b$.

The simplest normal curve is the case $\mu = 0$ and $\sigma = 1$, for which the equation is

$$y = \left( \frac{1}{\sqrt{2\pi}} \right) \cdot e^{-\frac{1}{2}x^2}$$

This special case is sometimes called the *standard* (or *normalized*) normal curve. Principles about normal distributions are often expressed in terms of this special case.

In the general case, we have the initial factor $\frac{1}{\sigma\sqrt{2\pi}}$ so that the total area under the normal curve is equal to 1, no matter what $\mu$ and $\sigma$ are. Having the total area equal to 1 corresponds to having the sum of all the probabilities equal to 1.

*Continued on next page*

1. Use a graphing calculator to show the standard normal curve, which is the case in which $\mu = 0$ and $\sigma = 1$.

2. Use a graphing calculator to show the normal curve for $\mu = 2$ and $\sigma = 3$.

3. Graph normal curves with $\mu = 2$ but using other standard deviations. What changes do you see?

4. Graph normal curves with $\sigma = 3$ but using different means. What changes do you see?

# Gifts Aren't Always Free

Craig's aunt is buying him a car for his high school graduation. He lives in a rural area, so a car will be very handy.

Craig knows he needs to work this summer, but he also wants to have some free time. He wants to figure out how many hours he needs to work.

Craig knows how much money he needs for everything except gasoline. He has figured out that he will be driving about 500 miles per week, and he knows that gasoline in his area costs $1.25 per gallon.

Craig has done some research on the kind of car he is getting. Specifically, he found a study that rated the fuel efficiency for each of a number of cars of this particular model and year. According to the study, the average of these individual ratings was 23 miles per gallon, and the standard deviation was 2.5 miles per gallon. Craig has not studied statistics and doesn't know what standard deviation means.

1. Explain to Craig what it means that the standard deviation is 2.5 miles per gallon.

2. Tell Craig how much he should plan on spending for gasoline per week, and why. You can assume that the variation in fuel efficiency among cars of this model is normally distributed.

3. Explain to Craig how normal distributions fit into all of this.

# Normal Areas

The diagram below shows the graph of the equation for the standard normal curve, which is

$$y = \left( \frac{1}{\sqrt{2\pi}} \right) \cdot e^{-\frac{1}{2}x^2}$$

This is the normal curve with mean 0 and standard deviation 1. The total area under this curve is equal to 1.

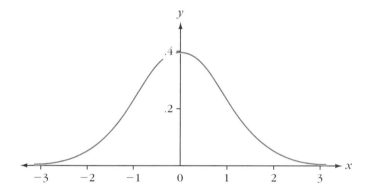

You know that the area below the curve between $x = -1$ and $x = 1$ is approximately .68, or 68% of the total area under the curve, and that the area between $x = -2$ and $x = 2$ is approximately .95, or 95% of the total.

Use these facts and the graph itself to estimate the answers to these questions concerning other areas and other percentages.

**1.** What percentage of the area is between $x = -0.5$ and $x = 0.5$?

**2.** What percentage of the area is between $x = -1.5$ and $x = 1.5$?

**3.** What interval symmetric about $x = 0$ will contain 50% of the area?

**4.** What interval symmetric about $x = 0$ will contain 80% of the area?

---

# The Normal Table

You have seen that for all normal curves, the area between $x = \mu - \sigma$ and $x = \mu + \sigma$ is approximately .68, no matter what the values of the mean $\mu$ or the standard deviation $\sigma$. Similarly, the areas of other regions symmetric about the mean depend only on how many standard deviations they extend from $\mu$.

Mathematicians have computed these areas precisely. Because these computations are not easy, the results are often put into a table for easy reference.

The table on the facing page gives the areas under the normal curve for various regions that are symmetric about the mean. In this table, $z$ represents the number of standard deviations that the area extends in each direction. The most commonly used values, for $z = 1$ and $z = 2$, are shown in **bold-faced** type.

For example, the case $z = 2$ refers to the area between $x = \mu - 2\sigma$ and $x = \mu + 2\sigma$, that is, the area within two standard deviations of the mean. The table entry for $z = 2$ is .9545, which corresponds to the fact that this area is about 95% of the total.

*Continued on next page*

Similarly, the table value .3829 for $z = 0.5$ means that about 38% of the area is between $x = \mu - 0.5\sigma$ and $x = \mu + 0.5\sigma$, that is, within half of one standard deviation of the mean.

| $z$ (number of standard deviations) | Area within $z$ standard deviations of the mean | $z$ (number of standard deviations) | Area within $z$ standard deviations of the mean |
|---|---|---|---|
| 0 | 0 | 1.7 | .9109 |
| 0.1 | .0797 | 1.8 | .9281 |
| 0.2 | .1585 | 1.9 | .9426 |
| 0.3 | .2358 | **2.0** | **.9545** |
| 0.4 | .3108 | 2.1 | .9643 |
| 0.5 | .3829 | 2.2 | .9722 |
| 0.6 | .4515 | 2.3 | .9786 |
| 0.7 | .5161 | 2.4 | .9836 |
| 0.8 | .5763 | 2.5 | .9876 |
| 0.9 | .6319 | 2.6 | .9907 |
| **1.0** | **.6827** | 2.7 | .9931 |
| 1.1 | .7287 | 2.8 | .9949 |
| 1.2 | .7699 | 2.9 | .9963 |
| 1.3 | .8064 | 3.0 | .9973 |
| 1.4 | .8385 | 4.0 | .99994 |
| 1.5 | .8664 | 5.0 | .9999994 |
| 1.6 | .8904 | | |

# More Middletown Musings

The situations in this assignment are similar to those in *Homework 6: Means and More in Middletown*, but for these questions, you will need the detailed information about the normal curve from *The Normal Table*. As before, you should assume that the data set for each situation is normally distributed.

1. As noted in the previous assignment, an analysis of the cost of rental apartments in Middletown shows a mean price of $650 per month with a standard deviation of $150 per month. Approximately what percentage of the renters pay between $530 and $770 per month?

*Continued on next page*

**2.** The Middletown Police Department decided to raise the score necessary to be eligible to become captain to 306 points. The mean score is 270 with a standard deviation of 15 points. Based on the new passing score, approximately what percentage of those who take the test will pass?

**3.** Against the best wishes of its membership, the executive board of the Middletown Track Club decided to pick a member at random to represent the club in the State Championship. Most members believe that the person representing the club should be someone who runs at least 40 miles per week. What is the probability that a member chosen at random will meet this criterion? (Recall that the club's survey showed that members run an average of 35 miles a week, with a standard deviation of 7 miles per week.)

*Note:* This question involves a *z*-value that is not in *The Normal Table*, so you should estimate the appropriate probability based on values that are in the table.

# Back to the Circus

You may recall this scenario from the unit assessment for the Year 1 unit *The Pit and the Pendulum*.

> A circus performer wants to ride a bicycle right up to a brick wall and stop dramatically very close to the wall without crashing. She wants to know when to apply the brakes.

The assessment asked students to propose a plan to collect and analyze data that would help her with her dilemma.

*Continued on next page*

One student proposed this:

> The performer should do an experiment. She should draw a line on the floor. Then she should ride at full speed toward the line and apply her brakes just when she reaches the line. She should do this as a controlled experiment, so that she always rides at the same speed, applies her brakes with the same pressure, has the same amount of air in her tires, and so on. Each time she stops, she should measure how far she goes past the line.
>
> She should use her results to tell her how far from the wall she should stop.

Suppose you carried out such an experiment many times and found that the mean of your stopping distances was 2 meters and the standard deviation was 0.3 meters.

If the performer is willing to hit the wall 5% of the time, how far away from the wall would you tell her to put on her brakes? (Presumably, on the rare occasions when she hits the wall, she'll be going very slowly at the time of impact, and won't get hurt.)

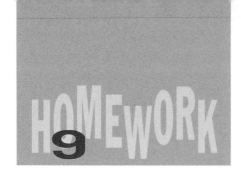

# Gaps in the Table

*The Normal Table* tells you the probability of getting a result within a given range for a data set that is normally distributed. For instance, for $z = 0.6$, the table gives a value of .4515, which means there is approximately a 45% chance that a given result will lie within 0.6 standard deviations of the mean.

Unfortunately, the chart you have only lists values for $z$ that are multiples of 0.1. So what do you do about "in-between" values, such as $z = 0.65$? That is, for normally distributed data, what is the probability of getting a result that is within 0.65 standard deviations of the mean?

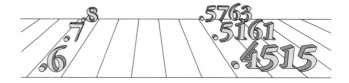

## The Intuitive Idea

Intuition might lead you to reason something like this.

> The value $z = 0.65$ is exactly halfway between $z = 0.6$ and $z = 0.7$. The value $z = 0.6$ has an associated probability of .4515, and the value $z = 0.7$ has an associated probability of .5161, so you might expect the probability associated with $z = 0.65$ to be exactly halfway between .4515 and .5161.

1. Test out this intuitive idea by answering these questions.

   a. Find the probability associated with $z = 1.8$ and the probability associated with $z = 2.0$.

*Continued on next page*

**b.** Find the number that is exactly halfway between the two probabilities you found in Question 1a.

**c.** Compare your answer in Question 1b with the probability in the table for $z = 1.9$. Are they exactly the same? Are they close?

## What Actually Happens

What you should have found is that the probability in the table for $z = 1.9$ is not exactly halfway—it's actually a little closer to the probability for $z = 2.0$ than it is to the probability for $z = 1.8$—but it's pretty close to halfway.

The example just described is a special case of a general approximation technique called **linear interpolation.** Although this method may not give the exact value, it will often give good approximations. This technique is especially useful for functions that can't be computed in any simple way, such as the function giving probabilities associated with a given $z$-value.

**2.** Here's an illustration of this technique with a function that's much simpler than the one represented by the normal table.

Consider the "squaring" function, that is, the function whose equation is $y = x^2$. This could be represented by the notation $f(x) = x^2$.

**a.** Find $y$ when $x = 7$. In other words, find $f(7)$.

**b.** Find $y$ when $x = 9$. In other words, find $f(9)$.

Using the technique of a linear interpolation, you would expect $f(8)$ to be about halfway between $f(7)$ and $f(9)$.

*Continued on next page*

**c.** Check this out. That is, find the number halfway between $f(7)$ and $f(9)$, and then compare that number to $f(8)$.

**d.** Use a graph of the function $y = x^2$ to explain why the number halfway between $f(7)$ and $f(9)$ was either higher or lower than $f(8)$.

**3.** Now examine what happens if you apply this technique to the function $g$ defined by the equation $g(x) = 2x - 1$.

**a.** Find $g(7)$ and $g(9)$, and then find the number halfway between these results.

**b.** Compare your answer to Question 3a with the value of $g(8)$.

**c.** What is it about the function $g$ that makes the technique give the exact value in this case?

One strength of the technique of linear interpolation is that it isn't limited to "halfway" points. Question 4 returns to the situation of probabilities associated with the normal distribution.

**4. a.** Use the technique of linear interpolation to estimate the probability associated with $z = 0.82$. (*Hint:* The value 0.82 is one-fifth of the way from 0.8 to 0.9.)

**b.** Use linear interpolation to estimate the probability associated with $z = \dfrac{4}{3}$.

# A Normal Poll

Clarence's younger brother, Henry, is one of two candidates running for president of his middle school. As it happens, Clarissa's younger sister, Harriet, is editor of the newspaper for the middle school.

Although neither Harriet nor Henry knows it, 60% of the student body plans to vote for Henry.

Harriet is more industrious than her big sister. She plans to take a 50-person poll at the school, selecting students at random. Based on which candidate gets a majority in her poll, Harriet will make a prediction about who will win the election.

For a poll of this size, the normal distribution gives a very good approximation for finding the probabilities of different outcomes (assuming that the overall population is large enough — see Question 3). The normal distribution that fits this situation best has mean $\mu = .6$ and standard deviation $\sigma = .069$.

1. Does it make intuitive sense that the mean for this normal distribution is .6? Why?

2. Use the normal approximation to find the probability that Harriet's poll will show Henry as the winner.

3. One guideline says that if you want to use sampling with replacement as a model for polling, your poll size should be no more than 5% of the overall population. How big must the school be if Harriet's poll fits this guideline?

# A Plus for the Community

The Community Recreation Center is holding a fair to get people more involved in the center and to raise some money.

One of the activities being planned is a "Wheel of Fortune." For each ticket you buy, you get to spin the wheel once. A spin of the wheel will win you either $1, $2, $3, or $10.

The $1 and $2 results each have a probability of .4, the $3 result has a probability of .15, and the $10 result has a probability of .05.

**1.** Suppose the center sold 1000 tickets and the results matched the theoretical probability distribution perfectly. That is, suppose 400 people won $1; 400 people won $2; 150 people won $3; and 50 people won $10. What would be the average amount that the center paid out per spin?

**2.** Would the answer to Question 1 be different if the center had sold 5000 tickets? What about other numbers of spins? Explain.

# DAYS 11-14

# Means and Standard Deviations

*Will Lawton reviews the steps for computing standard deviation in preparation for extending this concept.*

The central limit theorem guarantees that under suitable assumptions about poll size, the theoretical distribution of poll results approximately follows a normal curve. But which normal curve?

There is a different normal distribution for each possible mean and standard deviation. The next task of the unit is to relate these two parameters to the size of the poll and to the true proportion for the population from which the sample is taken.

# Mean and Standard Deviation for Probability Distributions

If you are given a set of data, the *mean* of the set is simply the average. That is, you add the items in the data list and divide by the number of items.

To find the *standard deviation* for a set of data, you take these steps.

**a.** Find the mean of the data items.

**b.** Find the square of the difference between each data item and the mean.

**c.** Add the squared differences.

**d.** Divide by the number of items.

**e.** Take the square root of this quotient.

*Continued on next page*

The terms *mean* and *standard deviation* can be defined in a similar way for probability distributions with a finite number of outcomes.

The definition involves these two stages.

- Creating a set of data that exactly fits the distribution.

- Finding the mean and standard deviation for this set of data.

The mean and standard deviation for the probability distribution are defined to be the mean and standard deviation of this set of data.

It's true that there can be different data sets, of different sizes, that exactly fit the probability distribution. But you can prove using the distributive property that all such data sets will have the same mean and have the same standard deviation. So defining mean and standard deviation in terms of a particular such data set does make sense.

In fact, the distributive property shows that you can use the probabilities directly, without creating a data set, to compute both the mean and the standard deviation. In many statistics books, the mean and the standard deviation are defined that way. The definitions can be expressed as shown here using summation notation.

$$\text{mean} = \sum P(x_i) \cdot x_i$$

$$\text{standard deviation} = \sqrt{\sum P(x_i) \cdot (x_i - \mu)^2}$$

where the variables $x_i$ represent the possible outcomes for the distribution and $P(x_i)$ represents the probability of outcome $x_i$.

As with data sets, the mean and standard deviation often are represented by the symbols $\mu$ and $\sigma$. The **variance** (for either a set of data or a probability distribution) is simply the square of the standard deviation and is often represented as $\sigma^2$.

# A Distribution Example

You've seen that the terms *mean* and *standard deviation* can be defined for a probability distribution in a way that is similar to their definitions for data sets. This assignment looks at an example of how that is done.

Consider the experiment of flipping three coins and counting the number of heads. There are four possible outcomes—no heads, one head, two heads, and three heads—and the probability distribution for this three-coin experiment can be expressed by these equations.

- $P(0) = \frac{1}{8}$

- $P(1) = \frac{3}{8}$

- $P(2) = \frac{3}{8}$

- $P(3) = \frac{1}{8}$

The simplest set of data that fits this distribution is 0, 1, 1, 1, 2, 2, 2, 3—that is, flipping the three coins eight times and getting no heads once, getting one head three times, getting two heads three times, and getting three heads once.

**1.** Find the mean for the data set 0, 1, 1, 1, 2, 2, 2, 3.

**2.** Find the standard deviation for this data set.

*Continued on next page*

**3.** Find the mean for the three-coin probability distribution using the formula

$$\text{mean} = \sum P(x_i) \cdot x_i$$

where the variables $x_i$ represent the possible outcomes of the experiment and $P(x_i)$ represents the probability of outcome $x_i$. (*Hint:* In this context, the variables $x_i$ are the outcomes 0, 1, 2, and 3, so the summation means $P(0) \cdot 0 + P(1) \cdot 1 + P(2) \cdot 2 + P(3) \cdot 3$.)

**4.** Explain why the formula for the mean in Question 3 gives the same result that you got in Question 1.

**5.** Standard deviation can be found using the formula

$$\text{standard deviation} = \sqrt{\sum P(x_i) \cdot (x_i - \mu)^2}$$

**a.** Write an expression, without using summation notation, for what this formula means in the case of the three-coin probability distribution.

**b.** Find the numerical value of your expression in Question 5a.

**6.** Explain why the formula in Question 5 gives the same result that you got in Question 2.

# The Search Is On!

You now know how the concepts of mean and standard deviation are defined for theoretical probability distributions.

In this unit, the focus is on the probability distributions that describe the results of polls of different sizes. We are assuming that the overall population is large compared to the size of the poll, so we are analyzing the probabilities as if polls are done using sampling with replacement.

Based on this assumption, the probabilities for different poll results fit the binomial distribution, which depends on two parameters.

• $n$, the number of trials (For polls, this is the size of the poll.)

• $p$, the probability of success (For polls, this is the fraction supporting the candidate in the overall population.)

The goal of this activity is to find formulas for the mean and standard deviation of the binomial distribution in terms of these two parameters. The approach here is first to find the mean and standard deviation for specific values of $p$ and $n$, and then to look for patterns. Here are two suggestions that will make it easier to find patterns in the data.

• Look at the *number* of votes a candidate gets in the poll rather than the *proportion* of votes the candidate gets.

• Look for a formula for the *variance* rather than the *standard deviation*. (*Reminder:* The variance is the square of the standard deviation.)

*Continued on next page*

Once you have a formula for variance, you will use it to get a formula for the standard deviation. (In a later activity, you will convert from a formula based on the number of votes to a formula based on the proportion of votes.)

## Your Task

Follow these steps to develop the formulas.

**1.** Choose a value for $p$ (the fraction of voters in favor of the candidate). For this value of $p$, choose several different values for $n$, find the mean and the variance of the number of "yes" votes for each of those values of $n$, and then develop formulas for the mean and variance in terms of $n$.

**2.** Once you have mean and variance formulas in terms of $n$ for one value of $p$, get formulas for other values of $p$.

**3.** Find a general formula for the mean and variance of the number of "yes" votes in terms of $n$ and $p$.

**4.** Use your variance formula to write a formula for standard deviation.

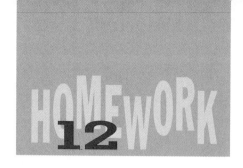

# Why Is That Batter Sneezing?

If polling is done for a two-person election using sampling with replacement, then the poll consists of independent repetitions of an event with only two possible outcomes. As you have seen, the set of probabilities associated with this type of polling is called the *binomial distribution*.

The same basic theory that applies to such polls applies to many other situations as well. Questions 1 and 2 each describe a situation that involves the binomial distribution.

1. A baseball player is batting .400, which means he has gotten a hit in 40% of his previous times at bat. (Ignore the complication of bases on balls and other situations in which a turn at bat doesn't figure into the player's batting average.)

   Based on this record, assume that for each future time at bat, the player has a probability of .4 of getting a hit.

   a. If he bats three times in the next game, what is the probability that he will get exactly one hit? Exactly two hits? Exactly three hits? No hits at all?

   b. Make a probability bar graph showing your results.

*Continued on next page*

**2.** Alida has the flu, but she has an important meeting today with five other people. She is concerned about giving them the flu, because she is in the most contagious period of the disease. Suppose that according to medical information about this type of flu, each of the people at her meeting will have a 30% chance of catching the flu from her.

**a.** What are the chances that no one at the meeting will become infected?

**b.** Find the probability that the number of people infected is exactly one, exactly two, and so on.

**c.** Make a probability bar graph showing your results.

**d.** If no one else at the meeting got infected, would you believe that Alida was in the most contagious period? Explain.

**3.** Make up another question that you find interesting and that involves the binomial distribution.

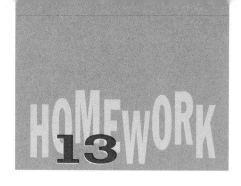

# Putting Your Formulas to Work

In *The Search Is On!*, you found formulas for the mean and standard deviation for the binomial distribution. If you use sampling with replacement, these formulas apply to the probability distribution of poll results.

You also know that if *n* is "big enough," the binomial distribution can be approximated by a normal distribution. Not surprisingly, this normal distribution has the same mean and standard deviation as the binomial distribution it approximates. Therefore, you can use the formulas from *The Search Is On!* for this normal distribution.

*Continued on next page*

In Question 1 of this assignment, you will put these formulas to use. Question 2 asks a more general question about the formula for standard deviation.

1. Remember that you are in charge of polls for Coretta. According to the poll that was taken before you started, she has approximately 53% of the vote. In other words, your sample proportion $\hat{p}$ in that poll was .53.

   You are about to do a new poll, and you want the results to be encouraging. (If it looks like she's winning, people may jump on the bandwagon, in terms of both volunteer work and campaign contributions.)

   a. Suppose Coretta really does have 53% of the vote (so the value of $\hat{p}$ from the earlier poll was exactly correct). If you now do a 300-person poll, what is the probability that your poll will show her to be in the lead? Explain how to use the normal distribution and the formulas from *The Search Is On!* to answer this question.

   b. What would be the answer to Question 1a if you did a 600-person poll instead? Explain.

2. Look at your formula for the standard deviation of the number of "yes" votes in an $n$-person poll. According to this formula, the standard deviation increases as $n$ gets bigger. This means that as the poll size gets bigger, so does the fluctuation.

   On the other hand, intuition suggests that a bigger poll should be more accurate, so shouldn't there be *less* fluctuation among big polls than among small ones? How do you explain the fact that the standard deviation is bigger for bigger polls?

# From Numbers to Proportions

You know that the important thing in an election is the proportion of votes that a candidate gets, not the actual number of votes. But the formulas found in *The Search Is On!* were for the mean and standard deviation of the *number* of votes for a given candidate in a poll.

The questions in this activity will help you find formulas for the mean and standard deviation of the *proportion* of votes for a candidate in a poll.

1. **a.** Imagine that you have done six 500-person polls for a 2-person election. Make up results for these polls, giving the number of votes in favor of your candidate in each poll.

*Continued on next page*

**b.** Use the six results from Question 1 to find the mean and standard deviation of the number of votes in favor of your candidate.

**2. a.** Compute the *proportion* of votes for your candidate for each of your six results from Question 1a.

**b.** Find the mean and standard deviation for this set of six proportions.

**3.** Compare the results for Questions 1b and 2b.

**a.** How does the mean for the *number* of votes compare to the mean for the *proportion* of votes?

**b.** How does the standard deviation for the *number* of votes compare to the standard deviation for the *proportion* of votes?

Now, use what you have learned in Questions 1 through 3 to tackle the main objective.

**4.** Find formulas for the mean and standard deviation for the *proportion* of votes the candidate gets in an *n*-person poll (in terms of $n$ and $p$, where $p$ is the true proportion).

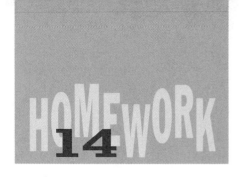

# Is Twice As Many Twice As Good?

Your growing expertise in polling has caught the eye of a candidate for City Council. He has a limited budget for polling, and you figure that given the funding, you can do a 200-person poll.

Based on previous elections, this candidate is fairly sure he has the support of 60% of the overall population. He would like to see a poll confirm this belief.

You point out that even if his overall support really is 60%, you can't guarantee that a poll will give this exact result. In response, he asks you to give him an interval within which you think the poll result will occur.

1. If the candidate really does have the support of 60% of the population, what interval around 60% has a 95% chance of containing your poll result?

2. Suppose you take your answer to Question 1 to the candidate, who decides he wants a more precise poll. He offers to increase the budget so you can poll twice as many people. He thinks this will allow you to cut the size of the interval in half.

   Is he right? If you don't think so, explain why not, and explain how your poll size would need to change in order to cut the size of the interval in half.

# A Matter of Confidence

*Tony Ryan, Mike Pettis, and Andy McGrane compare their results of having experimented with different values of p to determine what happens to $\sigma$ in each case.*

Unless a pollster talks to every person in the overall population, there's no guarantee that the poll results give a true picture of the population. Therefore, a crucial question for every pollster is, "How confident can I be that my poll results are 'fairly close' to the truth?"

Over the next few days, you'll see how to turn this idea of "confidence" into a precise mathematical concept.

# Different p, Different σ

Suppose you take a 20-person poll and get a sample proportion $\hat{p} = .60$. Of course, you would expect that the true proportion should be fairly close to this, but you can't be sure (unless your sample of 20 people is almost the entire population).

When you take a poll, there's a 95% chance that the sample proportion will be within two standard deviations of $p$, the true proportion. And if $\hat{p}$ is within $2\sigma$ of $p$, then $p$ is within $2\sigma$ of $\hat{p}$.

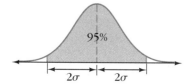

The interval of size $2\sigma$ around $\hat{p}$ is called a **95% confidence interval.** Unfortunately, the value of $\sigma$ itself depends on $p$, so you can't find this interval if you don't already know $p$. In this activity, you will explore this dilemma.

*Reminder:* For this activity, $n = 20$ and $\hat{p} = .60$.

1. Suppose $p$ is .55.

   **a.** What is the value of $\sigma$?

   **b.** What are the endpoints of the 95% confidence interval around $\hat{p}$?

   **c.** Is $p$ within the 95% confidence interval?

2. Now suppose $p$ is .80.

   **a.** What is the value of $\sigma$?

   **b.** What are the endpoints of the 95% confidence interval around $\hat{p}$?

   **c.** Is $p$ within the 95% confidence interval?

# Let's Vote on It!

Is there a burning issue about which you're curious how others feel? Here is your chance to ask some people—in fact, a whole "sample's worth" of people.

In this project, you and a partner will take a poll about some topic you choose. The topic needs to have only two sides, such as a yes-or-no issue, and should be a topic on which people are unlikely to be undecided.

Once you decide on a topic, you need to select an overall population from which to choose a sample. You should pick a population for which you can take a fairly random sample. For example, your population should not be "teenagers," because you can't possibly get a random sample of all teenagers. A more reasonable population might be "teenagers in your community."

*Continued on next page*

You also need to decide how to choose your sample. You cannot simply say, "Pick people randomly from the population." You need to give details. You should also decide on a way to let respondents maintain their anonymity. In particular, they should not be influenced by your presence.

The last part of the planning involves deciding on the size of your poll. You will do this a little later in the unit, when you know more about the impact of sample size.

Eventually, you and your partner will turn in a write-up on your project. That write-up should include these items.

• A clear statement of the question voters are voting on

• How and why you selected your overall population

• The procedure you used to select your people to sample so that it would be a random sample of the population

• The procedure you used to ensure that people would vote honestly, and the reason you think it was effective

• The size of your sample, and the way you determined that number

• The results of your poll

• Your conclusions based on your results

In addition to a write-up, you and your partner will make a 5-minute presentation to the class on your project. You should discuss the most interesting issues connected with your project during the presentation.

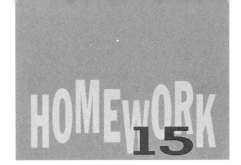

# Project Topics and Random Polls

*Let's Vote on It!* describes a major project for this unit. Although you will work on this project with a partner, in this assignment you will work on your own. You may decide to change some of the decisions you make in this assignment based on the discussion of the assignment and on your partner's ideas.

In this assignment, you will need to do these tasks.

- Choose a tentative topic and formulate a specific question

- Decide what your overall population will be

- Decide how you will choose a random sample from your population

- Decide how you will give participants enough anonymity so they will answer your question honestly

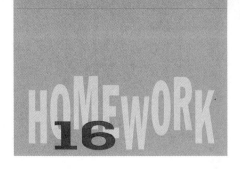

# Mean, Median, and Mode

When you gather data and get a variety of results, you often want to summarize your information using a single number to represent an "average" or "typical" result. Such a number is called a *measure of central tendency.*

The *mean,* which you have used throughout this unit, is one of the most commonly used measures of central tendency. Two others that you have probably worked with before are the *median* and the *mode.*

**1.** Review for yourself the precise meaning of the concepts of *mean, median,* and *mode.* (Look up the terms if necessary.) Then state the definitions in your own words.

**2.** A student received grades on various assignments, with each grade based on a six-point scale. The graph shows how often the student received each possible score.

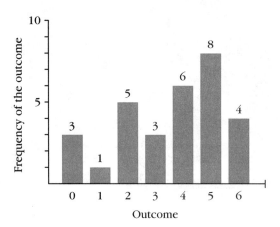

*Continued on next page*

**a.** Find the mean, median, and mode for the data in the graph.

**b.** Discuss what each of these measurements tells you about the student.

**3.** You often find it necessary to try to represent a situation with a single "typical" number. The measure of central tendency that is most meaningful will vary from situation to situation.

**a.** Make up a situation in which you think the *mean* would be the most meaningful measure of central tendency.

**b.** Make up a situation in which you think the *median* would be the most meaningful measure of central tendency.

**c.** Make up a situation in which you think the *mode* would be the most meaningful measure of central tendency.

# The Worst-Case Scenario

You've seen that the reliability of a poll depends on $\sigma$, the standard deviation of the distribution of sample proportions. But $\sigma = \sqrt{\frac{p(1-p)}{n}}$, where $p$ is the true proportion, so you can't find $\sigma$ if you don't know $p$. And the whole purpose of the poll is to find out the value of $p$. So what do you do?

What professional pollsters generally do is consider the "worst-case" scenario. That is, they use the largest standard deviation that a poll of size $n$ could have.

**1.** Pick a specific value for $n$. For that choice of $n$, experiment with different values of $p$ and see what happens to $\sigma$ in each case. Find the value of $p$ that gives the largest value for $\sigma$.

**2.** Try other values of $n$ and generalize your results.

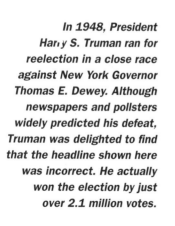

*In 1948, President Harry S. Truman ran for reelection in a close race against New York Governor Thomas E. Dewey. Although newspapers and pollsters widely predicted his defeat, Truman was delighted to find that the headline shown here was incorrect. He actually won the election by just over 2.1 million votes.*

# A Teaching Dilemma

Ms. Gordon is a new history teacher who is trying to develop some policies about grading. Her predecessor left her a copy of a test he had used for many years, together with the information that the mean test score had been 72 and the standard deviation had been 5.9.

Ms. Gordon has decided to use the test with her own students. She has no reason to think that her students will perform differently from those in previous years. In answering Questions 1 through 3, assume that her test scores are normally distributed with a mean of 72 and standard deviation of 5.9.

1. Suppose Ms. Gordon decides that students need a score above 85 to get an A. What percentage of her students will get A's?

2. Suppose instead that Ms. Gordon decides that she wants 3% of her students to get A's. What should she set as the minimum score for an A?

3. Finally, suppose Ms. Gordon wants 80% of her class to get C's. Suggest a reasonable range of scores for a grade of C that would probably contain about 80% of the test results. Is this the only possibility? Explain.

# What Does It Mean?

River City is thinking of letting homeless people sleep in City Hall overnight.

Some people who live near City Hall are against the plan because they don't want a lot of homeless people gathering near their homes. People who favor the plan point out that there are already homeless shelters in other neighborhoods and say that there is no reason why people living near City Hall should avoid having to deal with the problem.

Other people oppose the plan because they think the city should do more than simply let people sleep in City Hall; that is, the city should provide housing with amenities such as showers and cooking facilities. People who favor the plan counter by arguing that letting people sleep in City Hall is better than leaving them out on the streets and that no better facilities seem to be available.

The local newspaper reports that it took a random telephone poll of registered voters. According to the poll, 52% favor the plan, with a margin of error of plus or minus 4%. You should assume that this margin of error is based on a 95% confidence level.

1. What is the confidence interval for this poll?

2. Explain what it means to say that the poll has a 95% confidence level.

3. Approximately how many people were in the sample?

4. Based on this result, how confident can one be that more than 50% of the voters favor this plan?

# Confidence and Clarabell

**1.** The idea of a confidence interval is a crucial notion for working with polls and other kinds of sampling.

    **a.** In your own words, explain what a confidence interval is.

    **b.** Give specific examples of how the concept of a confidence interval might be used and how it is related to the concepts of *confidence level* and *margin of error.*

**2.** Clarabell and Bellaclar are having one of their famous debates.

Clarabell claims that if you are sampling a bigger population, you need to take a bigger sample. In particular, she claims that taking a 500-person sample makes sense if your overall population is 40,000 people. But she says this is much too small a sample for a place like River City, with 400,000 voters. Bellaclar doesn't think that the size of the overall population should matter at all.

Would you please clear up this matter for them?

# Polling Puzzles

Every pollster would like to have a high level of confidence and a small margin of error. And every pollster would love to be able to achieve this without polling a lot of people.

Unfortunately, these goals are incompatible, because confidence level, margin of error, and sample size are interconnected. As you will see in these questions, you can control two of these three parameters, but not all three at once.

1. Suppose a pollster wants a 2% margin of error with a 95% confidence level. How many people should be polled?

2. Suppose a pollster wants a 5% margin of error with a 97% confidence level. How many people should be polled?

3. Suppose a pollster wants to poll 400 people and have a 95% confidence level. What will the margin of error be?

4. Suppose a pollster wants to report a 3% margin of error with a 100-person poll. What will the confidence level be?

# How Big?

You and your partner should have a plan for how to choose people to vote in your project, *Let's Vote on It!* Now it's time for you to decide on how many people you want to sample for your project.

Discuss this issue with your partner. Think about how reliable and how precise you want your result to be. That is, what confidence level do you want, and what margin of error do you want? Keep in mind that if you are too demanding about these conditions, your sample size may become unmanageable.

Based on your decisions, find an appropriate sample size, and explain the calculations you did do to come up with that number. This number and your explanation will be part of the final write-up you do on your project.

In addition, you should turn in a statement including the items listed here.

- The name of your partner

- A statement of the topic for your poll

- A description of your overall population

- A discussion of how you will choose a random sample from your population and how you will give voters enough anonymity so that they will vote honestly

- The precise question you will ask participants

# Putting It Together

*Garnette Abbott and Jen Goodale enjoy the challenge of revisiting a problem from Year 2 and applying concepts learned in this unit.*

You now have all the necessary tools to make a report to Coretta, telling her what that original 53% poll result means. Before you do so, the unit takes a look back at a Year 2 problem about a suspicious coin.

The unit then focuses on your report for Coretta. It concludes with work and reports on the project *Let's Vote on It!*

# Roberto and the Coin Revisited

In the Year 2 unit *Is There Really a Difference?,* you considered the problem of Roberto and his brother's coin. Here is a description of the situation.

> Every time there was an extra dessert at Roberto's house, his older brother took out his special coin. He always let Roberto flip the coin, and he always called out, "Heads."
>
> It seemed to Roberto that his brother won more often than he should have with a fair coin. One day when his brother was out, Roberto found the coin and flipped it 1000 times! He got 573 heads and 427 tails.

Your task when you first encountered this problem was to decide if the coin was fair. That meant figuring out how likely it would be for a fair coin to have such unbalanced results.

*Continued on next page*

In *Is There Really a Difference?*, you used the $\chi^2$ statistic to see that these results would be extremely unlikely with a fair coin (so Roberto had reason to be very suspicious of his brother's coin). Now, you will use different mathematical tools to explain what's going on.

1. Although the situation of coin flips involves the binomial distribution, the analysis can be approximated by the normal distribution.

   a. Explain what it means to say that the binomial distribution can be approximated by the normal distribution.

   b. Use the normal approximation to find out how likely it would be for a fair coin to give results as unbalanced as 573 heads and 427 tails.

2. Based on Roberto's experience with his brother's coin, give 95% and 99% confidence intervals for the true probability of getting heads with that coin.

3. Do you believe this was a fair coin? That is, do you think the apparent preference for heads is because the coin is not balanced, or is it simply a coincidence? Explain your reasoning.

# How Much Better Is Bigger?

Is it always better to get a larger sample? In this assignment, you'll explore how changing the poll size can affect either the confidence level or the margin of error.

**1.** Pick three large, but quite different, poll sizes, and assume that you want a margin of error of 5%.

  **a.** For each poll size, find the confidence level that you would have for that margin of error.

  **b.** Describe how the confidence level changes as the poll size gets larger and larger.

**2.** Again, pick three different large poll sizes. (They can be the same as in Question 1.) This time, assume that you want a 95% confidence level.

  **a.** For each poll size, find the margin of error you would have for this confidence level.

  **b.** Describe how the margin of error changes as the poll size gets larger and larger.

**3.** Choose one of your examples and explain what your values for the confidence level and the margin of error mean in that context.

---

# The Pollster's Dilemma Revisited

It's time to return to the original problem of the unit, involving Coretta's campaign for mayor of River City.

Recall that a poll was taken before you joined the campaign. That poll surveyed 500 people and found that 53% of them intended to vote for Coretta.

The question you need to answer is this:

*What does this poll result mean?*

Write a report for Coretta explaining how confident she should be that she was leading at the time of the poll. Explain your answer in terms of confidence intervals, standard deviation, and any other ideas you consider appropriate.

# Finish Collecting Data for Project

Tomorrow, you will spend most of the class period working on your project. You need to complete your polling by then, so that you can make effective use of the time.

# The Pollster's Dilemma Portfolio

Now that *The Pollster's Dilemma* unit is completed, it is time to put together your portfolio for the unit. This has three parts.

• Writing a cover letter summarizing the unit

• Choosing papers to include from your work in this unit

• Discussing your personal growth during the unit

## Cover Letter for *The Pollster's Dilemma*

Look back over *The Pollster's Dilemma* and describe the central problem of the unit and the main mathematical ideas. This description should give an overview of how the key ideas were developed in this unit and how they were used to solve the central problem.

*Continued on next page*

In compiling your portfolio, you will be selecting some activities that you think were important in developing the key ideas of this unit. Your cover letter should include an explanation of why you selected the particular items.

## Selecting Papers from *The Pollster's Dilemma*

Your portfolio from *The Pollster's Dilemma* should contain these items.

- An assignment that shows the relationship among confidence interval, margin of error, and poll size

- An assignment involving standard deviation

- *POW 10: The King's Switches*

- Your work on the unit project, *Let's Vote on It!*

## Personal Growth

Over the past four years you have had several units that dealt with statistics and probability. What have you learned? What general themes have come up repeatedly? How are concepts from statistics and probability used?

Summarize your experiences and your knowledge about statistics and probability. You don't have to include specific activities from units, but you should discuss your growth over time in your understanding of these two important branches of mathematics.

# Supplemental Problems

The supplemental problems for *The Pollster's Dilemma* continue the unit's focus on sampling and related ideas. Here are some examples.

- *What Is Random?* and *Random Number Generators* both involve the important concept of randomness.

- *Three-Person Races* and *Another View of the Central Limit Theorem* concern generalizations of key ideas in the unit.

# What Is Random?

One of the basic assumptions of the central problem in this unit was that the voters in the poll were a random sample from the population of all voters.

The word "random" comes up in many contexts in mathematics. Your task in this activity is to summarize what you have learned about this concept.

You may find it helpful to review the situations in which you've used randomness or to consult a textbook on the theory of probability.

# Random Number Generators

Many graphing calculators and computers have a random number generator. As you have seen, this is a device that supposedly picks numbers at random. Using a random number generator allows you to conduct various probability simulations.

The manufacturer of a graphing calculator or computer needs to create a way for the machine to generate its random numbers, and the method may be different for different machines. Your task in this activity is to learn about how a random number generator really works. You may want to contact a manufacturer for information.

# The Tack or the Coin?

You may remember a situation from the Year 2 unit *Is There Really a Difference?* that concerned Roberto, Roberto's brother, and a suspicious coin. The details aren't important, but the main thing is that Roberto's brother was using a coin to decide which of them should get any extra dessert that there happened to be.

Roberto wasn't sure whether his brother's coin was fair, but he certainly didn't like the results he had seen in the past. He told his brother that the fate of the extra dessert would no longer be determined by that coin.

*Continued on next page*

Roberto's brother chuckled and gave Roberto a new option, which worked like this. They would take ten thumbtacks, shake them, and drop them on the ground.

- If more than five of the tacks landed point up, then Roberto would get the extra dessert.

- If fewer than five tacks landed point up, then Roberto's brother would get the extra dessert.

- If exactly five tacks landed point up, then they would drop the tacks again.

**1.** Play around with Roberto's brother's new option and see what happens. You may want to vary the number of tacks that you use each time. Record your results in an organized way.

**2.** Choose another sample size for the bunch of tacks, and repeat the experiment over and over until you think you have a feel for how often tacks land point up. Again, record your results in an organized way.

**3.** Make a prediction about how many tacks would land point up if you shook and then dropped 100 tacks on the ground.

**4.** Test your prediction for 100 tacks, and write about how it turned out.

**5.** Discuss how the number of tacks in the experiment and the number of times you do the experiment influence the reliability of your prediction.

# Three-Person Races

In the probability analysis you did for the central problem of this unit, you were told to assume that there were only two candidates.

Of course, many elections have more than two candidates, and the mathematical analysis is more complicated with more than two candidates. In this problem, you will examine the case of a 3-person race.

Suppose there is an election race with three candidates—A, B, and C. Assume that in the overall population, the candidates have these percentages of support.

- candidate A—40%

- candidate B—35%

- candidate C—25%

These numbers are called the **true proportions.** (Notice that the true proportions add up to 100%.)

*Continued on next page*

1. Suppose you select two people at random and ask them which candidate they are supporting.

   a. List the possible outcomes for the number of votes each candidate could get in such a poll.

   b. Find the probability of each possible outcome. Assume that the overall population is large enough that you can treat your poll as if it involves sampling with replacement. (*Suggestion:* Check your work by seeing if your probabilities add up to 1.)

2. Repeat Question 1 for a poll of three people.

3. Generalize your results to a poll of $n$ people. That is, find a formula for the probability that such a poll will have $r$ votes for candidate A, $s$ votes for candidate B, and $t$ votes for candidate C (where $r + s + t = n$).

   *Hint:* You've seen that for polls involving only two candidates, the probabilities for various poll results can be expressed using combinatorial coefficients and powers of the true proportions. Build on your work in Questions 1 and 2 to see how to adjust to the case of three candidates, using something similar to combinatorial coefficients.

# Generalizing Linear Interpolation

*Homework 9: Gaps in the Table* describes the method known as *linear interpolation* for finding "in-between" values for functions. Your task in this activity is to develop a general formula for using the technique of linear interpolation.

Assume that you have a function $g$ and that you know the values of $g(a)$ and $g(b)$. Also assume that $c$ is some number between $a$ and $b$.

What would you use as an estimate for the value of $g(c)$, based on linear interpolation?

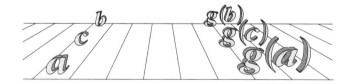

# Another View of the Central Limit Theorem

This unit has focused on a special case of the central limit theorem. This special case says, in brief, that if $n$ is "large enough," the binomial distribution can be approximated by the normal distribution.

In this activity, you will examine a case of the central limit theorem in which the original distribution is not binomial.

Consider the spinner shown here, in which the probability of spinning 1 is .3, the probability of spinning 3 is .5, and the probability of spinning 9 is .2.

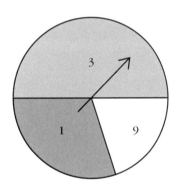

**1.** Make a probability bar graph for the outcomes of this spinner.

The situation becomes more complex as you spin the spinner more and more times and keep track of the results. For instance, if you spin this spinner twice, you might get two 1's, a 1 and a 3, a 1 and a 9, two 3's, a 3 and a 9, or two 9's.

Here, you'll consider different cases of $n$ spins (your graph in Question 1 was the case $n = 1$) and see what happens as $n$ increases.

**2.** Consider the case $n = 2$. That is, find the probability of each of the possible two-spin results.

To analyze the results of many spins, it's better to focus on the *average* result rather than the *sum* of the results.

*Continued on next page*

(This is analogous to looking at the *proportion* of votes that a candidate gets rather than the *number* of votes.) For instance, if you spin a 1 and a 9, your average result is 5.

**3.** **a.** Convert your results from Question 2 to averages. (If $n = 1$, the average is the same as the sum, so you don't need to convert the 1-spin results.)

**b.** Make a probability bar graph of the results from Question 3a, using the same scale as in Question 1. (You may want to redo your graph from Question 1 using a scale that works for both $n = 1$ and $n = 2$.)

**4.** Consider the cases $n = 3$, $n = 4$, and $n = 5$. Find the probability distribution for the average result in each case, and make a bar graph of the results in each case, again using the same scale. (*Note:* Some averages can be achieved in different ways. For instance, for $n = 5$, you can get an average of 2.6 by spinning four 1's and one 9 or by spinning one 1 and four 3's. Either outcome gives a sum of 13, which is an average of 2.6.)

**5.** Compare the probability bar graphs for the cases $n = 1, 2, 3, 4,$ and 5, and describe how the graphs are changing.

**6.** Suppose you approximate the distribution of average results for 100 spins using a normal distribution.

**a.** What would you expect for the mean of the normal distribution? Explain your answer. (*Hint:* What would you expect as the average for 100 spins? Why?)

**b.** What would you expect for the standard deviation of the normal distribution? Explain your answer.

# SUPPLEMENTAL
## PROBLEM

# It's the News

The central problem of this unit concerns election polls. Polls are used in many situations to get information about what people think and do. Such polls appear in newspapers regularly, although reports on the polls sometimes don't give as much information as they should.

Your first task in this activity is to find a newspaper or magazine article that reports on a poll.

Then summarize what the report says and discuss any shortcomings or weaknesses you see in the report. In particular, comment on any information that you think should have been included that would have helped you understand better what conclusions you could draw from the poll.

# Glossary

This is the glossary for all five units of IMP Year 4.

*Absolute value function family*

Informally, the family of functions whose graphs have the V-shape of the graph of the absolute value function defined by the equation $y = |x|$.

Example: The function defined by the equation $y = |2x + 1|$, whose graph is shown here, is considered a member of the absolute value function family.

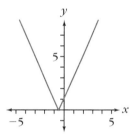

*Acceleration*

See **velocity.**

*Amplitude*

See **periodic function.**

*Asymptote*

Informally, a line or curve to which the graph of an equation draws closer and closer as the independent variable approaches $+\infty$, approaches $-\infty$, or approaches a specific value.

Example: For the function $f$ defined by the equation $f(x) = \frac{3}{x-1}$, both the horizontal line $y = 0$ (which is the *x*-axis) and the vertical line $x = 1$ (the dashed line in the diagram) are asymptotes. The graph approaches the line $y = 0$ as *x* approaches $+\infty$ or $-\infty$, and the graph approaches the line $x = 1$ as *x* approaches 1.

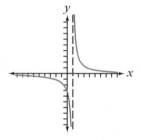

*Bias*

In sampling, the tendency of a sampling process to overrepresent or underrepresent a portion of the population being sampled. Avoiding bias is an important goal in sampling.

*Binomial distribution*

A probability distribution describing the result of repeated independent trials of the same event with two possible outcomes. If a particular outcome has probability *p* for each trial, the binomial distribution states that the probability that this outcome occurs exactly *r* times out of *n* trials is ${}_nC_r \cdot p^r \cdot (1 - p)^{n-r}$, where ${}_nC_r$ is the combinatorial coefficient equal to $\dfrac{n!}{r!(n - r)!}$.

Example: Suppose a weighted coin has probability .7 of coming up heads. If the coin is flipped 50 times, the probability of getting exactly 30 heads is

$$ {}_{50}C_{30} \cdot (.7)^{30} \cdot (.3)^{20} $$

Central angle      An angle formed at the center of a circle by two radii.

Example: The angle labeled $\theta$ is a central angle.

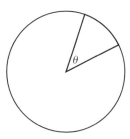

Central limit
theorem      A statistical principle stating that when samples of
a sufficiently large given size are taken from almost
any population, the means of these samples are
approximately normally distributed. See *The Central
Limit Theorem* in *The Pollster's Dilemma.*

Circular function      Any of several functions defined by placing an angle $\theta$
with its vertex at the origin and the initial ray of the
angle along the positive $x$-axis, as shown in the diagram.
If $(x, y)$ is any point different from $(0, 0)$ on the terminal
ray of the angle, then the sine, cosine, and tangent of $\theta$
are defined by the equations

$$\sin \theta = \frac{y}{r}$$

$$\cos \theta = \frac{x}{r}$$

$$\tan \theta = \frac{y}{x}$$

where $r = \sqrt{x^2 + y^2}$

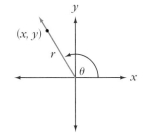

The circular functions also include the secant,
cosecant, and cotangent functions, which are defined
as other ratios involving $x$, $y$, and $r$. (The circular
functions are also called trigonometric functions.)

**Commutative**  An operation $*$ is commutative if the equation $a * b = b * a$ holds true for all values of $a$ and $b$. An operation that does not have this property is called *noncommutative*.

Example: The operation of addition is commutative because for any numbers $a$ and $b$, $a + b = b + a$. The operation of subtraction is noncommutative because, for example, $5 - 9 \neq 9 - 5$.

**Completing the square**  The process of adding a constant term to a quadratic expression so that the resulting expression is a perfect square.

Example: To complete the square for the expression $x^2 + 6x + 4$, add 5 to get $x^2 + 6x + 9$, which is the perfect square $(x + 3)^2$.

**Complex number**  A number of the form $a + bi$, where $a$ and $b$ are real numbers and $i$ is the number $\sqrt{-1}$. The number $a$ is the *real part* of $a + bi$, and $bi$ is its *imaginary part*.

**Components of velocity**  The velocity of an object is sometimes expressed in terms of separate *components of velocity*. For instance, a falling object that is also moving to the side has both a vertical and a horizontal component of velocity.

Example: In the diagram on the facing page, if a person is swimming across a river at a speed of 5 feet per second, in the direction shown by the solid line, then the "toward-shore" component of the swimmer's velocity is 5 sin 60° feet per second and the "parallel-to-shore" component of the swimmer's velocity is 5 cos 60° feet per second. (The "toward-shore" component can also be expressed as 5 cos 30° feet per second.)

Finishing shore

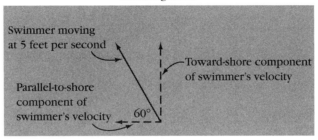

Starting shore

*Composition of functions*

An operation on functions in which the output from one function is used as the input for another. The composition of two functions $f$ and $g$ is written $f \circ g,$ and this function is defined by the equation $(f \circ g)(x) = f(g(x))$. A function formed in this manner is called a *composite function.*

Example: Suppose $f$ and $g$ are defined by the equations $f(x) = x^2$ and $g(x) = 2x + 1$. Then $f \circ g$ is defined by the equation $(f \circ g)(x) = (2x + 1)^2$.

*Confidence interval*

In a sampling process from a population, an interval around the sample mean that has a certain likelihood, called the *confidence level,* of containing the true mean for the population. If the interval is symmetric around the sample mean, then half the length of the interval is called the **margin of error.**

Example: The interval of values within two standard deviations of the sample mean is a *95% confidence interval,* because if that procedure is followed for many samples, it will contain the true mean 95% of the time.

*Conic section*     Any of several two-dimensional figures that can be formed by the intersection of a plane with a cone. The specific figure formed generally depends on the angle at which the plane meets the cone, and is "usually" an ellipse, parabola, or hyperbola.

*Constant function*     A function whose value is the same for every input.

*Correlation coefficient*     A number between $-1$ and 1, usually labeled $r$, that measures how well a set of data pairs can be fitted by a linear function. The closer $r$ is to 1, the better the data set can be fitted by a linear function with positive slope; the closer $r$ is to $-1$, the better the data set can be fitted by a linear equation with negative slope. If $r$ is not close to either 1 or $-1$, then the data set cannot be approximated well by any linear function.

*Cosine*     See **circular function.**

*Cubic function*     A function defined by an equation of the form $y = ax^3 + bx^2 + cx + d$ in which $a$, $b$, $c$, and $d$ are real numbers with a $\neq$ 0.

*Dependent variable*     See **function.**

*Directly proportional*     A relationship between two quantities or variables in which one of the variables is a constant multiple of the other variable.

Example: If an object has been traveling at 20 miles per hour, then the distance it has traveled is directly proportional to the amount of time it has been traveling. This can be seen algebraically as follows: If $d$ represents the distance (in miles) and $t$ represents the time elapsed (in hours), then $d$ and $t$ satisfy the equation $d = 20t$.

| | |
|---|---|
| *Discriminant* | See **quadratic formula.** |
| *Domain* | The set of values that can be used as inputs for a given function. |

Example: If $f$ is the function defined by the equation $f(x) = \frac{x}{x^2 - 1}$, then the domain of $f$ is the set of all real numbers except 1 and $-1$.

*End behavior*

The behavior of a function as the independent variable approaches $+\infty$ or $-\infty$. See *Approaching Infinity* in *The World of Functions*.

Example: For the function defined by the equation $y = 2^x$, the end behavior is that $y$ increases without bound as $x$ approaches $+\infty$ and that $y$ approaches 0 as $x$ approaches $-\infty$.

*Exponential function family*

The family of functions defined by equations of the form $y = a \cdot b^x$ in which $a$ is a nonzero real number and $b$ is a positive real number other than 1. If $b > 1$, the function is an *exponential growth* function; if $b < 1$, the function is an *exponential decay* function. Functions in this family are characterized by the property that a fixed change in the independent variable always results in the same *percentage* change in the dependent variable.

*Fibonacci sequence*

The numerical sequence 1, 1, 2, 3, 5, 8, 13, . . . , in which the first two terms are both 1 and each succeeding term is the sum of the two preceding terms. (For example, the sixth term, 8, is the sum of the fourth and fifth terms, 3 and 5.) The sequence is often represented using the *recursion equation*

$$a_{n+2} = a_{n+1} + a_n$$

*Function*

Informally, a relationship in which the value of one variable (the **independent variable**) determines the value of another (the **dependent variable**). In terms of an In-Out table, the independent variable gives the input and the dependent variable gives the output. In terms of a graph, the independent variable is generally shown on the horizontal axis and the dependent variable on the vertical axis.

Formally, a function is a set of number pairs for which two different pairs cannot have the same first coordinate.

Example: The equation $y = x^2$ expresses $y$ as a function of $x$.

*Greatest integer function*

See **step function.**

*Identity*

1. An equation that holds true no matter what numbers are substituted for the variables (as long as the expressions on both sides of the equation make sense).

   Example: The equation $(a + b)^2 = a^2 + 2ab + b^2$ is an identity, because this equation holds true for all real numbers $a$ and $b$.

2. For a given operation, an *identity* (or an *identity element*) for that operation is an element which, when combined with any element using the given operation, yields that second element as the result.

   Examples: The number 0 is the identity for addition because $x + 0$ and $0 + x$ are both equal to $x$ for any number $x$. Similarly, the number 1 is the identity for multiplication.

| | |
|---|---|
| *Identity function* | The function on a given domain whose output is equal to its input. This function is the identity for the operation of composition of functions and can be represented by the equation $f(x) = x$. |
| *Independent events* | Two (or more) events are independent if the outcome of one does not affect the outcome of the other. |
| *Independent variable* | See **function.** |
| *Inverse* | If an operation has an **identity,** then an *inverse* for a given element (under that operation) is an element which, when combined with the given one, yields the identity as the result. |
| | Examples: The number $-7$ is the inverse for 7 for the operation of addition because both $7 + (-7)$ and $(-7) + 7$ are equal to 0, which is the identity for addition. Similarly, the number $\frac{1}{5}$ is the inverse for 5 for the operation of multiplication. |
| *Inverse of a function* | Informally, the inverse of a function $f$ is the function that "undoes" $f$. Formally, the inverse of $f$ is its inverse with regard to the operation of composition. That is, the inverse of $f$ is the function $g$ for which both $f \circ g$ and $g \circ f$ are the appropriate identity functions, with $(f \circ g)(x) = x$ and $(g \circ f)(x) = x$. The inverse of $f$ is sometimes represented by $f^{-1}$. |
| | Example: If $f$ is the function defined by the equation $f(x) = 3x + 2$, then the inverse of $f$ is the function $g$ given by the equation $g(x) = \frac{x-2}{3}$. The fact that $g$ "undoes" $f$ is illustrated by the fact that $f(5) = 17$ and $g(17) = 5$. In terms of composition, we have $(f \circ g)(17) = 17$ and $(g \circ f)(5) = 5$. |

*Inversely
proportional*  A relationship between two quantities or variables in which one of the variables is obtained by dividing some constant by the other variable.

Example: If the length and width of a rectangle are to be chosen so that the rectangle has an area of 30 square inches, then the length will be inversely proportional to the width. This can be shown algebraically as follows: If $L$ represents the length and $W$ represents the width (both in inches), then $L$ and $W$ satisfy the equation $LW = 30$, so $L = \frac{30}{W}$.

*Isometry*  A geometrical transformation $T$ with the property that for any pair of points $A$ and $B$, the distance between $T(A)$ and $T(B)$ is equal to the distance between $A$ and $B$. Isometries do not change the size or shape of geometric figures, and include **translations, rotations,** and **reflections.**

*Least squares
method*  A method of determining a function from a given family that best fits a set of data. For a finite set of data points $(x_1, y_1)$, $(x_2, y_2)$, . . . , $(x_n, y_n)$, the least-squares method seeks the function $f$ (from the family) that minimizes the value of the expression

$$\sum_{i=1}^{n} [y_i - f(x_i)]^2$$

in which $y_i - f(x_i)$ represents the vertical distance between the graph of $f$ and the data point $(x_i, y_i)$.

*Linear equation*  For one variable, an equation of the form $ax + b = 0$, in which $a$ and $b$ are real numbers with $a \neq 0$. For $n$ variables $x_1, x_2, . . ., x_n$, an equation of the form $a_1 x_1 + a_2 x_2 + . . . + a_n x_n + b = 0$.

*Linear function*    For a function with one input variable, a function defined by an equation of the form $y = ax + b$ in which $a$ and $b$ are real numbers. (The special case of a constant function, in which $a = 0$, is sometimes excluded from the family of linear functions.) The definition is similar for functions with more than one input variable.

*Linear regression*    A process for obtaining the linear function that best fits a set of data. The equation for this function is the *regression equation* and its graph is the *regression line*.

*Logarithmic function family*    Informally, the family of functions defined by equations of the form $y = a + b \log x$ (or of the form $y = a + b \ln x$), where $a$ and $b$ are real numbers with $b \neq 0$.

*Loop*    In programming, a set of instructions that specifies the repeated execution of a given set of steps.

*Margin of error*    See **confidence interval.**

*Mean of a discrete probability distribution*    If a probability distribution has possible outcomes $x_1, x_2, \ldots, x_n$, and the outcome $x_i$ has probability $P(x_i)$, then the mean of the distribution is given by the expression

$$\sum_{i=1}^{n} P(x_i) \cdot x_i$$

The mean of the distribution is numerically equal to the expected value of the event that the distribution describes. See *Mean and Standard Deviation for Probability Distributions* in *The Pollster's Dilemma.*

*Nested loop*    A programming loop that occurs within the body of another loop.

*Normal curve*

The graph that represents a normal distribution. If the normal distribution has mean $\mu$ and standard deviation $\sigma$, then the equation of its graph is

$$y = \left(\frac{1}{\sigma\sqrt{2\pi}}\right) \cdot e^{-\frac{1}{2}\left(\frac{x-\mu}{\sigma}\right)^2}$$

Example: If $\mu = 0$ and $\sigma = 1$, the equation simplifies to

$$y = \left(\frac{1}{\sqrt{2\pi}}\right) \cdot e^{-\frac{1}{2}x^2}$$

This special case is called the *standard normal curve.* The diagram here shows the graph of this equation.

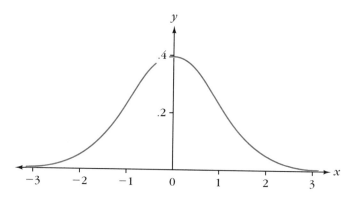

*Parabola*

The general shape for the graph of a quadratic function. Also see **conic section.**

*Parameter*

Often, a variable whose value is used to specify a particular member of a family of functions. (The term *parameter* has other meanings as well.)

Example: The family of quadratic functions consists of all functions defined by equations of the form $y = ax^2 + bx + c$, where $a$, $b$, and $c$ are real numbers with a $\neq$ 0. The variables $a$, $b$, and $c$ are parameters whose numerical values specify a particular quadratic function. The set of quadratic functions is called a *three-parameter family.*

| | |
|---|---|
| *Period* | See **periodic function.** |
| *Periodic function* | Informally, a function whose values repeat after a specific interval. Specifically, a function $f$ is periodic if there is a positive number $a$ such that $f(x + a) = f(x)$ for all values of $x$. The smallest positive value for $a$ is called the **period** of $f$. |

If a periodic function has a maximum and a minimum value, then half the difference between these values is the **amplitude** of the function.

Example: The function $f$ defined by the equation $f(x) = 3 \sin (2x) + 5$ is a periodic function with period 180°, because $f(x + 180°) = f(x)$ for all values of $x$. The graph shown here for this function illustrates its periodic behavior. The maximum value for $f$ is 8 [for instance, $f(45°) = 8$] and the minimum value is 2 [for instance, $f(135°) = 2$], so the amplitude of $f$ is $\frac{1}{2}(8 - 2) = 3$.

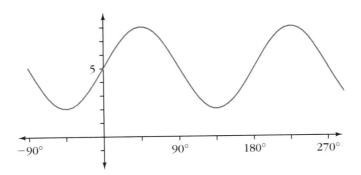

*Polar coordinates*

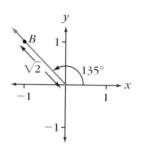

A system in which a point in the plane is identified by means of a pair of coordinates $(r, \theta)$ where $r$ is the distance from the origin to the point and $\theta$ is the angle between the positive $x$-axis and the ray from the origin through the point, measured counterclockwise. See *A Polar Summary* in *High Dive*.

Example: The point B in the diagram, whose rectangular coordinates are $(-1, 1)$, has polar coordinates $(\sqrt{2}, 135°)$ because the distance from $(0, 0)$ to $B$ is $\sqrt{2}$ and the angle from the positive $x$-axis to the ray through $B$ is $135°$. [*Note:* The point $B$ has other polar coordinate representations, such as $(-\sqrt{2}, 315°)$ or $(\sqrt{2}, 495°)$.]

*Polynomial function*

A function defined by an equation of the form $y = a_n x^n + a_{n-1} x^{n-1} + \ldots + a_1 x + a_0$, in which $a_n, a_{n-1}, \ldots, a_1$, and $a_0$ are real numbers. If $a_n \neq 0$, the polynomial has *degree n*. The family of polynomial functions includes **constant functions** (degree 0), **linear functions** (degree 1), **quadratic functions** (degree 2), and **cubic functions** (degree 3), as well as functions of higher degree.

Example: The function defined by the equation $y = 3x^4 - 2x^2 + 5x - 1$ is a polynomial function of degree 4.

*Power function*

Generally, a function defined by an equation of the form $y = ax^b$ in which $a$ and $b$ are real numbers. (In some contexts, restrictions are imposed on $b$, such as requiring that $b$ be an integer.)

Example: The function defined by the equation $y = 5x^{\frac{1}{2}}$ is a power function.

| | |
|---|---|
| *Principal value* | A term sometimes used in the definitions of the inverse trigonometric functions to identify a specific number whose sine, cosine, or tangent is a given value. |
| | Example: The equation $\sin x = 0.5$ has infinitely many solutions, but the solution $x = 30°$ is selected as the principal value, so that $\sin^{-1}(0.5)$ is defined to be $30°$. |
| *Probability distribution* | A set of values giving the probability for each possible outcome for an event. |
| | Example: If a fair coin is flipped twice and we count the number of heads, the probability distribution is $P(2 \text{ heads}) = \frac{1}{4}$, $P(1 \text{ head}) = \frac{1}{2}$, $P(0 \text{ heads}) = \frac{1}{4}$. |
| *Projection* | A process for representing a three-dimensional object by means of a two-dimensional figure, or any representation of a figure by a lower-dimensional figure. |
| *Pythagorean identity* | Any of several trigonometric identities based on the Pythagorean theorem. |
| | Example: The equation $\sin^2 x + \cos^2 x = 1$, which holds true for all values of $x$, is a Pythagorean identity. |
| *Quadratic equation* | For one variable, an equation of the form $ax^2 + bx + c = 0$ in which $a$, $b$, and $c$ are real numbers with $a \neq 0$. |
| *Quadratic formula* | A formula for finding the solutions to a quadratic equation in terms of the coefficients. Specifically, for the quadratic equation $ax^2 + bx + c = 0$ (where $a$, $b$, and $c$ are real numbers with $a \neq 0$), the solutions are given by the quadratic formula expression $\frac{-b \pm \sqrt{b^2 - 4ac}}{2a}$. The expression $b^2 - 4ac$ in this formula is called the **discriminant** of the equation. |

| | |
|---|---|
| *Quadratic function* | A function defined by an equation of the form $y = ax^2 + bx + c$ in which $a$, $b$, and $c$ are real numbers with $a \neq 0$. |

*Radian*

The measure of a central angle of a circle that intercepts a portion of the circumference whose length is equal to the radius of the circle. A radian is approximately equal to 57°.

Example: In this diagram, the length of the arc from $A$ to $B$ is equal to the length of the radius $\overline{OA}$ of the circle, so angle $AOB$ measures one radian.

*Random*

A term used in probability to indicate that any of several events is equally likely or, more generally, that an event is selected from a set of events according to a precisely described probability distribution.

*Range*

The set of values that can occur as outputs for a given function.

Example: If $f$ is the function defined by the equation $f(x) = x^2$, then the range of $f$ is the set of all nonnegative real numbers.

*Rational function*

A function that can be expressed as the quotient of two polynomial functions.

Examples: The function defined by the equation $y = \frac{3}{x}$ is a rational function, as is the function defined by the equation $y = \frac{x^2 + 3x - 7}{2x^3 + 4x + 1}$. A polynomial function is a special type of rational function. For instance, the function defined by the equation $y = x^3 - 2x^2 + 3$ can be expressed as a quotient of polynomials by writing the equation as $y = \frac{x^3 - 2x^2 + 3}{1}$.

*Rectangular coordinates*

A system in which a point is identified by coordinates that give its position in relation to each of the mutually perpendicular coordinate axes. In the plane, these axes are usually called the *x*-axis (horizontal) and *y*-axis (vertical). The horizontal coordinate is given first.

Example: In this diagram, point *A* has coordinates $(3, -2)$ because it corresponds to the number 3 on the *x*-axis and the number $-2$ on the *y*-axis.

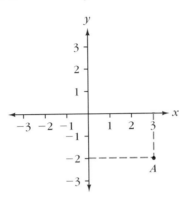

*Recursion*

A process for defining a sequence of numbers by specifying how to obtain each term from the preceding term(s). An equation specifying how each term is defined in this way is called a *recursion equation*.

Example: The sequence 1, 3, 5, 7, . . . (the sequence of positive odd integers) can be defined by the recursion equation $a_{n+1} = a_n + 2$ together with the *initial condition* that $a_1 = 1$.

*Reflection*

A type of isometry in which the output for each point is its mirror image. A reflection is sometimes called a "flip."

Example: The diagram here illustrates a reflection in which the *y*-axis is a *line of reflection*. The triangle in the second quadrant is the reflection of the triangle in the first quadrant. In three dimensions, the role of a line of reflection is replaced by a *plane of reflection*.

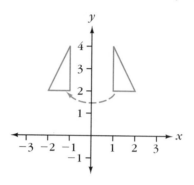

*Rotation*

A type of isometry in which the output for each point is obtained by rotating the point through an angle of a given size around a given point.

Example: The diagram below illustrates a 90° rotation counterclockwise around the origin. Each point of the lightly shaded triangle is moved to a point that is the same distance from the origin as the original point, but which is 90° counterclockwise (with respect to the origin) from the original point. The diagram shows the "paths" of two of the vertices of the lightly shaded triangle.

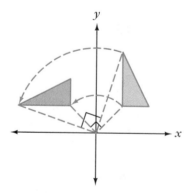

| | |
|---|---|
| *Sample mean* | The mean for a sample taken from a population. The sample mean is often used to estimate the **true mean** for the population. |
| *Sample proportion* | In a sample from a population, the fraction of sampled items that represent a specific outcome. The sample proportion is often used to estimate the **true proportion.** |

Example: If an election poll of 500 voters shows 285 voters favoring a certain candidate, the sample proportion for the poll is $\frac{285}{500}$, which may be expressed as .57 or as 57%.

| | |
|---|---|
| *Sampling* | A process of selecting members of a population and studying their characteristics in order to estimate or predict certain characteristics of the entire population. The selected members of the population comprise the *sample.* |

In selecting the sample at random from a population, we sometimes consider a member of the population ineligible for further selection once it has already been selected. This is called *sampling without replacement.* If members of the population are eligible for repeated selection, this is called *sampling with replacement.*

| | |
|---|---|
| *Sine* | See **circular function.** |
| *Sine family of functions* | The family of functions whose graphs have the same shape as the graph of the sine function. These functions can be written in the form $y = a \sin (bx + c) + d$, where $a$, $b$, $c$, and $d$ are real numbers with $a$ and $b$ not equal to 0. This family includes the cosine function, because $\cos x = \sin \left(x + \frac{\pi}{2}\right)$. |

*Standard deviation of a discrete probability distribution*

If a probability distribution has possible outcomes $x_1, x_2, \ldots, x_n$, and the outcome $x_i$ has probability $P(x_i)$, then the standard deviation of the distribution is given by the expression

$$\sqrt{\sum_{i=1}^{n} P(x_i) \cdot (x_i - \mu)^2}$$

where $\mu$ is the mean of the distribution. See *Mean and Standard Deviation for Probability Distributions* in *The Pollster's Dilemma.*

*Step function*

Informally, a function whose graph consists of horizontal line segments.

Example: The **greatest integer function,** written $[x]$, is defined by the condition that $[x]$ is the largest integer $N$ such that $N \leq x$. The diagram here shows the graph of this step function.

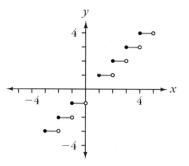

*Tangent*

See **circular function.**

*Transformation*

1. A *transformation of a function* is any of certain changes to a function that shift the graph vertically or horizontally or that stretch or shrink the graph vertically or horizontally.

2. A *geometrical transformation* is a function whose domain is the set of the points in the plane or the set of points in 3-space, in which the image of each point is another point (possibly the same point). An **isometry** is a special type of geometrical transformation.

*Translation*

A type of isometry in which the output for each point is obtained by moving the point a fixed amount in each of the coordinate directions. A translation is sometimes called a "slide."

Example: In the diagram here, the line segment connecting $(3, 2)$ and $(5, 1)$ is being translated 3 units to the right and 4 units down, so that its image under the translation is the line segment connecting $(6, -2)$ and $(8, -3)$.

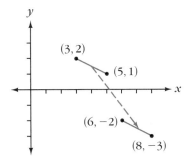

*True mean*

The mean for a population. See also **sample mean.**

*True proportion*     In a population, the fraction of items that represent a specific outcome. See also **sample proportion.**

Example: If 600 out of 1000 balls in an urn are red, then the true proportion of red balls is $\frac{600}{1000}$, which may be expressed as .6 or as 60%.

*Unit circle*     A circle of radius 1, especially the circle in the coordinate plane with radius 1 and center at the origin.

*Variance*     The square of standard deviation. For a finite set of data $x_1, x_2, x_3, \ldots, x_n$ with mean $\mu$, the variance is given by the expression

$$\frac{1}{n} \sum_{i=1}^{n} (x_i - \mu)^2$$

*Velocity*     A combination of the speed and direction of a moving object. If an object is moving vertically, we generally consider upward motion as having a positive velocity and downward motion as having a negative velocity. The rate at which the velocity of an object is changing is the object's **acceleration.** A positive acceleration corresponds to an increase in velocity.

## Student Book Interior Photography

**3** Oxnard High School, CA; Jerry Neidenbach; **5** Tony Stone Images; **7** Hillary Turner; **14** Capuchino High School, CA; Chicha Lynch, Hillary Turner, Richard Wheeler; **20** Tony Stone Images; **23** PhotoEdit; **27** PhotoDisc; **30** Capuchino High School, CA; Chicha Lynch, Hillary Turner, Richard Wheeler; **34** SuperStock, Inc.; **37** FPG International; **38** Capuchino High School, CA; Peter Jonnard, Hillary Turner, Richard Wheeler; **41** Tony Stone Images; **43** The Image Bank; **44** FPG International; **45** FPG International; **48** Capuchino High School, CA; Peter Jonnard, Hillary Turner, Richard Wheeler; **52** PhotoDisc; **53** SuperStock, Inc.; **54** Capuchino High School, CA; Chicha Lynch, Hillary Turner, Richard Wheeler; **55** Hillary Turner; **62** Stock Boston; **68** Capuchino High School, CA; Chicha Lynch, Hillary Turner, Richard Wheeler; **70** Tony Stone Images; **72** Tony Stone Images; **78** Capuchino High School, CA; Peter Jonnard, Hillary Turner, Richard Wheeler; **77** The Image Bank; **79** The Image Bank; **80** PhotoEdit; **82** SuperStock, Inc.; **85** Leo de Wys, Inc.; Tony Stone Images; **87** FPG International; **91** Capuchino High School, CA; Peter Jonnard, Hillary Turner, Richard Wheeler; **93** SuperStock, Inc.; **98** Corbis/Bettmann; **99** FPG International; **102**; Leo de Wys, Inc.; **104** SuperStock, Inc.; **110** Leo de Wys, Inc.; **113** Capuchino High School, CA; Peter Jonnard, Hillary Turner, Richard Wheeler; **114** Hillary Turner; **118** Hillary Turner; **119** Hillary Turner; **121** Aptos High School, CA; Anthony Pepperdine; **124** Hillary Turner; **129** The Image Bank; **130** SuperStock, Inc; **131** SuperStock, Inc; **133** Brookline High School, MA; Terry Nowak, Lynne Alper; **140** SuperStock, Inc.; **142** Capuchino High School, CA; Peter Jonnard, Hillary Turner, Richard Wheeler; **143** Stock Boston; **149** Tony Stone Images; **150** Stock Boston; **153** Stock Boston; **159** Shasta High School, CA; Dave Robathan; **161** Leo de Wys, Inc.; **163** FPG International; **176** SuperStock, Inc.; **182** PhotoDisc; **184** Capuchino High School, CA; Chicha Lynch, Hillary Turner and Richard Wheeler; **187** SuperStock, Inc.; **188** The Image Bank; **190** Foothill High School, CA; Cheryl Dozier; **208** Animals, Animals; **210** The Image Works; **215** Capuchino High School, CA; Dean Orfanedes; **216** FPG International; **222** Hillary Turner; **233** Hillary Turner, Richard Wheeler; **236** Corbis/Bettmann; **241** Hillary Turner, Richard Wheeler; **242** Brookline High School, MA; Terry Nowak, Lynne Alper; **243** Hillary Turner; **257** Foothill High School, CA; Cheryl Dozier; **258** Tony Stone Images; **259** Leo de Wys, Inc.; **262** Palm Press/©Harold E. Edgerton; **265** Capuchino High School, CA; Dean Orfanedes, Hillary Turner,

Richard Wheeler; **280** FPG International; **281** FPG International; **282** Capuchino High School, CA; Dean Orfanedes, Hillary Turner, Richard Wheeler; **284** Hillary Turner; **291** Capuchino High School, CA; Chicha Lynch; **292** Corbis/Bettman; **293** PhotoEdit; **300** San Lorenzo Valley High School, CA; Sandie Gilliam, Lynne Alper; **307** PhotoEdit; **308** Capuchino High School, CA; Peter Jonnard, Hillary Turner, Richard Wheeler; **310** Hillary Turner; **312** Tony Stone Images; **314** Hillary Turner, Richard Wheeler; **315** San Lorenzo Valley High School, CA; Sandie Gilliam, Lynne Alper; **320** SuperStock, Inc.; **335** San Lorenzo Valley High School, CA; Sandie Gilliam, Lynne Alper; **341** Foothill High School, CA; Madeline Rippe, Cheryl Dozier; **348** Leo de Wys, Inc.; **357** The Image Bank; **359** Comstock; **361** PhotoDisc; **365** Capuchino High School, CA; Chicha Lynch, Hillary Turner, Richard Wheeler; **373** FPG International; **377** Brookline High School, MA; Terry Nowak; **386** Capuchino High School, CA; Chicha Lynch, Hillary Turner, Richard Wheeler; **395** Hillary Turner; **400** PhotoEdit; **409** Santa Cruz High School, CA; George Martinez, Lynne Alper; **414** SuperStock, Inc.; **415** SuperStock, Inc.; **416** FPG International; **417** The Image Bank; **420** SuperStock, Inc.; **421** SuperStock, Inc.; **423** Patrick Henry High School, MN; Jane Kostik; **429** The Image Bank; **430** Black Star; **431** SuperStock, Inc.; **434** The Image Works; **436** Foothill High School, CA; Cheryl Dozier; **445** FPG International; **447** The Image Bank

## Cover Photography

*High Dive* Corbis and Comstock; *Know How* Tony Stone Images, Inc.; *As the Cube Turns* Hillary Turner and Rick Helf; *The World of Functions* Hillary Turner and Richard Wheeler; *The Pollster's Dilemma* Corbis.

## Front Cover Students

*The World of Functions* first row: Hilda Chavez, Mary Truong, Tom Hitchner, Enrique Gonzales.  Second Row: Kermit Bayless, Jr., Kei Takeda, Ryan Alexander-Tanner, Rena Davis.